The Dreyfus Affair
and the American Conscience, 1895–1906

The Dreyfus Affair

and the
American Conscience,
1895–1906

Egal Feldman

Wayne State University Press

DETROIT 1981

Library of Congress Cataloging in Publication Data

Feldman, Egal, 1925–
    The Dreyfus affair and the American conscience, 1895–1906.

    Bibliography: p.
    Includes index.
    1. Dreyfus, Alfred, 1859–1935. 2. France—Foreign
opinion, American. 3. Public opinion—United States.
I. Title.
DC354.8.F44   1981   944.081′902′4   80–6233
ISBN 0–8143–1677–8

In memory of my parents, Chaya and Moshe

Contents

Preface

American historians have treated their social history in splendid isolation. Apart from studies of diplomatic entanglements, an arena in which the United States became increasingly enmeshed toward the end of the nineteenth century, American consciousness and perceptions of the critical issues of the European world have been generally ignored.

Because of the international attention that the Dreyfus affair commanded, it offers the historian an occasion to monitor and evaluate American observations of the legal, political, and social customs of France during a very critical period. Such an exercise reveals much of what Americans thought, not only of Europe, but of themselves. How did Americans in the age of McKinley and Roosevelt, expansionism and progressivism, perceive the crisis in France, and what do such perceptions tell us about American estimates of their own life and institutions?

■ My indebtedness to the staffs of numerous libraries and archives is great, and thanks are especially extended to the American Jewish Archives, the American Jewish Historical Society, the Archives of the Archdiocese of Baltimore, the Houghton Library of Harvard University, the Library of Congress, the Library of the Catholic University of America, the Massachusetts Diocesan Library, the New York Public Library, the Illinois Historical Society, the Ohio Historical Society, the St. Paul Seminary Library, the State Historical Society of Wisconsin, the Wilson Library of the University of Minnesota, the Yale University Library, the YIVO Institute for Jewish Research, and the interlibrary loan division of the University of Wisconsin–Superior.

I also extend my gratitude for financial support for research and travel granted to me on several occasions over the past decade by the University of Wisconsin–Superior; to Mrs. Grace Collins, who skillfully typed the final drafts of the book; to the helpful advice of Mrs. Jean Owen, of Wayne State University Press; and to my wife, Mary, who patiently read and commented on many versions of the manuscript.

I

America
and the Case of
Alfred Dreyfus

no case has ever excited such universal and profound interest
throughout the civilized world. Every government, every military
officer, every judge, every lawyer, every layman in every country has
followed with intense interest and anxiety every stage of this trial.
JAMES B. EUSTIS, 1899

Before the Dreyfus "affair,"
France led in civilization
Now all that is left over there
is her automobilization.
Automobile Magazine, October 1899

The arrest of Alfred Dreyfus, an obscure artillery captain, late in 1894,
on the charge of treason, was at first not a major preoccupation in the
United States. It was a foreign event which had no direct bearing on
America's internal or external interests. Yet by 1898 the case of Alfred
Dreyfus was known in every American city and hamlet.

The French Intelligence Bureau, the Statistical Section, as it was
called, had as its principal function spying on the German embassy,
especially on the activities of its military attaché, Colonel Louis Von
Schwarzkopen. By 1892, through the services of a cleaning woman, who
provided the contents of the German embassy's wastepaper baskets to
the office of French intelligence, it was clear that French military information was being leaked regularly to the Germans.[1]

In the summer of 1894 a document, retrieved from the German
Embassy by this process, arrived at the Statistical Section. Its contents

appeared especially alarming. This was the memorandum soon to become celebrated as the *bordereau*, or schedule, so-called because it was a covering letter for a set of memoranda. Written on both sides of thin, transparent paper, it contained what appeared to be a list of vital military data. The *bordereau* was delivered to Major Hubert Joseph Henry, who was then assisting Colonel Jean Sandherr, the head of the Intelligence Bureau. After some weeks, Henry notified the head of the general staff, Raoul de Boisdeffre, and the secretary of war, General Auguste Mercier, of his discovery. After a hasty and somewhat superficial deliberation, the espionage chiefs concluded that the *bordereau* was the work of a probationary staff officer, one who was probably in the process of completing his staff schooling. Since most of the references in the *bordereau* were to matters of French artillery, it was surmised that the officer was attached to that branch. Examining the list of probationaries, Sandherr and Henry, both anti-Semites, were suddenly struck by the name of Captain Alfred Dreyfus, a Jewish officer. Without a further inquiry the intelligence officers concluded triumphantly that the traitor must have been a Jew and so informed General de Boisdeffre, who in turn passed the story to General Mercier.

The last thing Mercier, who was new and insecure in his post, wanted was a prolonged and embarrassing scandal. Quick action in breaking a spy case which involved Germany, France's traditional enemy, might also pay handsome political dividends. With little hesitation, therefore, he decided to proceed against Dreyfus. On October 15, 1894, Dreyfus was ordered to appear before the minister of war. The unsuspecting victim found himself confronted by a group of superior officers. One, Major Mercier Du Paty de Clam, pretending that he had injured his finger, asked Dreyfus to write a letter for him, the contents of which dealt with the text of the *bordereau*. Du Paty and the others present, convinced of Dreyfus' guilt and proud of the trap which they had set for him, expected an immediate confession. A loaded revolver lay on the table to give the traitor an honorable and expeditious exit. Much to the consternation of Du Paty, Dreyfus made no confession, nor did he appear perturbed as he proceeded to take dictation. Despite the failure of the experiment, however, Du Paty charged him with the crime of high treason and ordered him jailed. Accompanied by Major Henry, Dreyfus, still protesting his innocence, was escorted to the Cherce-Midi military prison. While in prison he was subjected to a continuing interrogation; after all, no motive or clear proof of Dreyfus' guilt was yet established. His home was invaded and meticulously searched for incriminating data; his wife was severely warned not to say anything to anyone about her husband's incarceration.

To establish Dreyfus' guilt, the services of Alphonse Bertillon, a well-known authority in crime detection and reputed to be a handwriting expert, were procured. An admirer of the military and eager to support the conviction, Bertillon evolved a strange theory, which he called "auto-forgery," to explain the differences between the characters on the *bordereau* and those produced by Dreyfus in the October interview. Dreyfus, Bertillon explained to the generals, had clearly forged his own handwriting, while introducing into it a sufficient variation to confuse matters. Despite the disagreement of other handwriting experts with Bertillon's hypothesis, his conclusions were accepted by Du Paty, and he so notified the minister of war.

Meanwhile, hints of these unusual occurrences were leaked to the press. Early in November, the *Libre parole*, a Parisian anti-Semitic tabloid, announced the arrest of a Jewish officer, Alfred Dreyfus, on the charge of treason, and reported that he had made a full confession of his crime. As a result of this awkward development (the public was already demanding Dreyfus' blood), General Mercier, in his desire to appease the multitude, determined to win a quick conviction of Dreyfus by courtmartial, which was ordered for December 19, 1894.

Despite the protests of Dreyfus' counsel, Edgar Demange, it was decided that the trial would remain closed to the public. During the subsequent private proceedings, the military judges examined a "secret dossier" compiled from miscellaneous data supplied by the Statistical Section, consisting of a collection of material on French spies and their activities, which was to be ascribed to Dreyfus. This dossier, put together by Mercier himself, with the cooperation of Boisdeffre and Sandherr, was communicated only to the judges when they convened for deliberations. Neither Dreyfus nor his attorney were allowed to examine this dossier, but Dreyfus was convicted of treason on December 22 on the basis of it. Within the next few weeks he was subjected to a public military degradation, then exiled for life to Devil's Island. Frenchmen now slept better, regretting only that French law, in a momentary humane gesture had some time ago abolished the death penalty for such acts of treachery.

Americans, like most Frenchmen and others throughout the world, if they did catch a glimpse of these happenings, must have also cast a sigh of relief that a traitorous villain had been caught in the act. Except in rare instances, the guilt of Dreyfus was seldom questioned during the first months after his conviction. However, from the early days of the case, Mathieu Dreyfus, the prisoner's brother, was exerting every effort to unravel the mystery that lay behind his brother's arrest, to expose the true culprit, and to bring about a new trial for Dreyfus. The first break in the case resulted from an unexpected event. Because of poor health, Sandherr, the chief of intelligence, resigned from his office on July 1, 1895, and was replaced by Major Georges Picquart, a young and brilliant officer, soon to be promoted to the rank of lieutenant-colonel. Early in the spring of 1896, a suspicious-looking special-delivery letter, a *petit bleu*, was received in the office of French Intelligence. It was written in the hand of Major Ferdinand Walsin Esterhazy, a French officer with a shady reputation. Suspecting him to be another traitor, Picquart examined his handwriting and was surprised by its similarity to that of the *bordereau*. It suddenly occurred to Picquart that the wrong man might be serving a life sentence on Devil's Island. When he shared these suspicions with his superior, General Boisdeffre, he was instructed to drop the investigation. When he persisted with his inquiry, he was removed from Intelligence and, on December 12, sent to a dangerous assignment in North Africa.

Picquart's post was filled by his subordinate, Lieutenant Colonel Hubert Joseph Henry. Henry immediately began to defame Picquart's character, forging letters for the "secret dossier" to strengthen the case against Dreyfus. In Africa Picquart, sensing that a plot was being hatched against him and fearing for his life, asked for a leave and hurried to Paris to disclose his suspicions about Esterhazy's guilt and Dreyfus' innocence to a lawyer friend, Louis Leblois.

Fearful of the consequences that might result from a reopening of the Dreyfus trial, the War Office launched a campaign to clear Esterhazy's name. The general staff also made every effort to cast suspicion on Picquart's activities and to brand him an untrustworthy soldier. With the willing cooperation of Esterhazy, a courtmartial, designed to clear his name, was planned for early January, 1898. It was difficult to keep all these undertakings concealed; the case was generating enormous attention. Esterhazy's staged courtmartial, and his unanimous acquittal, divided France into hostile factions. It was clear that a vast majority of Frenchmen hailed Esterhazy as a hero and saw in his acquittal a major victory for the integrity of the army. The French right, viewing itself as the defender of the Republic, rejoiced in the victory over what it called the "Jewish Syndicate" and its German and intellectual allies.

On the other hand, the "revisionists," as the supporters of the prisoner and proponents for his retrial were called, though fewer in number and temporarily dazed, were far from defeated. A significant turning point in their fortunes came unexpectedly with the publication of an open letter to Félix Faure, the president of France, entitled *J'accuse.* Written by the novelist Émile Zola, it transformed the Dreyfus case into the Dreyfus "affair." Although the letter resulted in Zola's prosecution and conviction for libel, forcing him to flee to England, it also set in motion a chain of events—a confession of forgery and the suicide of Henry, a public and parliamentary agitation which shook the French Republic to its core, and, most significant, a reopening of the Dreyfus case by the French High Court of Appeal in September, 1898. Dreyfus' return to France for the trial in Rennes in June of the following year and his second courtmartial sent vibrations throughout the Western world.

■ The priority which Americans granted to the Dreyfus event by 1898 reflected the world-wide attention that the affair was beginning to claim. There were special, uniquely American elements which stirred people in the United States. At the turn of the century a revolution in the management and technology of communication in general and of journalism in particular had made it possible for the first time for important European events to be transmitted clearly, expeditiously, and inexpensively to American newspaper readers.[2] The story of the Dreyfus case provided the American public with exciting reading; like "Cuba Libre," the anti-Spanish rallying cry launched by New York's yellow press, it sold newspapers to a nation that consumed newsprint voraciously. And like the case of Cuba, it would not have received the hearing that it had without the thorough coverage extended to it by America's dailies.

Much has been written about the aggressive marketing and competitiveness of the yellow journalism of the turn of the century, about its dispensation of vulgarity, sensationalism, and crime. True as such allegations might be, an important factor in the success of the new-style journalism was its ability to select and elaborate upon those events which also carried the greatest moral weight with its thousands of readers. In this context the Dreyfus issue was judged to be an excellent candidate. To report on the French case, American newspapers engaged the services of skilled and imaginative correspondents who wrote about it with uninhibited passion. James Creelman, one of the best of their number, spoke for the rest when he wrote about "that form of American journalistic energy which is not content to merely print a daily record of history, but seeks to take part in events as active and sometimes decisive agents."[3]

Shifts in American legal perspectives also helped make the Dreyfus affair more relevant to Americans. A surge of admiration for the Anglo-American system of common law was in part responsible for this new perception. A more careful study of the law, its origins, its relationship to historic and societal events, became a popular pastime among a rising new breed of lawyers. Much of this fermentation occurred while the trials of Alfred Dreyfus were commanding universal attention. The Dreyfus affair constituted an event which provided American lawyers with a timely opportunity to debate the relative merits of French and American law.

The Dreyfus affair had also important religious consequences. It posed challenging questions about the nature and degree of anti-Semitism, and it stirred up ancient animosities between Protestants and Catholics in the United States and abroad. Among liberal Protestants there was a growing commitment during these years to a social rather than an individual salvation. For them the creation of a freer, more equitable society became a significant religious objective. They were prompt to take notice and probe into the causes of human injustice, wherever it occurred. American Protestants of all shades of opinion were also conscious of the influx of hundreds of thousands of Roman Catholic immigrants from southern and eastern Europe. In a period of increasing secularization, it was a disturbing occurrence but also a challenge to American Protestant leaders at a time when Protestant confidence in its dominant numerical position in American religious life was being reduced. It became tempting to view an anti-Semitic or an anti-Protestant movement in France, a predominantly Roman Catholic country, as one more piece of evidence of the inability of the Roman church to conform to what was to many the tolerant spirit of Protestantism and Anglo-Americanism.

Obviously, these were not the most pleasant years for American Roman Catholics. To suspicions which confronted them at home were added charges of irreverence, modernism, and "Americanism" from the European Catholic community. These internal and external tensions molded a peculiarly American-Catholic response to the Dreyfus affair which differentiated it from that of other Americans. To American Jews, divided between the older German-speaking settlers and more recent arrivals from eastern European ghettos, the Dreyfus affair came less as news than as a reminder of the blessings of their new-found freedom in the United States as well as life's persistent precariousness for their European brethren.

In an era when the United States was emerging from a century of relative insularity, aspiring to play a meaningful, if not an heroic, role in the world, it was only natural that the attention of Americans would be attracted to major political and social crises abroad. Not all Americans celebrated their nation's military and imperial achievements, and many pointed to the crisis in France as an example of the risks that strident militarism could pose to the survival of a democratically inclined citizenry. Still, in an age of growing Anglo-American friendship and common pride of destiny, the Dreyfus affair could not have come at a more propitious moment. Few other events could have better supported the rising conviction of a generation of native-born Americans, and many newcomers as well, of the superiority of Anglo-American political and social institutions.

In short, America's perception of and response to the Dreyfus affair was a composite matter, one which helped arouse a variety of emotions, anxieties, and aspirations. Prosperous and secure at home, growing in power and prestige abroad, thoughtful Americans had an opportunity to re-examine their political and social values, to reflect upon their virtues and prejudices, their strengths and weaknesses. The French event also demanded a response to the question of whether a Dreyfus case could victimize America.[4] These and related issues will be described and discussed in the pages that follow.

II

Émile Zola:
The Citizen against
the State

Such cowards, hypocrites, and flatterers as the members of military
and ecclesiastic courts the world could produce by the million every
year. But it takes five centuries to produce a Joan of Arc or a Zola.
MARK TWAIN, 1898

the stern Muse who utters definite judgments will remember that a
man of letters left his work, in the fullness of wealth, success, and
glory, to struggle, almost alone against the world, to save an innocent
man, and that he did it to obey his conscience and to serve the truth.
GUSTAVE GEFFROY, 1902

It was not Émile Zola's role as novelist but as fighter for justice that
earned him recognition in the United States. Few individuals symbol-
ized in a more dramatic way the lone citizen pitted against the massive
bureaucracy of state. For a moment Zola was not merely part of the
Dreyfus affair; he *was* the affair, and Americans (with a few significant
exceptions) followed his tribulations as if he were one of their own. His
novels were well-known in the United States; by 1900, about fifty of
them were being offered to the public by American publishers, but they
were not universally applauded. The movement in literature which he
launched found few imitators. Zola's frankness about matters of sex and
sensuality made American readers uncomfortable, and many condemned his work.[1]

J'accuse was not the first piece that Zola wrote in defense of Dreyfus.
He had taken an interest in the case in 1897. Esterhazy's staged court-

martial and subsequent acquittal infuriated him, and he became determined to strike back at the corrupt proceedings and unjust verdict.[2]

Anticipating Zola's dramatic outburst, the *New York Times*, on the day of the publication of the famous open letter, reported to its readers that Zola had taken on the government and army of France: "The French law does not take a jocose view of assaults upon character," said the *Times*. Was Zola aware of the implications of his allegations, it asked. When he "accuses four French officers of high rank, including the Minister of War of perjury, and challenges them to sue him, it must be presumed that he knows what he is about."[3]

Americans were not prepared for the verbal abuse showered upon the novelist and the violence that erupted throughout France in his name. Asked by an American reporter why he had taken it upon himself to challenge the Esterhazy verdict, Zola replied: "As a firm believer in the innocence of Dreyfus, . . . I had to keep the agitation going, because nobody with any sense of justice and of humanity can rest until this fearful error has been rectified."[4]

Obviously Zola's accusations against France's highest political and military officials for engineering and concealing one of the momentous crimes of the century constituted an insult that could not go unchallenged. Yet, in order to avoid reopening the Dreyfus case, the French cabinet acted cautiously. It lodged a charge of criminal libel against Zola, based upon a single passage in *J'accuse* in which Zola accused the court-martial of acquitting Esterhazy on order. The cabinet hoped in this way to limit the ensuing court action to the Esterhazy affair.[5]

The trial of Émile Zola, which opened in Paris on February 7, 1898, was carefully observed by the American press. The explosion of the *Maine* in the Havana harbor coincided with but did not eclipse American interest in the trial, which also provided the public with the rare opportunity of observing a French court in session through their daily newspapers. "In the audience were several notabilities and many ladies, especially actresses, most of whom were provided with sandwiches and bottles of wine," it was reported on the opening day of the trial. A correspondent from Paris remarked: "The public—and only a very few were admitted without tickets—were squeezed together like herrings in a barrel. The heat was suffocating, and every half hour or so fainting women were carried outside." The second day was more instructive. The unruly audience flung off all reserve and "applauded uproariously at every passage of the evidence that met with its approval, laughed at the judge," and "hissed unpopular witnesses." Americans soon agreed that "the whole scene was profoundly disgraceful," especially the "dangerous and menacing mob" which had collected outside the courtroom and whose ceaseless shout was "Down with Zola!"[6]

As the trial progressed, Zola, who was described as wearing "his usual nosenippers, dressed in a dark gray overcoat" with a tall silk hat and blood-red dogskin gloves, appeared to be under considerable stress. "It is neither too much nor too little," observed an American lawyer, "to describe this trial as being what most French trials are, a roaring farce." A trial characterized by "exciting encounters . . . between various persons in a court," a "succession of shrieks, of screams, and of general hysteria, mixed of course with much shrugging of shoulders," was difficult for Americans to comprehend. The peculiarity of the French justice presented by the trials of Dreyfus and Zola "is calculated to sicken and nauseate the people of . . . the United States."[7] Because of his predilection for exaggerated gestures and lengthy rhetoric, even Zola himself became the butt of American criticism, though few doubted the justness of his cause. A friendly observer questioned the appropriateness of Zola's closing peroration:

> Dreyfus is innocent; I swear it. I stake my life upon it. At this solemn hour, before the tribunal that represents human justice, before you . . . before the entire world, I swear that Dreyfus is innocent. . . . Let it all fall to the ground, let my works perish, if Dreyfus is not innocent. Everything seems to be against me,—the two chambers, the civil power, the journals of large circulation, the public opinion that they poisoned. But with me there is only an idea, an ideal of truth and justice. And I am perfectly at ease; I shall triumph. I did not wish my country to remain in falsehood and injustice. Here I may be condemned; but some day France will thank me for having helped to save her honor.[8]

At the end of the fifteen-day trial the jury retired; it reappeared after a thirty-five-minute deliberation, as Zola had himself foreseen, with a verdict of guilty. The announcement caused an eruption of delirious joy among the spectators. "The air was filled with cries of 'Long live the army! . . . To the door with the Jews! Death to Zola!' amid which Zola cried: 'These people are cannibals!'" Found guilty of libel, both Zola and the publisher of the *Aurore*, Georges Clemenceau, whose newspaper dared to print *J'accuse*, were each accorded the maximum penalty: one year in prison for Zola, four months for the publisher, and a fine of a thousand francs each.

The trial did not damage Zola's image in the United States, where he was now viewed as a hero. James B. Eustis, a former ambassador to France and a greater admirer of French customs than most of his American contemporaries, wrote: "Émile Zola was only known before the Dreyfus case as a scholarly writer of novels of questionable taste. Today he ought to be crowned as the bravest citizen in the French Republic. To him the insolent arrogance of the officers of the general staff of the army had no more terrors than the intimidations of the judge who presided at his trial and who made himself conspicuous by his outrageous rulings."[9]

American thoughts about France turned sour. Its former position declined drastically in public estimation. Carl Schurz concluded that "in France the government, and even the courts of justice, are at the mercy of a most dangerous combination of revolutionary influences capable of causing explosions of an incalculable mischievous character." The proceedings of the trial he found startling: "It is not too much to say that if a detailed and strictly truthful report of it . . . had appeared in a work of fiction, the verdict of the unbiased reader would be that while a novelist may ask us to accept many improbable things, he should not ask us to believe that such an undisguised, ruthless perversion of justice was possible in a high tribunal of a civilized nation calling itself a republic at the close of the nineteenth century."[10]

Zola appealed his conviction, partly on the ground that the minister of war had acted illegally in ordering his prosecution, a task that should have been undertaken by a military court. Much to the annoyance of Frenchmen, the sentence was annulled and a new trial ordered. Throughout France anti-Semitic cries were raised against the tribunal, accusing its justices of selling out to the "Jewish Syndicate." The new trial, to be removed from Paris to Versailles, was scheduled to begin on July 18, 1898. In a separate process, Zola was also found guilty of using libelous language about three handwriting experts in *J'accuse* and was condemned to two additional months in prison and a further fine of seventeen thousand francs.[11]

Things looked bleak for the novelist. Walter Littlefield, an able observer of the Zola affair for the *New York Times*, predicted that the second trial was "likely to be as fully sensational in character" and "conducted in a manner which will confirm the doubts of foreigners as to the justice of French legal procedure."[12] It was common knowledge that the presiding judge, Samuel Perivier, was convinced of the guilt of Dreyfus, while the jury, drawn from Versailles, was to be stacked with "citizens two-thirds of whom are half-pay or retired officers of the army," hardly an advantage to Zola. Everything, Littlefield wrote, pointed to "a more one-sided trial than the first, with overwhelming odds against the defender of Dreyfus."[13]

But why should Americans be startled at lopsided justice in France, asked Frederick W. Whitridge, a political and constitutional authority. The constitutional guarantees to which Americans were accustomed were alien to the people of France. "If a private citizen is unable to safely challenge the decisions of his governors, or direct public attention to their errors, where is the substance of the democracy?" Unlike Americans, who believe that the state is the "aggregation of its citizens," those in authority in France view their state in more mystic categories as "something above the community" and their army as "not the servant but the incarnation of the state." Neither was it simple for Americans to comprehend the "immense caste and racial feeling which segregates the army from the people and puts it above the law. . . . It is this which causes us to wonder whether the French republic and ours belong in the same class."[14]

Joseph H. Choate, president of the American Bar Association, concurred in these sentiments. He informed a national gathering of lawyers in the summer of 1898 that the Zola trial was characterized by a "reckless and cruel disregard of every principle of right and justice known to us," one that was "surely without precedent in modern history. . . . However satisfactory such a method of administering criminal justice may be to the French people, who cling to it through all changes of government, it could only excite horror and disgust throughout the Anglo-Saxon world."[15]

Zola, meanwhile, prodded by his legal advisors and friends, who were also convinced that justice in France was impossible and that a jail term would be of no service to the cause of Dreyfus or to himself, reluctantly agreed to flee to England. As Ernest Visetelly, his biographer and friend, recalls, "A few toilet articles were pressed upon him, and his wife emptied her purse into his; then, after dining, he drove to the Northern Railway Station, where he caught the express starting for Calais at nine P.M. He secured a compartment which had no other occupant, and journeyed to London." Since his safety in London was uncertain, he did not remain there long but was hurried off to a retreat provided by a friend in Wimbledon and, later, to more desolate surroundings. His disappearance from France surprised many. Some Americans thought he was in Switzerland; others placed him in Norway, Belgium, and elsewhere. Only his wife and a few close friends, including a representative of his New York publisher, knew of his location and would pay him occasional visits at his English retreat.

Zola remained in hiding for almost a year. He returned to France on June 4, 1899, in time to witness the excitement of the preparation for Dreyfus' second courtmartial. By that time the political outburst which he had helped to arouse had exceeded his wildest dreams. Colonel Henry's confession of forgery and his subsequent suicide pushed the question of revision of Dreyfus' sentence into the hands of the Supreme Court of Appeal. It had taken up the question in September, 1898, and recommended a revision of the judgment the following June. American journalists followed the French court's deliberations in detail, and its decision delighted Americans, who tended to read into it more hopeful signs than were justified: "Dreyfus Case Won at Last" was a typical newspaper announcement early in June. The yellow press appeared to be even more carried away: "Out of the darkness has come light; out of the morass of falsehood and race prejudice have come truth. . . . out of threatened revolution has come respect for the law. Reason and justice have triumphed in France," announced the *New York Journal*. The *Journal* was convinced that "the verdict is practically an acquittal. In accusing the foul brood of forgers and perjurers that subjected an innocent man to inhuman tortures, the court proclaims the innocence of Dreyfus."[16] Even the more reflective *Nation* announced, "never was there a more notable demonstration of the truth" and predicted with assurance that Dreyfus "will be sent before a new court-martial, which will not dare resort to the monstrous methods of its predecessors."[17]

That Zola's solitary stand against the highest French authorities was largely responsible for the attainment of the revision of the judgment against Dreyfus was not forgotten. Zola "aroused the sentiment of the world on behalf of justice," said a St. Louis paper: "Neither the army nor the government of France could withstand the pen of one man pointed with truth and wielded in defense of right."[18] Fully conscious of the difficulties that still lay ahead, however, Zola was far from serene: "I am fighting a great fight, which is by no means ended. I cannot write anything until the case is over," an American newspaper quoted him as saying.

His personal reactions to events in France were solicited in the United States. Some months earlier, Robert H. Sherard of the *American Monthly Review of Reviews* posed a series of questions to the novelist, especially regarding his thoughts about the mounting tide of anti-Semitism in France. Zola tended to belittle it. "I cannot believe," he remarked, "that France, the great, generous, enlightened nation, will tolerate such a movement a century after the French Revolution and the Declaration of the Rights of Man." Those involved in arousing such sentiments, he said, "cannot stir the people of France." He characterized hatred of the Jews as a "hypocritical form of socialism. . . . the Jews have been made to represent[,] in the eyes of the ignorant and the have-nots, the capitalists, against whom the demagogues have always directed the furies of the proletariat." The movement, he acknowledged, had taken him by surprise. It

> stupefied me—that there should be a return to fanaticism, an attempt to light up a religious war in this epoch of ours, one hundred years after the revolution, in the heart of our great Paris, in the days of democracy, of universal toleration, at the very time when there is an immense movement being made everywhere toward equality, justice, and fraternity. A handful of madmen, cunning or idiotic, come and shout in our ears every morning "Let us kill the Jews. Let us devour the Jews. Let us massacre them. Let us exterminate them. . . ." Is it not inconceivable? Could anything be more foolish? Could anything be more abominable?[19]

After his return from exile Zola's attitude toward American reporters underwent a change. His recent experiences, he admitted, had shaken him severely. "The 18th of July, 1898," was "the most dreadful day of my life," he confided to a New York reporter. "On that day it was that I . . . forsook all that I loved and tore myself from all the associations dear to my heart and mind. . . . This sudden parting was surely the most terrible, the greatest sacrifice for the soul." His flight to England, he explained almost apologetically, grew out of the necessity to "gain time" for the friends of Dreyfus. "We wished to delay the case . . . in the hope that the truth would then become clearer." But "to go away in utter darkness," he explained remorsefully, "to see the lights of France fade away in the distance . . . with the mob of knaves and fools yelling slander and insults at me" was the most painful experience of his life. "These were terrible hours, from which my soul came steeled, invulnerable in future to unjust attacks. Can you conceive what torment it was for me in the long months of banishment, to be stricken from the ranks of the living, to be daily expecting the awakening of justice, which every day was deferred?"

Now that his task was nearing completion, Zola explained, he wished "no applause and no rewards." For him it was sufficient to have been involved in a "cause so beautiful, so human!" His greatest reward, he said, lay in the knowledge that he had helped to drag an innocent man from "the grave in which he was buried for four years." The idea of seeing Dreyfus finally free, "of pressing his hands, fills me with extraordinary emotion which brings tears to my eyes." Perhaps even more important was the knowledge that he had been proven right. "Do you recall the scandalous outcry with which my letter to the President of the Republic was received? I was a libeler of the army, a bought creature, a wretch without a country. Writers friendly to me turned from me in horror." He challenged his critics to re-read his "poor letter." "I am ashamed of its moderation, its opportunism—I might almost say its cowardice. . . . It appears childish, like the conception of a dull writer compared to the majestic truth." He was happy that each of his accusations had been confirmed: "None of the men I accused can deny his guilt any longer. . . . What I predicted is now clear." As for the legal case against him, he was indifferent to its outcome. Now that he was well on the way toward achieving his objective, his own trial had "no further purpose," and it interested him no more.[20]

Such interviews were rare, however. When invited by a group of American newspapers to report on the progress of the Rennes court-martial, with a generous stipend for his services, his reply was unusually curt: "Not for millions!" "Positively . . . I will not write of the Dreyfus case for any newspaper whatsoever—at least not until the coming trial is over."[21] What was more, he was annoyed at the circulation of rumors about his future plans:

> I learn that a man in New York boasts that he has a contract with me to write a play about Dreyfus. Another talks of my making a lecture tour through the United States. I learn, too, that certain newspapers have recently published articles signed with my name and are announcing that they will publish other articles by me. All such statements are absolute impositions. I have never authorized these statements nor the publication of these articles.[22]

He was irritated with the rumor circulating in the United States about an agreement between him and a theatrical agent, Edmond Gerson, to write a five-act play about the Dreyfus affair. Gerson, it was announced, "transmitted 10,000 francs to Zola as part payment." Zola in return was said to have agreed to "begin work on the play in a few weeks." The play, yet unnamed, was to open in New York in January, and there was a strong possibility, according to the rumor, that Zola himself would take a leading role. According to the report, the expectation was that the play would be a sensation.[23]

Despite Zola's reluctance to write for American newspapers, an effort was made, especially by New York's yellow press, to assure readers that the papers were in communication with him. The *New York Journal*, for example, featured cabled dispatches from Zola which gave his views about the Rennes trial. Most probably, some of these cables were not written by Zola; the *Journal*'s readership demanded instant satisfaction of its curiosity about Zola, however, and so it was provided.[24]

Zola's hopes for the outcome of Dreyfus' second courtmartial quickly turned sour. "There has not appeared even one impartial witness against Dreyfus," he commented to an American reporter on August 20. "In all the annals of political crime there is no more deeply depraved case on record. . . . In my studies of human nature I have sounded very low depths of depravity, but this trial reveals lower depths than any the most unbridled imagination could put forth."[25]

Zola's disillusionment at the verdict, which, by a vote of five to two once again found the prisoner guilty, bordered on despair. Even the "pardon" granted to Dreyfus by the president of France ten days later was of little consolation. His letter to Lucie Dreyfus, the captain's wife, which was translated and reprinted in the United States, indicated his bitterness and determination to continue the fight for total justice. "Peace be to the martyr who has such need for repose," he wrote. "As for us, Madame, we shall continue the fight. . . . We shall exact rehabilitation of the innocent man less for the sake of him, who has already so much glory, than for France, which would assuredly be killed by this excess of infamy. . . . You may depend on those who have restored to your husband his freedom to restore him his honor."[26]

In the following weeks Zola became once again the crusading journalist, striving for Dreyfus' complete rehabilitation. With "The Fifth Act" reminiscent of *J'accuse*, Zola struck out at the verdict. Placarded throughout Paris in bold black type, one American newspaper commented: "the celebrated novelist has again entered the arena in the fight for truth and justice." It was a warning and a call for action to the people of France: "The Rennes trial was only the fourth act. . . . great God! what will the fifth act be? What new tortures and sufferings will it bring!"[27]

■ Like many other participants in the Dreyfus drama, Émile Zola did not live to see its conclusion. He died on September 29, 1902. As a writer, however, his reputation was now larger than ever. As Gustave Geffroy recalled shortly after Zola's death, what was most striking was the knowledge that "a man of letters left his work, in the fullness of wealth, success, and glory, to struggle, almost alone against the world, to save an innocent man, and that he did it to obey his conscience and to serve the truth."[28]

An unsuccessful attempt was made to create a literary monument in Zola's name in the United States. When Zola's widow put up his extensive book collection for sale in 1903, a prominent book collector from Minneapolis, James Carleton Young (1856–1918), who aspired to erect in that city a library in Zola's name "in which every work will bear an inscription by its author," was one of the first on hand. Young purchased from the collection more than eight hundred autographed volumes, autograph letters, manuscripts, and "several thousand volumes by dead and living writers in virtually all languages." His project, however, was never consummated.[29]

But it was not Zola's books that really mattered to Americans. "All this posthumous dedication of his name to glory is not in recognition of his service to French literature," commented the *New York Times* in 1906, when it learned of the decision to transfer Zola's remains to the Panthéon, there to rest with other French notables. "That service, indeed, could not in his lifetime secure him membership in the French Academy. . . . It is based on the fact that Zola, at a critical moment, with the utmost courage, and at marked risk, raised his voice to demand that justice be done to Captain Dreyfus."[30] Mark Twain's comment that while France could generate yearly millions of "cowards, hypocrites, and flatterers as members of military and ecclesiastic courts," it took her "five centuries to produce a Joan of Arc or a Zola"[31] was typical of public sentiment. Most significant, however, was the fact that it was the Zola event which made Americans aware of France's legal and moral decline, to which we now turn.

III

Dreyfus,
Anglo-Americanism,
and the Common Law

The whole business, in whatever aspect we regard it, undoubtedly
soothes our sense of self-satisfaction, so that we thank heaven that we
are not as the Frenchmen are.

JOHN T. MORSE, JR., 1898

In nothing, perhaps, does the substantial identity of the two branches
of the old stock appear so much as in the doctrine and practice of
law.

JAMES BRYCE, 1907

When Émile Zola chose England as a place of refuge, he must have had
some awareness of the blossoming friendship between England and the
United States. That this intimacy coincided with the Dreyfus affair was
of no minor significance, for it colored and in part determined the view
that Americans held of France and her domestic tribulations. It was
through British eyes that Americans saw much of what was transpiring
in France. British news dispatches and British reporters provided
American readers with most moving accounts of the Dreyfus story and
comments on them. To an important degree these sources helped shape
an American perspective of the Dreyfus affair.[1]

Underlying this shared interest in French events was a rediscovery
of a common Anglo-Saxon heritage, a "unique partnership"; proposals
were even made for an alliance or reunion of the English-speaking
people. On both sides of the Atlantic this spirit captivated the popular
imagination. Its proponents beckoned "the Pulpit, the Press, the Bar,
and the Stage, to help the great Anglo-Saxon peoples consummate their

destiny in one combined effort to perform the duty with which God has charged them." An English-speaking alliance, argued John R. Dos Passos, a spokesman for Anglo-Americanism, "would mark an epoch in the world's history" with untold benefits for all mankind.[2]

To be sure, the hyphenated terms "Anglo-Saxonism" or "Anglo-Americanism" did not impress *all* Americans. To Irish-Americans or more recent arrivals from eastern Europe, such designations were either annoying or meaningless. For others, they implied more forceful but not necessarily identical sentiments. But to a significant minority on both sides of the Atlantic they suggested expansionism, imperialism, and the necessity to conquer and educate the weak and backward races. This aura of self-righteousness, urgency, and mission appealed to some of the best minds in the Anglo-American community.[3] "Terrible as war may be," declared Joseph Chamberlain in 1898, it would be "cheaply purchased if in a great and noble cause the Stars and Stripes and the Union Jack should wave together" over an Anglo-Saxon alliance. In the United States Albert Beveridge, a prominent senator from Massachusetts, thundered: "God has not prepared the English speaking people . . . for a thousand years for nothing but vain and idle self-admiration. No! He has made us the master organizers of the world to establish system where chaos reigns."[4]

A popular question of the day was whether America and England together could whip the entire world, if not militarily, then at least spiritually. There was little disagreement in Protestant circles that upon the English and American peoples lay the responsibility for the "evangelization of the world."[5] As the historian Harvey Wish notes: "Chauvinism and racialism became substitutes for religion in this secular age. . . . Blood rather than mere culture alone was the new touchstone." In the United States the religious leader Josiah Strong, the New England writer John Fiske, the naval historian Alfred Mahan, the political scientist John W. Burgess, Ambassador and Secretary of State John Hay, President McKinley himself, and such distinguished senators as Albert J. Beveridge, Henry Cabot Lodge, and Chauncey M. Depew aided in the conversion of an influential section of American public opinion to the doctrine of Anglo-Saxon superiority.

Abhorrent as all this might appear to later generations, it ought to be recalled that the rhetoric of Anglo-Saxon and Anglo-American superiority and bellicosity contained a nobler dimension. Anglo-American fervor was experienced most intensely during the years of progressivism and reform at home. Some of its most enthusiastic devotees aimed their Anglo-American crusade at a grand moral objective, the coming of a "golden age" of universal peace, prosperity, freedom, and justice. They firmly believed that only the united forces of the English-speaking people could achieve success in this enterprise. Alliance with England was seen as an act of altruism, a "common cause . . . on behalf of humanity." "When England and America together, shall say, in the presence of any wrong—'this must stop'—it will stop."[6] Still, implicit in this thinking was the conviction that non-English people lacked the proper moral incentives and political talents to lead mankind out of the darkness.

It was against the backdrop of such contradictory sentiments that English-speaking observers of the Dreyfus affair shaped their opinions of French society. The affair supported their conviction of political superiority. "We thank Heaven that we are not as the Frenchmen are," was a sigh frequently heard. "The political development of France," H. C. Foxcroft, an English journalist, observed, "despite all appearances to the contrary, is far less advanced than our own; while as regards judicial experience she stands, by the inexorable logic of events, much where we stood two centuries ago."[7]

■ Anglo-American understanding, however, grew out of more than romantic attachments and racial notions; it was also rooted in the reality of foreign entanglements. In the United States and England the Dreyfus issue coincided with critical international involvements which caused both countries to draw closer together. America's declaration of war against Spain, hardly a popular event in Europe, was especially resented in Latin Roman Catholic countries. England was almost alone in its support of the American position in the short conflict. This gesture was not lost on the American public and went a long way to assure Americans that they had rediscovered a trusted friend. "It should be remembered," observed Dos Passos, that such advocacy "subjected England to the risk of being involved in serious complications with the other nations of Europe. . . . There was never an occasion in history when national gratitude was more justly due from one nation to another."[8] It mattered little to Americans that British self-interest was behind such friendly conduct. Ostracized from the European concert of powers, England had turned westward for diplomatic friendship, and with the disintegration of the Chinese empire, the United States and England also found common Asian objectives in their support for an open-door policy in China.[9]

Even more important was the Anglo-French crisis over the fate of the city of Fashoda, on the upper Nile, in the fall of 1898. Throughout that year French forces had been pressing into northern Africa, laying claim to the upper Nile valley as a link between their possessions in West Africa and those at the entrance to the Red Sea. Suddenly at Fashoda they found themselves facing a stubborn and determined British army. This rather minor disagreement caused a major international crisis: 1898 was the year of the Esterhazy courtmartial, the Zola affair, and the Henry suicide, and the conflict over Fashoda took place, by coincidence, at the very time when Dreyfus was dispatched to Devil's Island. "By a strange twist of events," writes Roger G. Brown, "the destinies of Captain Jean-Baptiste Marchand [the French commander at Fashoda] and Captain Alfred Dreyfus became momentarily linked between January and November of 1898."[10] The anxiety which the Fashoda struggle created in England was translated into violent attacks on France for its mishandling of the Dreyfus issue. At the same time, the competition between the two powers in Africa intensified French resentment of such criticism by a party which was threatening its African claims. Sir Thomas Barclay recalls in his reminiscences that in England "pro-Dreyfusism raged as an anti-French fever, with a violence only second to that of the anti-Dreyfus fever in France."[11]

Rather than risk a military confrontation with England, France recalled her troops from the upper Nile. Torn internally by the Dreyfus affair, castigated by world opinion, the country was in no position to act decisively against England. At the same time, British policymakers, viewing France's internal instability as dangerous, determined to put up a show of military and naval strength. In short, "the Fashoda incident became the Fashoda crisis because of the condition of French politics."[12] The twin sentiments of Anglo-American unity and Anglo-American disdain for the legal and social institutions of France which were created by these events and the Dreyfus case were to remain strong even after Anglo-French differences over Fashoda were completely resolved.[13]

■ While England was flexing its muscles in Africa, the United States was experiencing a golden age: in rapid succession its people tasted military and naval victory, the acquisition of a colonial empire, and acceptance by world opinion as a major power. But, as indicated above, these achievements abroad did not diminish American aspirations toward democratization of the social order at home and creation of a better life for all citizens. The symptoms of this "Progressive Age" manifested themselves, as Richard Hofstadter observes, "in two quite different moods. The key to one of them was an intensification of protest and humanitarian reform. . . . The other mood was one of national self-assertion, aggression, expansion. The motif of the first was social sympathy; of the second, national power. . . . The capacity for sympathy and the need for power existed side by side."[14] American concern for the fate of Dreyfus mirrored these two objectives. His ordeal drew a response rooted in this heritage of social consciousness and humanitarianism as well as in inflated notions of American moral, social, and legal superiority.

In America, as in England, the Dreyfus affair was diagnosed as a symptom of the debased conditions of Latin and Catholic Europe. "The so-called Latin races," complained a Boston newspaper, are "more barbarian than Roman." It was not totally lost on Americans that the Spanish-American War had been unpopular in Catholic circles, or that France's attitude toward America during the "Splendid Little War" was cool at best.[15] Although France remained officially neutral in the conflict, the French public in general sided with Spain. French newspapers condemned American intervention in Cuba as "an act of international piracy" and McKinley's war message as "a declaration of war of the new world against the old." Gestures of sympathy for Spain were invariably mixed with questions about American objectives: "Who knows on what side the cabinet of Washington will direct its blows, what power it will attack, what new territory it will attempt to seize?"[16]

Horace Porter, the American ambassador to France, reported such feelings to Washington in a dispatch of May 24, 1898. "Some are influenced stupidly by a fear that the United States, after finishing with Cuba, will at once seize upon all French colonies in the new world," he wrote. France's uneasiness was also conditioned by the "claim of England that an Anglo-Saxon Alliance is to be formed to menace and hold in control the acts of European Powers." This rumor, Porter claimed, carried "considerable weight with the more impressionable element in France and has greatly excited many of the people." Furthermore, he said, animosity towards the United States emanated from the most influential classes—royalists, bankers, the clergy, and radical intellectuals. "At the opening of our dispute with Spain they used all manner of hard names toward us and represented Americans to be largely a nation of loafers," said an American commentator, and the United States naval attaché in France wrote to President McKinley in the fall of 1898, "In general every hand here is against us."[17]

■ The Anglo-American consensus about the affair, which centered about a legal procedure, expressed itself most vividly through a transatlantic dialogue concerning the juridicial heritage of the English-speaking people. Legal thinkers on both sides of the Atlantic praised the superiority of English common law, the common foundation for the inevitable progress of English-speaking civilization. The vicissitudes of the Dreyfus case served as a barometer to measure the intensity of their mutual faith in their institutions: such legal fiascos could not have occurred in the United States or England. The Anglo-American legal base, it was said, enabled each country to act more humanely, more justly, and more responsively, in accordance with the highest aspirations of a free people.[18] (It may be noted that in such self-congratulatory exercises Americans tended to overlook or minimize imperfections in their own legal practices—the denial of justice to the poor, women, and minorities and the toleration of vigilante groups, lynch law, and the Ku Klux Klan.[19])

As a consequence of this consensus of views and mutual disgust at the news from France, English and American jurists now exchanged visits and speaking engagements. Prominent lawyers and judges of both countries became well known on both sides of the Atlantic. Lord Russell of Killowen, for example, was no stranger to America when he was appointed lord chief justice of England in 1894.[20] Two years later he was invited to deliver the annual address before the American Bar Association at Saratoga Springs. In his address to the association, when he touched on the blessings of peace, especially "peace between the two great divisions of the English-speaking world," the orator, according to his biographer, "contrived to import tears into his voice, and such was the sympathy he evoked that many signs of emotion were displayed by the audience"—a peculiar display from a gathering of lawyers, but it underscores the intensity of the Anglo-American bond. An American lawyer remarked some years later that "to his appearance among us . . . I attribute very largely the growth of friendly relations between England and America—one of the most significant facts of the present time."[21]

Lord Russell represented England on the Venezuela Arbitration Commission, to which Chief Justice Melville W. Fuller of the United States Supreme Court was also appointed. The commission convened in France while the Rennes trial was in progress. At Queen Victoria's request, Russell attended the proceedings of Dreyfus' second courtmartial to convey his impressions of the trial to her. A close student of the Dreyfus affair, Russell had followed its legal ramifications carefully throughout the years. Although he differed with many of his countrymen about the degree of anti-Semitism involved in its origins and was critical of the bellicose tone which many English newspapers assumed toward France (Russell was an Irish Roman Catholic), it was nevertheless his belief, as he stated in the report to the queen, that "the facts now disclosed are of such a startling and significant character that it is impossible any longer for honest men to repose faith in the implicated heads of the army or to acquit them of treachery and duplicity."[22]

The legal nexus with Great Britain had also its American side. The appointment in 1899 of Joseph H. Choate, president of the American Bar Association, as ambassador to England was not without symbolic significance. In his address read to the 1899 convention of the bar, Choate reminded the group of lawyers that "the Common Law lies at the foundation of individual liberty in both countries alike."[23] The annual gathering, at which the Dreyfus case was discussed at some length, also heard Sir William R. Kennedy, a justice of the English High Court of Justice, express the hope that "to whatever region of the earth God-given responsibilities send the children of our mighty race, whether under the Flag of England or under the Stars and Stripes, they may plant there, on a sure foundation, . . . the pillar of strong and impartial justice, as becomes the faithful servants of Him who is the infinity of Just Judge."[24]

When the British ambassador to the United States, James Bryce, a constitutional historian in his own right, delivered the principal address to the annual convention of the American Bar Association in 1907, he entitled his paper "The Influence of National Character and Historical Environment on the Development of the Common Law." He was not the first of his generation to make the comparison between the "legal ideas and legal methods of ourselves whose minds have been formed by the study of the Common Law and the ideas and methods of the lawyers who belong to the European continent."[25] Despite the lengthy separation of England and the United States, observed Bryce, the legal basis of both peoples did not change:

> An American Counsel in an English Court, or an English counsel in
> an American court, feels himself in a familiar atmosphere, and
> understands what is going on. . . . You read and quote our law
> reports . . . we read and quote yours. . . . In nothing, perhaps, does
> the substantial identity of the two branches of the old stock appear so
> much as in the doctrine and practice of the law. . . . It is a bond of
> union and of sympathy whose value can hardly be overrated. . . .
> There is nothing of which you and we may be more justly proud
> than that our common forefathers reared this majestic fabric which

has given shelter to so many generations of men and from which there have gone forth principles of liberty by which the whole world profited. . . . So may it ever be both in America and in England."[26]

IV

The Indictment of
French Jurisprudence

In France . . . there are no rules of evidence. . . . Witnesses have
appeared before the judges and have spoken their minds freely.
They have not presented evidence. They have given their own opinions. They have expressed the opinions of others. They have
repeated conversations that they have heard at second or third hand.
All this is called testimony in France.

New York Times, February 25, 1898

An American or Englishman, when he crosses the Straits of Dover to
France, often feels that he is half way to China. Trials of this kind
tend to confirm the impression that the French people . . . in regard
to their development, are midway between the English and the
Chinese.

American Law Review, 1898

It has been said that no institution in the United States has been held in
greater esteem than that of the judiciary, no principle considered a more
indispensable component of a democratic society than the guarantee of
equality before the law to each individual.[1] This conviction, though hon-
ored as frequently in the breach as in practice, provided Americans with
a yardstick with which to measure the temper of other societies, and the
Dreyfus affair provided them with just such an opportunity. Senators,
congressmen, and the president himself were showered with cables
from anxious constituents demanding that official action be taken in
response to the unjust second verdict of 1899, though there is no indication that President McKinley complied with such petitions. Congress
had adjourned for the summer holiday, but a New York newspaper was
convinced that had it been in session a strong congressional protest
would have been lodged on behalf of Dreyfus. The governor of New

History repeats itself
L'histoire se répète. Comparaison entre Simpson et Dreyfus.

The Indictment of French Jurisprudence   27

York, Theodore Roosevelt, remarked that it was a "rare thing for the whole nation to watch the trial of a single citizen of another nation."[2] Yet, as Hannah Arendt observes, it was hardly novel for the generation of the nineties to be stirred by a miscarriage of justice. Such behavior was "typical of the nineteenth century," she writes; "men followed legal proceedings . . . keenly because each instance afforded a test of the century's greatest achievement, the complete impartiality of the law."[3]

Viewed from this perspective, one might say that the Dreyfus affair belonged as much to America as it did to France. The mistreatment of Dreyfus, commented the *Nation*, "was committed theatrically in the face of the whole world." In that age of innocence Americans believed that France was, or at least should be, seriously concerned with their opinions in the matter. "It is incredible that the Court of Cassation [the French Supreme Court of Appeal] will do injustice," remarked the *New York Times*, with "all the world looking on, with the evidence all displayed, and with the public judging the judges." "If Dreyfus is crushed his country will be crushed with him and France will be the scorn of the civilized world."[4]

In an era of growing insistence upon the social responsibility of the courts, legal soul-searching, and reassessment of traditional constitutional principles, an important judicial event, regardless of where it occurred, commanded an inordinate amount of attention. Compelling questions were being raised in the United States about the relation of law to society, the evolution of the court system, comparative jurisprudence, and the traditional ways of arriving at just decisions. Laymen too were more curious than ever about the structure and operation of the law. Its intricacies had become public property, and discussions about its complexity and meaning became a popular pastime. Roscoe Pound, the generation's great legal teacher, urged lawyers to respect the public's right to know, to clarify "what law is and why law is and what law does and why it does so." Good law, he believed, must hold its own at the bar of public opinion: "Today the reasons behind the law must be such as appeal to an intelligent and educated public. There must be reasons behind it, as there must be behind everything that is imposed upon the people of the present." An irrational or incomprehensible system of jurisprudence has no place in a modern, pragmatic society, said Pound. Courts, according to George Kirchwey, the dean of the Columbia University Law School, "are set in their high places as interpreters of the popular sense of justice, not as interpreters of obscure oracles."[5] In this context, it is understandable that Americans would react so strongly to reports of legal mismanagement in France.

■ The matter of the authorship of the *bordereau*, the pivotal document and the principal piece of evidence in the case against Dreyfus, suggests how conjecture and confusion befuddled America's image of Gallic judicial behavior. The *bordereau*, a list of vital military data written on an onionskin type of paper, was found shredded in the wastepaper basket of the German military attaché by a French agent. French Intelligence claimed that it was written by Dreyfus, since the handwriting appeared very similar to his. Handwriting experts were summoned to support this assertion. Although they disagreed among themselves, Dreyfus was found guilty largely because of the testimony of one of these "experts," Alphonse Bertillon.

The truth was that Bertillon, associated for many years with the Paris police, was not a handwriting expert at all, but an authority on criminal identification—to be more specific, a specialist in the field of statistical anthropometric measurements. An admirer of the French military, Bertillon, when first called in on the case, was given to understand that apart from the *bordereau*, there was already a considerable body of evidence against Dreyfus. Although pompous and opinionated, he was not the type to challenge the military. It required little more than a similarity of handwritings to convince him that the *bordereau* was in Dreyfus' hand.

Prior to 1897 Bertillon's reputation was very high in criminal investigation circles in the United States, where his contributions to legal anthropometry were held in high esteem. His system of identification, which preceded the more modern method of fingerprinting, was based on a minute classification of bone measurements, such as the width of the prisoner's head and other personal characteristics. It was described by an American admirer as *"scientific and absolutely infallible."* Bertillon, Americans were told, *"has never mistaken one single prisoner for another."*[6]

Given his international reputation, it is not surprising that Bertillon was invited to pass judgment on questions of chirography. At the 1894 courtmartial Bertillon explained to the army chiefs in elaborate and scientific-sounding language his certainty that the *bordereau* was written in Dreyfus' hand. Although none present were able to follow his argument, the military judges were quick to support his assertions rather than those of the dissenting experts, not only because of his reputation in the field of criminal apprehension but also because it was his testimony that they really wished to hear. For this reason he was invited by the prosecution to testify against Dreyfus in all the subsequent trials which grew out of the case. In each of these trials Bertillon clung stubbornly to his original thesis that Dreyfus was the author of the *bordereau*. His testimony became increasingly verbose, contradictory, and unintelligible. Americans were at first intrigued by his testimony and his elaborate theories, but their opinion soon changed. By 1899 his courtroom orations were a standing joke in the United States, and he was being referred to as the "prince of quacks," a "scientific ass" whose "trunkful of demonstrations would adorn the comedy stage."[7]

Bertillon suggested that Dreyfus had forged his own handwriting, a proposal considered by American observers as "inconceivable." For treating his theories with seriousness, Americans described the French as suffering from "*bordereau* on the brain." Bertillon's frequent courtroom appearances were designated as "grotesque," and his testimony, Americans agreed, "would not be considered for a moment in an American or English court" and like everything else about the Dreyfus case, was "utterly without coherence or logic."[8]

The most sophisticated analysis of Bertillon's testimonies was developed by Frank P. Blair, an American criminal lawyer, who observed that the Frenchman's theory had flowered in stages, between 1894 and 1899, reaching full bloom at the Rennes courtmartial "in a disquisition of seven hours."[9] Bertillon, noted Blair in an essay on the Frenchman's work, proceeded from his assumption that Dreyfus was "a shrewd man, a skillful man, a man of extensive technical learning, a man of resources," obviously not one "likely to plunge into treasonable practices without taking minute precautions." Dreyfus, Bertillon believed, would certainly not "write an incriminating letter like the *bordereau* without first disguising his hand," but not in the way ordinary mortals would: Dreyfus would avail himself of the ultimate protection. His forgery, Bertillon explained, would "have to show that the handwriting differed from his own," and, in the event that the compromising document were found in his possession, he had cleverly fortified himself with an additional alibi, one which would "enable him to set up as a defense a conspiracy against himself, an 'alibi de machination.'" This he would accomplish by shifting suspicion to his brother, Mathieu, thereby compelling their joint trial in the civil rather than the military courts. This ingenious construction Bertillon designated "auto-forgery," that is to say, he explained, Dreyfus forged his own handwriting, "intending, if arrested, to show that it was not his natural hand, but a counterfeit thereof." "In short," continued Blair, "the difference between Dreyfus's natural hand and that of the *bordereau*, admitted by Bertillon, was according to him, artfully put in by Captain Dreyfus to throw off suspicion; while the absolute similarities were put in to enable him, in a proper case, to claim they were traced from his own handwriting, and therefore, done by someone else."

Blair took note of Bertillon's admission that "it required vast ingenuity to conceive such a plan" and his modesty in neglecting to mention
"the ingenuity required to unravel it." This amazing hypothesis, con-
fessed Blair, "cannot be said to clarify the subject at all" but tended
rather to confuse the issue. Its exposition left judges, lawyers, and juries
exhausted and bewildered and raised serious doubts about Bertillon's
mental stability. As Blair put it, "I do not mean to imply that [insanity] is
M. Bertillon's mental condition; but certainly a neurologist would
regard his [pattern of thought], if coupled with other symptoms, as an
unfortunate sign." At any rate, concluded Blair, the world was in Bertillon's debt "for a new idea, the conception of a man forging his own
handwriting!"[10] It was not until the middle of 1906, however, that Bertillon's quackery was fully and officially exposed. On June 22 the *New
York Times* reported that a committee of prominent French scientists had
concluded that Bertillon's handwriting theories "were absolutely without scientific value," being based "not only upon vague probabilities, but
on false documents."[11]

■ The Bertillon incident was but one illustration of the confused image
of French legal behavior taking shape across the Atlantic; in fact, much
that was connected with the Dreyfus affair became increasingly incomprehensible, even ludicrous to Americans. Courtroom scenes were
referred to as "a mockery of justice," "an opéra-bouffe performance."
Even Americans with no special training in the law thought it peculiar
that witnesses were allowed to indulge in lengthy and irrelevant digres-
sions or were given the right to remain silent under interrogation. The
denial of cross-examination to counsel was also found unacceptable, as
was the unprofessional behavior of the French judiciary in molding its
decisions to appease a public clamor.[12] Cynicism was mixed with resentment in the United States during the Rennes courtmartial. "Ridiculous
and undignified—it was an instrument of insolence toward the accused
and his defender"—so one editorial ran:

> Seen from this distance, the whole proceeding was a burlesque
> more extravagant than ever figured in Offenbach's wildest fancy. The
> witnesses for the prosecution were excused from the task of stating
> facts and from the responsibility of confining themselves within the
> bounds of relevancy. They were prosecutors, special pleaders, denun-
> ciators and demagogues to supplement their ignorance. They flew
> into frantic and violent harangues. Instead of evidence they gave
> imprecations. Baffled, discomfitted, and contradicted, in a manner

which would have thrown them out of court in this country. . . . In the history of the civilized world, there has not been an incident so shameful and disheartening.[13]

The temptation to caricature rather than condemn Dreyfus' second trial was strong. A typical dramatization follows:

> Judge: Did you say your name was Alfred or Alphonse Dreyfus? Be careful how you reply.
> Dreyfus: Alfred Dreyfus is my name.
> Judge: Ah, ha. Why did you say "Alfred Dreyfus is my name," instead of "My name is Alfred Dreyfus"?
> Dreyfus: Really, *mon colonel,* I don't—
> Judge: You hesitate. You look confused. I note the fact that you uncrossed your legs when I asked you this question. That is proof of an uneasy conscience. What have you to say?
> Dreyfus: I can't—
> Judge: He can't. This is a confession. He is guilty. (sensation)
> Dreyfus: No, *mon colonel,* I am innocent.
> Judge: If you are innocent, perhaps you will tell where you were the night before last at fifteen minutes past ten?
> Dreyfus: In jail.
> Judge: Where were you on January 11, 1896?
> Dreyfus: In jail.
> Judge: Where were you on the night of March 3, 1897?
> Dreyfus: In jail.
> Judge: Where were you when the Suburban was run in 1898?
> Dreyfus: In jail.
> Judge (triumphantly): Always in jail, yet this *canaille* claims to be innocent. Once more, where were you on the 29th of February, 1899?
> Dreyfus: In jail.
> Judge: *Sacrebleu!* You convict yourself. There was no 29th of February, 1899.[14]

The conviction stunned Americans. "We rub our eyes to see clearer, [if] we are still living in modern, not medieval, times as such monstrous injustice might indicate. It seems incredible that the defiance of conscience, reason, and justice could take place in the last part of the last year of that century which we are fond of regarding as the most civilized of all epochs." It mattered little that Dreyfus was being tried by a military court. To Americans all courts were equal, all trials alike and subject to identical moral strictures; each was expected to dispense justice according to due process, equitably and impartially and in a manner comprehensible to Americans.[15]

■ Few events provided Americans with a better opportunity to compare their own courtroom practices with those of a foreign nation than the Dreyfus case. From the point of view of comparative jurisprudence, the event could not have occurred at a more propitious moment, for the study of the evolution and differentiation of legal institutions had become a popular exercise for both students and practitioners of law. The true jurist, noted an authority on legal education in 1899, must approach his calling from two directions: first, through the understanding of "the law of his own country," by probing its origins and evolution, and second, by comparing it with the legal practices of other nations.[16]

Still, it is difficult to avoid the impression that contemporary interest in comparative legal systems had been aroused not solely by detached scholarly curiosity but rather by a wish to trace the long historic ascent of Anglo-Saxon law so as to document the superiority of the English common law over the Roman systems. Such exercises were popular contests, with the victor predetermined in the minds of both writer and reader.

It was this type of thinking which prompted the British jurist Lord Bryce to explain with pride to an American audience that Anglo-American legal institutions were characterized by a greater degree of "exactitude" than the law of other people. Safeguards under the common law, he said, "prevented the mistreatment of accused persons and that recourse to torture . . . common in Continental Europe." Common law instilled in the legal profession "the feeling that an accused person ought to have a fair run for life or freedom." Unlike French courts, English-speaking courts were marked by the "self-restraint which experienced counsel impose on themselves when conducting a case" and "by the care . . . which the judge takes to let the prisoner have the benefit of every circumstance in his favor. . . . How different things are in some parts of the European continent is known to you all."[17] Other commentators pointed out that the common law lacked the "despotic spirit and tendencies which France . . . inherited from the imperial jurisprudence." It was more responsive to the will of the people. Unlike the law of the non-English Europeans, "it did not descend . . . from an ancient and foreign wisdom or authority. . . . It did not come from above but from all around."[18] Anglo-American practitioners were not the docile servants of power, as in countries like France, where the physical force of the executive ruled and determined the law. They were guided by precedents and knowledge of the law.

This growing interest in comparative legal systems, with particular emphasis on French legal proceedings in the Dreyfus case, was reflected in the law journals, which expanded their discussions of French juridical matters.[19] They traced for lawyers and laymen the development of the French judicial system from the chaotic conditions of the ancient regime to the less than perfect edifice rebuilt under the Code of Napoleon. Americans were unclear about the precise meaning of the term "revision," frequently employed in press accounts: did it mean reopen, or review? They were bewildered by the contrary reports that dribbled through the wire services about the progress of the case. As one legal authority explained, in France "every accused person is looked upon as guilty. This wrong tendency is not the result of intentional ill-will upon the part of anybody, but is a consequence of a badly ordered judicial system." It was also regrettable, Americans were told, that the French courts permitted an excessive number of lawyers to be admitted as advocates, many of whom were of mediocre ability, too easily swayed by political winds and administrative pressures, and too weak to "soar above the level of the agitated community and hold the balance evenly between small and great, weak and strong, iniquity and right."[20]

Some Americans were puzzled about the structure and operation of the Court of Cassation, the French High Court of Appeal, as they read of its deliberations over the feasibility of "revision" of the Dreyfus case in 1898 and 1899. One writer described it as consisting of

> a Chief Justice and a public prosecutor, who are on equal footing, three presiding judges, forty-five counsellors [i.e., judges] and six attorney-generals. All of them receive higher salaries than the judges of other courts. They sit in a splendid court, decorated by the best modern painters. When they demand it, they have a guard of picked soldiers. They are dressed in red gowns and ermine mantles. All of them try to appear dignified, and the majority of them are most serious. The advocates who plead before them form a body apart from the rest of the bar, and in jurisdiction the decrees rendered within those sacred walls have almost the weight of law, despite the fact that they are often contradictory.

Unlike the Supreme Court of the United States, it was explained, the French high tribunal was divided into three distinct bodies, or chambers: a civil chamber, a criminal chamber, and a chamber of indictments, with a president or chief justice presiding over all and a president for each. In special circumstances, as in the Dreyfus case, the three chambers convened as a single body.[21] As the national supreme court of appeal, the Court of Cassation sat in Paris. Appeals were directed to it from inferior courts but would be entertained only on a point of law, that is, on an error in an indictment, writes Joel Benton, an American lawyer. The Court of Cassation was also designated a school of jurisprudence, since it had a bar of its own not connected with the other courts. As in the United States, its justices were appointed by the chief of state and could be removed only for misconduct. Its wheels ground slowly; even a simple case brought before it, noted Benton, was subject to endless delays that "would take pages to describe, no matter how simple, certain, and plain your case may be." Since courts remained closed from August to November, except in unusual circumstances such as the Dreyfus case, and did not begin work before eleven in the morning, French judges, according to the American commentator, were not overworked. What is more, Benton informed his American readers, "an advocate at the bar cannot do any ordinary business. He cannot be a doctor or teacher: he can be an actor only if he acts without pay. But he can be in Parliament—a deputy or a senator. An advocate cannot ask for fees— the client must offer them. So says the rule—but, before the suit is begun, the advocate knows well how to get around it."[22]

As Americans compared these divergent legal practices, they became increasingly dismayed at the vast gulf that separated them from France. One frequently mentioned source of alarm was the French rule of law which, it was believed, made a presumption of the guilt of the accused, so that the burden of proof lay on the defense, not the prosecution. Americans were also struck by the partisan behavior of French judges, who might side with a plaintiff or a defendant and then, from this position, badger and browbeat witnesses even before the details of the case had been presented in open court. According to the *Nation*, a French judge performed the dual role of an American district attorney and the jury: "His power is almost absolute over counsel and prisoner." However, in terms of his ability to control the behavior of courtroom audiences and the decorum of its proceedings, likened by one journalist to "a general beer-garden," the French judge was deemed a failure.[23]

A serious indictment of French judicial behavior, in American eyes, was provided by the method employed in the interrogation of witnesses. Before a question could be put to the witness, it had first to be put to the presiding judge. If the judge thought the question irrelevant or objectionable he could refuse to put it to the witness. "Thus French lawyers can ingeniously frame argumentative questions favorable to their side which the jury hear even if these cannot be answered" by the witness. Furthermore, as witnesses were called to testify they were permitted to veer from the facts and indulge in "hearsay observations, and . . . to express opinions or practically make speeches to the jurors." In French criminal courts, observed an American political analyst, "witnesses are neither examined nor cross-examined by counsel although they were permitted to insult one another or digress into irrelevant disquisitions."[24] During the Zola trial even Picquart, who was generally admired in the United States, was accused of being overly verbose in his testimony. In their closing summations, both prosecution and defense lawyers included material which in the United States would have been considered irrelevant and ruled out of order: "Each was a studied oration, dealing in a flood of statements and arguments that were perceptibly outside of the evidence." Speeches were unusually lengthy, extending for several days and frequently interrupted from the spectators' gallery.[25] Even Maître Labori, the defender of Zola, was not immune from criticism. In the midst of the Zola trial, Whitridge complained that Labori

> read an article from the *Libre Parole* saying that he, Labori, was only a naturalized Frenchman, that his father was a German, his mother an English Jewess, and his own wife the divorced wife of Pachman, a German who still visited his children at Labori's house; and, having read the article, the lawyer categorically denied the statements it contained. The incident deserves to be particularly considered. We cannot understand it. Nothing could better illustrate the danger of our endeavoring to estimate French institutions by our own standards.[26]

Even more serious, from an American perspective, was the apparent absence of any comprehensible set of rules of evidence: "the testimony was a most extraordinary mixture of fact, froth, inference, hearsay and conjecture, revealing how the safeguards of personal liberty, which have been embedded in the fundamental law of every English-speaking state since 1688, may, in France, be trampled upon and outraged." Everything is let in, or everything is let out, "according to the mere discretion of the presiding judge or the court," commented an American lawyer. The framers of the French criminal code, explained the president of the American Bar Association, carried away by their wish to alter the rules of evidence which existed under the Roman law "and, for fear of making others equally ridiculous . . . made none at all, but left everything to the judges."[27] The *Nation* remarked with displeasure that the Rennes courtmartial "has not been confined to the subject of the inquiry at any time, but has ranged through the whole earth and the things under the earth. . . . The rules for the admissibility of evidence," it reminded its readers, "constitute the foundation of the whole structure of jurisprudence, and they are just as necessary, just as indispensable, in a military trial as in any other. . . . Tested by the rules of evidence, the case against Dreyfus has already vanished." In French courts, said the *New York Times*, "witnesses have appeared before the judges and have spoken their minds freely. They have not presented evidence. They have given their opinions. They have expressed the opinions of others. They have repeated conversations that they have heard at second or third hand. All this is called testimony in France."[28]

Gossip, rumor, and "inner conviction," Americans were informed by the *Times*, had replaced evidence in the French judiciary. "The theory is," explained V. M. Rose, an American lawyer, "that whatever tends to show that [the defendant] is a bad man will tender it more probable that he has committed the particular crime with which he is charged." A trial in France, Rose observed, opened with a detailed review of all the "sins, real or imputed, of the prisoner, committed during a whole lifetime."

> Having started out with the assertion that the prisoner is guilty not only of the crime charged, but of many others as well, the judge then proceeds to interrogate him concerning every evil or suspicious circumstance attending his whole life . . . suggested by mere love of scandal and gossip, or invented by malice. . . . This would be a hard ordeal for the best man that ever lived; as no one could be ready to disprove on the spur of the moment all false reports that might have circulated concerning him either through mistake, spite, recklessness, covering his whole life. . . . Prisoners, confused and terrified, under such circumstances often succumb wholly, and answer at random, not knowing what they are saying.

Upon what grounds was a verdict rendered in France, Rose asked:

> Is it on the opinions of witnesses concerning the guilt or inno- cence of the accused? Or the slashing articles in the newspaper which the jurors have diligently read? Or on a multitude of idle and more or less conflicting rumors? Or on the prevailing sentiment of the audience as manifested in the courtroom? Or on the testimony of witnesses knowing the facts of which they speak? No one can tell.

Rose believed he was justified in the conclusion that, in regard to France, rules of evidence "may be classified along with the snakes in Ireland: there are none."[29]

■ Equally puzzling and ominous to some American sensibilities was the function of the French magistrate, the *juge d'instruction*, whose task was described as being somewhat vaguely analogous to that of the grand jury in the United States, that is, to prepare a preliminary examination and report on the prisoner. It was in the exercise of this responsibility, however, that all comparison with American practices came to an end. James B. Eustis described it as "a process of mental torture," in which "the accused is required to incriminate himself by his own testimony."[30] Through this method data was compiled into a dossier and presented to the trial judge.

The *New York Evening Journal* described the *juge d'instruction* as "neither judge, grand jury, public prosecutor, chief of detectives nor friend of the family; yet he touches on all these characters in one day's work." A person accused of an offense in France immediately falls into the clutches of this "amiable personage," whose first duty is to "overwhelm him with a mass of doubts and fears." His second duty is to "lead him to confess that he is guilty." His third duty is to "lay neat traps for him, so that he may be tripped up nicely at the trial." Unlike what was experienced in the United States, "when a man is accused of anything in France the first thing is to throw him into close confinement. Often he does not know of what he is accused. He sits in his cell. . . . He may not see his friends. He may not see his lawyer. . . . He may see no newspapers." The prisoner's only contact is with the *juge d'instruction*. If by chance the obstinate prisoner refuses to speak to this agent, he may well linger on in his cell for months until the necessary dossier is compiled.[31] The accused has no ability to defend himself during the preliminary stages of his indictment: "The right of bail, the writ of *habeas corpus* and all those other guarantees to secure the rights, and safeguard the personal liberty of the citizen against arbitrary acts of the Government, which are provided for in our Constitution, having been borrowed by us from the English Law, are not to be found in the French Constitution."[32]

If the French government chooses to oppress "a citizen by his illegal arrest and imprisonment, no matter what may be its duration, it is considered his affair, and not that of his fellow-citizens," *Harper's Weekly* explained, and cautioned Americans about falling into the clutches of French law:

> How many of our traveling pleasure-seekers, sojourning for a gala-day in Paris, realize that an enemy or a policeman . . . might easily divert their visit from one of gayety to one of penalty? An arrest is an

easy matter. It is easy here and in London, but practically it is not so
common an indulgence of the Anglo-Saxon as of the French police.
But once the accused is behind the cell door the matter takes on a
different aspect in France from that to which we are accustomed. . . .
There is no reason known to the French law for informing the
accused of the nature of the charge which has led to his incarceration. All that is necessary to keep him in prison for an indefinite time
is an understanding between the policeman and the magistrate—the
Judge d'Instruction. It is for this embodiment of French law and
French justice to discover some reason for depriving the victim of his
liberty, and in the meantime the victim must remain in ignorance. He
is not to know the charge that is made against him; but from time to
time he is haled before the *Judge d'Instruction* and examined as to his
life, his secret thoughts, his relations to society—in short he is probed
for hidden crimes, or for evidence of the truth of the charge which
some policeman may have lodged against him. . . . The accused is
kept in close confinement. His house is searched. His desk is broken
open. His private papers are carried to the magistrate, to whom the
postoffice authorities also deliver his mail. If he were an American or
an Englishman in his own land, he would be before the open courts,
as soon as he applied, on a writ of *habeas corpus* and the government
would be compelled to state the charge against him. In France he is
in the power of a practically irresponsible despot.[33]

Informed of such practices, Americans concluded that the system of
French law had not yet attained the character of a civilized, Western
society.[34]

■ In 1898 and 1899 the case of Alfred Dreyfus became a topic of discussion at the annual convention of the American Bar Association. The
lawyers in attendance, generally noted for the conservatism of their language, did not hesitate to denounce French judicial behavior. One delegate justified such criticism on the grounds that since "we have our
independence here and are removed by the ocean from the countries of
the Old World," American lawyers had a moral obligation to express
their opinion and judgment on the matter. An American point of view,
asserted another lawyer, would carry a "greater weight than if it had
proceeded from any of the kingdoms or republics of the continent of
Europe." It did not seem to matter to members of the American bar that
their comments concerned judicial proceedings of a military rather than
a civil court. A delegate from North Carolina, F. H. Busbee, expressed
it this way: "A court-martial is a legal and constitutional tribunal, and

the fact that it is composed of army officers, does not render it any less a regular court."[35]

Disenchantment with the French judiciary induced the editors of the *American Law Review* to urge the International Law Association to change the location of its annual meeting for 1900 from Rouen. "The French are incapable of understanding the meaning of justice," they argued: "The touch of the soil of France is to the feet of an upright lawyer of another nation, pollution." When a correspondent from Nova Scotia protested at the abrasive rhetoric, the editors of the *Review* retorted with evident anger: "We are not in the habit of speaking with bated breath about such matters as the Dreyfus affair. We do not abate one jot or tittle of the language used."[36]

Intertwined with this critical view of French jurisprudence was a desire to reassert the superiority of Anglo-Saxon legal institutions through the vehicle of the Zola and Dreyfus trials:

> Trials of this kind tend to confirm the impression that the French people, although we must accord to them the position on the whole of being a gallant and self-respecting people,—are in many respects, in regard to their development, midway between the English and the Chinese. . . . The peculiarity of French justice presented by the trials of Dreyfus and Zola is calculated to sicken and nauseate the people of other nationalities, and especially of England and the United States.[37]

Such trials, delcared Joseph Choate, might be satisfactory to the people of France, but for Americans they could only "excite horror and disgust." After observing the judicial treatment of Zola, he could not repress the cry, "Thank God! I am an American." "This single event, so shocking to our sense of justice and right," he went on, "has done more, I am happy to believe, than whole volumes of argument to strengthen and perpetuate our faith in our wholly different system of procedure for the ascertainment of facts on which life, liberty or property are to be brought in judgment."[38]

There was a general consensus in the American press that the procedure against Dreyfus could not have taken place in England or the United States: "It is practically impossible under the Anglo-Saxon system," said *Harper's Weekly*. Americans were disappointed in France. Notwithstanding its great revolution, a true spirit of change had failed to permeate the fabric of its social existence. "They turn kings and emperors off their thrones, they upset governments, but they never think of reforming the system on which rest the relative rights of the government and the governed." The *New York Times* added: "The French people and we do not travel along the same legal road toward justice."[39]

American editorials urged repeatedly that France mend its ways and erect "the safeguards of innocence that exist in other civilized countries." "Common justice is the first and most indispensable condition of a free country's existence." The tragedy of France was far from irrelevant to the thought of the English-speaking world, which viewed the debasement of a democracy as a universal concern.[40]

The American collapse of confidence in the moral and legal standards of France culminated in the extreme demand that extraterritorial privileges be accorded to Americans residing in France. Such exhortations were not widespread or even hotly urged, but the fact that they were even heard in a few reputable circles underscores the depth to which French jurisprudence had sunk in the popular imagination. The demand was first raised in connection with the trial of Émile Zola, on which occasion the *New York Times* remarked that "if Zola, a French citizen of some wealth and much repute, could be made the victim of irresponsible power exercised from behind the cringing shoulders of French judges and jurymen, what certainty, what probability even, is there that a foreigner's rights will be respected in the French tribunals, or that he will not be dealt with in any way that gallic prejudices or fears may dictate?" Extraterritorial judicial procedures were already employed in oriental nations, so that the precedent was there, said the *Times*:

> Civilized nations do not allow their subjects to be tried in the courts of China because they doubt both the power and inclination of a semi-civilized race to try an alien fairly. In short, the need for extraterritorial courts is recognized and their establishment is insisted upon wherever the ordinary principles of right and equity, as understood by real Occidentals, are not observed by the local officials. Who will say that extraterritorial courts are not needed in France? If an American or an Englishman should by chance be tried and punished as Zola was, the spectacle would be unendurable, and yet that fate may befall any one of the many Americans and Englishmen temporarily residing in the so-called republic.[41]

The *Nation* also concluded that the chief lesson drawn from the Dreyfus event was that "there is no judicial system, outside that of England and the United States, under which a political or military prisoner, or indeed any one charged with a criminal offense, can be sure of a fair trial." Every effort must be exerted to avoid recourse to a French tribunal. The American response to French judicial misbehavior, sug-

gested one editorialist, could most appropriately be expressed by insti-
tuting consular jurisdiction: "Without doubt France has placed herself
in that category, and such a demand would be the logical rejoinder to
the verdict."[42] It was a harsh indictment, but it mirrored the intensity of
American feelings about France in the summer of 1899.

V

Dreyfus and American
Anti-Militarism

We have in France a perfect specimen of what we might call an attempt at a de-civilized state—that is, a state in which military are taking the place of civic ideals.

A. G. SEDGWICK, *Nation*
August 16, 1898

Thus it was to "save the honor of the country" that the truth was suppressed and lies, forgeries and perjuries were put forward in its stead. It was to "save the honor of the country" that an innocent man was condemned to a punishment crueler than death. . . . that is the military and official idea of honor.

New York World, August 17, 1899

Not all Americans jolted by the absence of what they considered proper judicial norms in France argued from the same premise. Some, as we have seen, interpreted French legal disarray as a logical outgrowth of a vitiated Gallic-Roman culture. Others, and their number included some of the most distinguished citizens at the turn of the century—reformers and men of letters—were Dreyfusards but were not totally captivated by the blustering Anglo-Saxonism of many of Dreyfus' American supporters. They took small comfort in the military and imperialistic adventures launched in the name of Anglo-Saxon progress. They viewed the Spanish-American War and subsequent imperial experiments as crimes. "Don't yelp with the pack," Williams James, one of the most distinguished of this group, counseled his Harvard undergraduates in 1898. Although it attracted a diverse cluster of people, the core of this group of anti-militarists and anti-imperialists had been educated in Eastern universities and had family roots deeply imbedded in seven-

42

teenth-century New England. Its members saw themselves as a republican aristocracy, custodians of American cultural and political values, with an indisputable right to lead their country. Many of these critics of modern American tendencies were in their sixties, politically independent, and experienced; they were particularly harsh with those who were introducing a combative and expansive mood into American life.[1] These collective voices rose to a crescendo in the last three years of the century, the years in which the Dreyfus event was occupying world imagination. They attacked France as consistently as they did militarism in general and American imperialism in particular. They too were proud of their Anglo-Saxon racial heritage and held as high hopes for its future as did their Anglo-American brethren, but their aspirations and visions of what was best for their fellow-citizens were quite different.[2]

They stirred up controversy in America, organized an anti-imperialist league with chapters in numerous cities, made speeches, distributed literature, and by 1900 could claim thirty thousand members and more than half a million fellow-travelers.[3] Like those they opposed, they were not out of tune with their age; the degree of their impact and influence upon America was not overwhelming, but they added an element of moral vitality to American criticism of France. The revelation that in the French republic significant judicial issues were being resolved on the basis of military expediency and that generals rather than courts were dictating judicial decisions moved them profoundly.

It is interesting that even those who took a measure of personal pride in their country's recent imperial and military achievements were susceptible to anti-military rhetoric. A pervasive suspicion of the military, especially when coupled with ominous hints of its possible involvement in civil matters, was deeply imbedded in the American psyche. The nation's newly won prominence in international affairs as a result of its resounding victory over Spain did little to mitigate this innate caution about things military. Popular aversion to peacetime standing armies was a fact of life accepted, with some bitterness, by American military leaders, and the war with Spain did little to change this view. As a result of that conflict the United States Army was increased from twenty-five thousand to sixty-five thousand men, still tiny by European standards. Lieutenant-Colonel James S. Pettit of the Eighth Infantry remonstrated that "a great many of our people would oppose any substantial increase in our military organization. The masses are indifferent. Labor organizations are not friendly to the militia, and political parties cater to their wishes to obtain their votes. . . . The lessons taught by the Spanish-American War have almost if not entirely been forgotten."[4] The *Army and Navy Journal* was annoyed that Americans were being "ruled by an arbitrary and irresponsible popular opinion which, through a certain sublimated optimism which is at once benevolent and baneful, treats military service as inconsequential and renders it well-nigh impossible to maintain the rigorous discipline which is indispensable to an effective army."[5]

Americans, it appeared, accepted their army only as a necessary burden, preferring, if at all possible, to keep it invisible, isolating it "politically, intellectually, socially and . . . physically."[6] Unlike the situation in Europe, where standing armies had an importance unknown in the United States, special efforts were made to keep the American military from involvement in the formulation of domestic and foreign policies: "The army was still on the periphery of world politics. Its tradition was purely continental." Strung out along the western frontier, it was little heard of and even less seen, and Americans preferred to keep it that way.[7]

Given this deeply ingrained suspicion of things military, it is easy to understand why the Dreyfus event aroused feelings of hostility toward militarism in general and toward the French military in particular. From the American perspective, there was little question as to the true culprit in the affair: it was the French army. G. W. Steevens expressed a popular view when he observed that "in one respect alone can France claim pity—that she became bankrupt in justice through honouring too large a draft of her darling child, the army." He found something pathetic about the adulation Frenchmen accorded their army, which had only recently been humiliated on the field of battle, "crumpled up, shot down . . . and carried into captivity." He was startled to learn that in France "the daily passage of the regiment empties every shop, and leaves the whole street tingling with pride and enthusiasm and love." What was the explanation for this peculiar behavior, Steevens wondered. Could it be that "France feels a sort of yearning to comfort her army as a mother might comfort an unsuccessful son?"[8] The French Revolution, it appeared, had little effect upon such matters in France. "The French," editorialized a Boston daily, "are as instinctively a military people at the end of this century as they were at the beginning of it, and are as ready as they were then to allow their worship of the sabre and epaulettes."

Returning to New York from a vacation in France, Senator Chauncy Depew described to his constituents the deep infatuation which he witnessed between France and her military. "The Army is the darling of

France," he told a reporter. "Every speech begins with fulsome praise of the Army. All politicians bow to it, and say 'You are the hope, the strength, the salvation of France.' . . . We cannot conceive in our country of the Army thus dominating and dictating." Even John Dos Passos conceded that France's militaristic values could prove unsettling to the Anglo-American accord: The "entire conception and development of the Army," he declared "is contrary to true republican principles."[9]

It was inevitable that a people so captivated would refuse to admit that its army was capable of error or misdeeds. Consequently, they looked away while the French military chiefs "banded themselves together in a fraternity of crime and hate" to persecute "an innocent man in order that a traitor might be screened."[10] Incompetent in war, the French generals were pictured as equally inept in their dealings with civilian society. This was shown in their handling of the Dreyfus matter:

> The Dreyfus case was their own game, and they had all the cards; but . . . they could not play a single one correctly. Wherever it was possible to bungle or vacillate, they bungled and vacillated.
>
> They first admitted in the press that Dreyfus was condemned on secret documents—that is, illegally—and then denied it in the Chamber. They first contended that Dreyfus wrote the incriminating *bordereau* because it was like his natural handwriting, then that he forged it, because it was more like Esterhazy's. . . . They filled the air with asseverations of their loyalty to the Republic while they were openly violating its fundamentals. . . . The great international result of three years of government by generals is that France has virtually showed herself unfit for war by sea or land—afraid of England, terrified by Germany, the vassal of Russia—all but a second rate power.[11]

It was almost impossible to hear a flattering comment about the French General Staff in the United States. Its behavior, it was said, conjured up visions of "the decline of the Roman Empire, of the days when the Praetorian Guards were putting the Government up at auction." A visit of Admiral Dewey to France shortly after his great victory at Manila Bay prompted the *New York Times* to suggest that Frenchmen observe him carefully so that they might compare him with "the 'heroes' now prosecuting Dreyfus."[12]

Many Americans were puzzled by the support Frenchmen offered their patently corrupt military establishment. They displayed little sympathy for a nation that covered its eyes and refused to admit any wrongdoing, which persisted in clinging desperately to the skirts of its military irrespective of its behavior. Americans believed themselves to be a patriotic people, but the blind chauvinism of the French was beyond their comprehension. James Eustis explained that "the dual cry of *Vive la France* and *Vive l'Armée* has a deep significance. Every Frenchman patriotically believes that the honor of both is in his individual safe-keeping." The premise that the "honor" of the French army required the sacrifice of an innocent individual was repugnant: "It would be incredible that any Frenchman should suppose that military honor needs the sacrifice of an innocent man." "To have strangled justice, suppressed freedom of speech, exiled or insulted her noblest—and to have done it to preserve stainless an honor which was all the while covering itself with pitch!" the *Nation* found beyond belief. "Instead of the old motto, 'Let justice be done though the heavens fall,'" said the *Nation*, the French were saying "Let the army remain unsuspected though justice fall."[13]

The admission of Colonel Henry's widow that her husband had forged some of the documents used to convict Dreyfus, and her statement that he had done so to "save the honor of the country," also aroused astonishment. Such loyalty many Americans could not respect. "Thus it was to 'save the honor of the country' that an innocent man was condemned to a punishment crueler than death. . . . that is the military and official idea of honor."[14] The French, it was argued, had embraced a dangerous syllogism—that "the honour of the heads of the army, is the honour of the army, and therefore France." In practice, this obviously meant that "a general can do no wrong. . . . It comes, of course, in practice to the divine right of generals."[15]

This French concept of honor troubled Americans, and the repeated use of the term in press dispatches generated ridicule. "Th' throuble is, mong colonel . . . that it ain't been Cap Dhryfuss that's been on thrile, but th' honor iv th' nation an' th' honor iv th' ar-amy," said Mr. Dooley. After learning of the decision to pardon Dreyfus following his second conviction in September, 1899, a journalist complained: "Dreyfus was convicted to satisfy the 'honor' of the French Army. Now he will be pardoned to satisfy the honor of the French people. The whole business is dishonorable."[16]

As they read about and pondered French events, some Americans sensed in these occurrences a peculiar relevance to their own lives. John P. Altgeld, the liberal ex-governor of Illinois, saw in France's obsession with armed forces the tragic consequences of unbridled national support of a large standing army whose honor "must be maintained if a nation will be imperial." Dreyfus, he warned, was a "vicarious sacrifice" to the alleged honor of the Army of France. Fearful of the growth of their own armed forces, Americans pointed to the "melancholy condition of France" as an example to be avoided. A large standing army will poison the foundation of justice and will endanger the republic. "The military of France is a warning to the United States."[17] To the question of whether a Dreyfus case could happen in America, Americans responded that the depressed status of their army ensured against such a calamity. In at least this one area of public life, commented the widely read *Independent*, Americans appeared relatively safe. "The antagonism between the Army and the Government are happily absent in America," it said; there was no "great gulf between the army and the people as in France, where the officers inherit the traditions and sentiments of the extinct monarchy."[18]

■ As Americans reflected on the risks to a democratic community when its civil custodians bow to its military chiefs, their anxiety reflected a long-established American concern. "The tradition of antimilitarism has been an important factor in the shaping of some two hundred years of American history," Arthur A. Ekirch reminds us. Civil supremacy has long been a powerful element in the American notion of freedom. Imperialistic ventures and naval expansion in the nineties notwithstanding, this view did not alter: the war with Spain and the conquest of the Philippines did not enhance the reputation of the army or grant its generals a more powerful voice in matters of public concern.[19] "Militarism is especially dangerous in a republic," remarked a St. Louis newspaper. "If, in America, a military caste is allowed to grow . . . it will gradually overshadow the civil authority and in the end employ the logic of force which leads straight to the subversion of free institutions. The military of France is a warning to the United States."[20]

This fear was first evident in America during the trial of Émile Zola. "The army won a great victory in the trial," announced one newspaper, "but the civil administration of France received a deadly blow from which it will not speedily recover." The ease with which the French army was able to trample upon the civil law prompted an American constitutional lawyer, F. W. Whitridge, to wonder whether "the French Republic and ours belong in the same class, and are equally entitled to the name of Republic."[21] A. G. Sedgwick, an anti-military intellectual, warned Americans that

> whenever the state has been in the past essentially military the Anglo-Saxon notion of a fair trial has never obtained a foothold. . . . The Dreyfus case makes it extraordinarily plain exactly how a thoroughly

military community must view criticism of a trial which raises a doubt
about the procedure adopted by a state. What they have in their
minds is the ideal, not of justice, but of discipline. We have in France
a perfect specimen of what we might call an attempt at a de-civilized
state—that is, a state in which military are taking the place of civil
ideals. By making everyone a soldier, they have confirmed Frenchmen in the notion . . . that a trial is not machinery for the ascertainment of truth so much as a mode of discipline, and that consequently
an acquittal is defeat for the state, and tends to promote breaches of
discipline, even if none in the case itself has been committed. . . . The
peculiarity of the Dreyfus case is that it is the very type and exemplar
of the unfair trial of subject by despot, which the old militarism fastened on half the world, and the new militarism dangles before our
eyes as proof that an age of blood and iron and wrong has again
dawned.[22]

Within the context of these fundamental misgivings, the guilt or
innocence of Dreyfus became a "subordinate question." The real issue,
as some Americans saw it, was whether the French government would
submit to the dictation of the army and, if so, whether the French
republic could long survive under such conditions. As the *Outlook* put it,
such a state of affairs was "absolutely incompatible with self-government. The military power has usurped the civil power, military methods
have taken the place of judicial methods, and France is today under a
tyranny in the form of an irresponsible power behind the Government."
H. L. Nelson, editor of *Harper's Weekly*, shared the view that there was
"much more in the Dreyfus Affair than the question of the right and
the wrong involved in the unfortunate captain's conviction." At stake, he
was convinced, was the longevity of French civil institutions.[23] Should
the Court of Cassation rule in favor of Dreyfus, warned one editorial,
anything might happen:

> The Dreyfus affair, with its portentous ramifications, has shaken
> the fabric of free institutions to its centre and threatens the complete
> subordination of the civil to the military power. The fundamental
> question, which France may be expected to answer . . . is whether it is
> possible for a parliamentary government, representing faithfully the
> people and strictly obeying the constitution and the laws, to subsist
> side by side with a huge standing army, [constituting] an imperium in
> imperis.[24]

What brought France to this critical state of affairs? Armed to her
teeth, living in mortal dread of her neighbors, France could not risk

behaving differently toward Dreyfus, explained a Boston lawyer, Richard W. Hale. To the French military, according to Hale, "Whether Dreyfus is guilty or not is of incomparably less importance than the question whether all our systems of espionage and all our military secrets involved in the case shall be dragged out into a glaring light which will destroy their efficiency." He was critical of France's refusal to "jeopardize all by asking why? and wherefore? and when? and how? and who? when grave reasons of state make the answers inconvenient." Ever since the crushing defeat at the hands of Prussia in 1870, James Eustis explained, France had existed under the terrible apprehension which "produced the strange spectacle of a people, who are really ardent Republicans, living under a Republican form of government, worshipping their army with an almost idolatrous admiration, because they consider it as the only strong arm upon which they can lean in the hour of danger."[25]

Understanding these conditions, the *Nation*, though disappointed, was not surprised at the testimony of the officers at Rennes. It concluded that they "were expected to convict, just as they might be expected to execute any disagreeable military duty to which they were assigned," such as blowing up "a house filled with women and children if it were necessary to save the army." In short, "the Dreyfus verdict is the army vindicating the army. It is French 'military justice,' which the world now understands to be the grossest injustice under the forms of law."[26]

It was precisely the longstanding camaraderie between the two countries that made it so hard for Americans to look on what the *New York Times* called "the terrible misfortune that has befallen France." Americans had long believed that in France, as in the United States, government rested upon the will of the people, and that the army could not be an "instrument of oppression." Now, said the *Times*, "it is suddenly revealed in France that the army to a most extraordinary extent is infected with a cruel and degrading sentiment of injustice and blind selfishness, and that its Generals are capable of the most dishonorable oppression."[27]

The military domination of justice was especially disturbing to Americans because French public opinion stood "behind the army in this monstrous conviction. . . . solid as a stone wall" and "aggressively hostile as a brigade with fixed bayonets."[28] From the courtmartial that tried Dreyfus, or from courtsmartial in general, Americans anticipated little else. "After all," editorialized the *Outlook* when it learned of the Rennes decision, what could one expect of a group of officers, all of whom

were of lower rank than the guilty generals to whom they were
bound in obedience, first by their oath of allegiance, but also by every
military tradition, by the habits of a lifetime, and by the ambition for
preferment. Hence, to save these generals, already convicted by steal-
ing, lying, and forgery, the judges again condemned an innocent captain. Rank tells in 1899 as it did in 1894. . . . Expediency, not evidence, conquered them. To please the majority of Frenchmen, and to
please the army, the judges yielded more even than did Pilate himself; they crucified afresh an innocent victim.[29]

A prominent journalist, Julian Ralph, concurred: "We had here seven
judges of the mental calibre which leads men to choose soldiering as a
profession. These seven men had been machinized, woodenized, by a
lifetime's subjection to the iron discipline of military life. For four years
it had been Article One of their military faith to believe Dreyfus guilty."
It was obvious that a French courtmartial could not be relied upon to
determine questions of law. Inescapable to many Americans was the fact
that Dreyfus, presumably innocent, had been convicted twice of treason
by a courtmartial while Esterhazy, the real traitor, had been acquitted by
the same body. "It was French military justice that was in question,"
declared an observer of the Esterhazy trial. "French military justice
could not be vindicated by a new appeal to its own operation. It could
be vindicated only by some investigation undertaken outside of itself
and by other methods than its own."[30]

As it became increasingly evident that Dreyfus would not be acquitted in the second trial, the courtmartial was severely castigated in the
American press. Its judges "did not come to the trial in a judicial temper," it was declared. "They brought with them the prejudices of their
caste, its clannishness, its sensitiveness to prevalent army sentiment."
The judges could not shut out "the thought of what the effect of a judgment in favor of the detested Dreyfus is likely to be upon their own
future relations with their brother officers and their military superiors,"
said the *Hartford Courant*. It was a "revolting spectacle," said the *New York
Evening Telegram*, to witness "a veritable squadron of generals of division
taking advantage of the privilege of their rank to transform presump-
tions and impressions into 'proofs.'"[31] E. L. Godkin of the *Nation*
remarked with annoyance that the courtmartial which tried Dreyfus was
"composed in the main of officers who had never given any attention to
legal matters, who had no judicial experience whatever, who knew nothing about any rules of evidence or about nature of proofs." He was surprised at "the oddity of leaving a matter that came near bringing on a
civil war to the decision of . . . officers of or below the rank of colonel,

forming exactly the kind of court to which would have been referred a private soldier's theft of a pair of boots." Even American military courts, he believed, were best designed to adjudicate minor military offenses, such as drunkenness, insubordination, or cowardice in the field. Military people had neither the necessary training in the law nor the professional commitment to it which would allow them to cope with complex judicial issues. A military tribunal could not be expected to "lay aside the respect for authority which is naturally inspired by military training" and its dependence, both for promotion and comfort, upon superiors.[32]

At the same time, Americans refused to exempt military courts from proper legal behavior. "No greater mistake can be made," declared the *Washington Post*, "than to imagine that there is any contradiction between the rules regulating the procedure of court-martial and the ordinary laws of the land."[33] American military tribunals were perceived more positively. Americans thought more highly of and expressed a greater faith in the workings of their own military justice than they did in France's. The legal authority Arthur Ameisen was almost alone in his observation that if a Dreyfus case occurred in the United States the Supreme Court would be powerless to order a retrial.[34] Most American writers held that the Dreyfus case could never have occurred in the United States. "We do not believe that because a leakage was discovered in the General Staff of the United States Army, supposing the United States Army to be in possession of a 'general staff,' there could thereupon ensue so wanton and unscrupulous an assault upon a member of the General Staff. . . . We think better than that of the code of ethics inculcated at West Point." Americans preferred to believe that their system of military justice operated more equitably than in France, that it was bound by proper legal procedures, and that its courts were staffed by better trained lawyers.[35] Colonel John I. Rogers, an authority on military law, assured a gathering of Pennsylvania lawyers in 1902 that American military processes were undergoing continuous review and refinement, resulting in a code of law unmatched in the world.[36] He recognized with some distress the existence of an undercurrent of public disrespect for military legal practices, acknowledging that there was even a degree of justification for such popular bias.

> To the trained lawyer, sworn to uphold the Constitution and laws
> of both nation and state, who regards precedents and forms as the
> palladiums of personal and proprietary rights, there is something
> repulsive about Military Commissions and Drum-Head Court-
> Martial, seemingly organized to convict, proclamations of martial law

"in disaffected districts," suspensions of the *habeas corpus*, the substitu-
tion of Military Governor and Provost Marshals for legislatures,
Executives and Judiciary and disappearance of civil processes and
trial by jury down the barrel of the rifle or the scabbard or the
sabre. . . . spectacles of the hanging by the thumbs, and of the half
shaven sconce and plucked off buttons of the convict, as he makes his
exit out of camp to the tune of the "Rogues" March, and of that still
more modern and refined inventive cruelty, "the water cure" . . . are
not calculated to remove earlier and well-grounded impressions, that
military law and its tribunals are outside the pale of Civil Law and
only tolerated, in times of war, on the plea of necessity.

Still, the principle not to be overlooked, cautioned Rogers, was the
American safeguard, built into the structure of military legal practices,
that placed it "at all times . . . in strict subordination to the civil power."[37]

Edgar S. Dudley, professor of military law at the United States Military Academy, stressed to his students at this time the importance of
abiding by proper rules of evidence in military trials. "Hearsay evidence" or "opinion evidence" is not admissible in a courtmartial. "The
opinions of witnesses are . . . not evidence," he cautioned the future
officers. "In every case the fact in issue is to be proved, either by the
evidence of those who speak from their own actual or personal knowledge of its existence, or it is to be inferred from other facts satisfactorily
established."[38] Perhaps the accounts of the French courtmartial aired in
American periodicals, coupled with a greater public concern for legal
matters in general, were making the United States military sensitive to
its own legal shortcomings and were compelling it to scrutinize and
sharpen its juridical practices to conform to American judicial ideals.

VI

Picquart and Labori

Col. Picquart is the real hero of the Dreyfus case. . . . His bold bearing, his quick sense of personal honor, and his love of justice, leading him to risk reputation and life in behalf of a man whom he never knew, have marked him out for admiration from the first.

Nation, August 24, 1899

Lawyers everywhere should uphold the hand of their brethren when they are nobly engaged in the work of their profession. And may God forbid that the day should ever come in any land under any flag or at any time when a lawyer who does his duty, even if it be in defending the worst criminal, and is stricken down for so doing, shall not receive a word of cheer and sympathy from his brethren in America.

F. C. DILLARD
Report of the Twenty-Second Annual Meeting of the American Bar Association
August 29, 1899

America's critical stance towards the military and legal institutions of France was not totally unanimous, nor was it rooted in any rigid Francophobe ideology; it simply reflected a deep sense of disappointment at the treatment of Dreyfus and his supporters. The Dreyfus affair focused American critical views; Anglo-American rhetoric, belief in the superiority of the common law, and anti-militarist sentiment were not tools specially designed to attack French behavior but instruments which could be employed conveniently should the occasion arise. The Dreyfus affair offered just such an occasion. At the same time, American opinion was flexible, guided by a sense of fair play, and ready to commend the heroism and personal sacrifice of that minority of Frenchmen who supported the cause of Dreyfus. Such praise was given not only to individuals like Émile Zola, an intellectual who stood outside the ruling establish-ment, but also to members of the French military and bar. In the latter category, two individuals struck Americans most strongly, Lieutenant-Colonel Georges Picquart and Maître Fernand Labori. By applauding their forthrightness and gallantry, Americans also underscored their disillusionment with France.

■ Lieutenant-Colonel Picquart's tragic and heroic experiences epito-mized for Americans the corruption into which the French generals had descended. He served as a reminder that in France a soldier *could* serve the cause of truth and decency, but at a terribly high price. Picquart was born in Strasbourg in 1854, a descendant of an old Lorraine family. He was educated at St. Cyr and at the general staff school, where he was early recognized as a brilliant student. His rise was rapid; he gained his captaincy in 1880 and joined the War Office staff three years later. While serving in Tonquin in 1885, he was decorated; in 1888 he was promoted to major; and he was to be appointed to a professorship at the Military School (École Militaire) in 1890. He rejoined the War Office in 1893, succeeding Colonel Sandherr as head of Intelligence, and was pro-moted to lieutenant-colonel in 1896.

A meticulous, discreet, and dedicated officer, with a command of six languages, Picquart appeared ideally suited for intelligence work. One American admirer recalled that Picquart's discretion was so great that he had been chief of intelligence for six months before his mother knew of his appointment.[1] Although he was the youngest lieutenant-colonel in France, he was highly respected in French military circles. A devout Roman Catholic, a bachelor, intensely patriotic, with anti-Semitic lean-ings, he was the last person one would expect to challenge the Dreyfus verdict. Furthermore, like the staff that surrounded him, he was at first firmly convinced of the captain's guilt.

Not long after Picquart assumed his new position, a spy brought to his attention a *petit bleu* (a special-delivery letter frequently used in local correspondence in Paris at that time). An examination indicated that it was written by Ferdinand Walsin Esterhazy, a commandant of infantry in the Third Army Corps, to the German military attaché, Colonel Schwarzkoppen. The short message indicated that the writer was pro-viding confidential information to the German embassy. Further inquiry revealed that Esterhazy's handwriting was identical to that of the *border-eau*, the celebrated document which led to Dreyfus' arrest.[2]

Astounded by this discovery, Picquart made discreet inquiries about

Esterhazy. He learned that Esterhazy had an unsavory reputation, drank heavily, gambled frequently, and led a generally dissipated existence. When he reported his findings and suspicions to his superiors, he was told to drop the matter lest he embarrass the General Staff. However, Picquart pressed on with his investigations, and the more he did so, the greater his conviction that the wrong man was on Devil's Island.

His persistent inquiries alarmed his superiors, who proceeded to watch his movements closely, "as cats watch a mouse," observed the *Outlook*, "fearful as to what sudden spring he might make, as to what he might uncover. They did not propose to be exposed, not they; yet they saw with increasing consternation that their exposer was more and more bent on bringing the true culprit to justice." To protect themselves, they removed Picquart as head of Intelligence and replaced him with his subordinate, Lieutenant-Colonel Hubert Joseph Henry. Henry proceeded to forge more letters to fatten the Dreyfus dossier. Meanwhile, Picquart was posted to a series of distant assignments, first to the Italian border, then to Algiers, and finally to a dangerous mission in Tunis. Though disappointed and frustrated, he obeyed his orders without a murmur until he learned that his correspondence was being tampered with, that malicious rumors were being circulated about his personal life, and that Henry had been given a permanent appointment as chief of intelligence. At this point Picquart became concerned about the meaning of all this activity and also began to fear for his own safety.

So that his discoveries would not be lost, Picquart, while back in Paris on a short leave, consulted with an old school friend, Maître Louis Leblois, a prominent lawyer and a close friend of Auguste Scheurer-Kestner, vice-president of the French Senate. Picquart gave Leblois a sealed envelope containing an account of his findings and his suspicions of Esterhazy, instructing Leblois to employ the evidence only in the event of his death.[3] The details of the meeting, which Leblois related to Scheurer-Kestner, were leaked to the military. Some months later, in a parallel development, evidence of Esterhazy's authorship of the *bordereau* was discovered by a friend of Dreyfus' brother Mathieu. This information was submitted to the military. Faced by the weight of the evidence against Esterhazy, the military authorities with great reluctance ordered a courtmartial for Esterhazy, and Picquart was ordered home from his African post to testify.

When the War Office learned of Picquart's consultations with Leblois it was incensed. Such an action was believed a serious infringement of the laws concerning military secrets. As head of Intelligence, Picquart, they believed, should not have consulted a friend, and a civilian at that, about secret military matters. Picquart's indiscretions angered the War Office far more than did the revelations about Esterhazy. Before he returned from Tunis to testify, his Paris apartment was searched. When he arrived in France he was put in jail. "While the chief witness was thus treated," the *Outlook* complained, "Esterhazy had every freedom, and was permitted to remove his papers to London."[4]

Many American newspapers viewed the Esterhazy courtmartial which began in January, 1898, as a farce. General Georges de Pellieux, the presiding judge, it was reported, "took the ground that the *bordereau*, being part of the Dreyfus dossier, could not be introduced in the Esterhazy case. He took into consideration Esterhazy's depositions alone, and would not consider those of Mathieu Dreyfus, Picquart and Senator Scheurer-Kestner." Other witnesses at the trial were described in the American press "as pliant tools" who gave only the testimony they were expected to give. The whole inquiry was turned against Picquart. On the second day of the trial he was arrested, and Esterhazy was acquitted. It was this staged courtmartial that prompted Zola to write *J'accuse*, and it was only as a result of Zola's own trial in February, 1898, that Picquart's discoveries became public knowledge.[5]

Picquart was the chief witness against Esterhazy at the Zola trial, and in his testimony he described his discovery of the *petit bleu* and the efforts of his superiors to block his investigations. Witnesses were produced by the prosecution, among them Colonel Henry, who accused Picquart of forging the *petit bleu*. Zola's counsel, Fernand Labori, was not permitted to cross-examine Henry and Picquart's other accusers. At the conclusion of the Zola trial Henry and Picquart fought a duel, in which Henry was slightly wounded.

These events received considerable press coverage in the United States.[6] Many Americans were concerned about the fate of Picquart and were angered at the attempts to silence and humiliate him. Like Zola, he was viewed as a martyr to the cause of justice. His sacrifices were seen as brave and costly efforts to ensure the supremacy of the civil law. Americans were further shocked to learn that Esterhazy had been allowed to escape from France following his trial, while Picquart was discharged from the army and then jailed.

In the following weeks the crusade launched against Picquart by General Émile Zurlinden aroused considerable interest in the United States. Zurlinden, who was serving as minister of war, suddenly announced his resignation to assume the post of military governor of Paris. An anti-Semite and a staunch supporter of the General Staff, Zurlinden now proceeded to launch a vicious persecution of Picquart. He based his attack on accusations which included the charges that Picquart had given secret information from the Dreyfus file to his lawyer friend Leblois and that he had forged the *petit bleu*.[7] These charges, the *Outlook* explained, had been brought against Picquart by Zurlinden while he was still minister of war, but in order to take direct control of the prosecution, he had resigned his position and arranged to be appointed military governor. "In that capacity," said the *Outlook*, "he is now practically directing the prosecution which he ordered as Minister." Picquart, who had been arrested by the civil authorities, was now transferred to the military and lodged in the Cherche Midi, the fortress in which Dreyfus was held four years earlier. His secrets, Americans were informed, would be better secured from public view in a military than in a civilian jail. The *Times* remonstrated: "History does not chronicle any more outrageous violation of the civil law by military law."[8]

Learning of his impending transfer to a military jail, Picquart announced to reporters that if he were to be found dead in his cell, the cause would not be suicide. The *New York Times* quoted him on September 22, 1898: "I wish to declare that . . . I have no idea of commiting suicide." The *Outlook* remarked that Picquart's "secret confinement in a military prison by the direction of the Military Governor of Paris, show that the French Republic has practically ceased to exist; for such methods are absolutely incompatible with self-government. The military power has usurped the civil power, military methods have taken the place of judicial methods, and France is today under a tyranny in the form of irresponsible power behind the Government."[9]

The announcement that Picquart would be tried by a courtmartial created a further sensation. The purpose of this latest move was to disgrace Picquart publicly. As a convicted forger and an accomplice of an accused traitor, his testimony in the civil courts would be useless, and the courtmartial would prevent his appearance before the Court of Cassation, which at that moment was deliberating the question of revision. "I do not know whether the real intention of this scheme is clear," wrote a well-known English correspondent, M. de Blowitz, "whether the reader yet sees the motive behind it—namely, to throw doubt in advance on Colonel Picquart's deposition, and whether it is realized that this is taking place openly in a country which calls itself a land of light. . . . It makes one shudder." The *Philadelphia Press* editorialized that "not even the Dreyfus case itself is an example of so flagrant a case of injustice, malign and fanatical." Should Picquart be condemned, commented another editorialist, "the verdict will sound throughout the world as the funeral knell of individual liberty and security, creating in France such anger and hatred as nothing can appease."[10]

The courtmartial which Zurlinden prepared for Picquart did not materialize: much to the elation of American observers, the Court of Cassation ordered it postponed indefinitely. The announcement was celebrated as a defeat for the French General Staff, especially for Zurlinden, who was emerging as an arch-villain in the affair. "It is difficult to account for his conduct," said the *New York Sun* on December 12: "It is much easier and more reasonable to assume that he is the head, or the instrument of a desperate conspiracy to achieve certain ends of revenge, of the concealment of crime and perhaps of inordinate ambition."[11] Letters of sympathy and encouragement were showered upon Picquart during the Christmas season. Americans were informed that the famous prisoner was spending his time reading Carlyle's *History of the French Revolution* in English.

Early in March the Court of Cassation ordered Picquart's case returned to a civil court. "In reluctant and tardy obedience to this order," reported the *New York Sun*, on March 16, "the accused was . . . transferred from a military to a civil prison. This is a victory for justice and a grievous blow to the anti-revisionists, by whom Picquart is hated even more bitterly than Dreyfus himself," the *Sun* editorialized. It was a pivotal decision, for "if Colonel Picquart is tried promptly and is acquitted of forging the *petit bleu*, before the whole Court of Cassation shall arrive at a decision in the Dreyfus case, that decision can hardly fail to be in favor of Dreyfus."[12] In April Picquart was called to testify before the Court of Cassation, and his testimony was widely reported in the United States and was hailed as an important breakthrough in the Dreyfus affair. And when he was finally released from prison after the court decided that there was no case against him, American delight was boundless:

> No one has been persecuted as Picquart has been for defending
> Dreyfus and for letting the light in upon the foul work of Esterhazy
> and others. . . . During all this time Picquart had the manliness to
> withstand every pressure toward covering up the truth. His honesty
> and bravery have been amply proven. His was an intelligent honesty
> and his an intelligent bravery. His eyes were wide open, not only to
> the truth, which has now happily become evident to most people in
> France, but also to the certain risks he was running. Let us hope that
> his countrymen will remember that he has been no ordinary hero
> and martyr, and, in a characteristic generosity in acknowledging

injustice, demand for him an exalted rank in the army he has served so well.[13]

Concerned Americans urged that Picquart be reinstated in the army with full military honors. A simple pardon was not enough: "Picquart is free, but his military career is ruined, because he had the courage to proclaim his belief in the innocence of a persecuted man. Unless he is restored to his former rank in the army, the work of justice which France has now undertaken, will be left incomplete."[14] His testimony on behalf of Dreyfus at the Rennes trial had been carefully monitored in the American press. "He spoke clearly, forcibly and rapidly. . . . There was no longer any doubt of the influence of this master mind upon the seven judges behind the black table," wired one reporter from Rennes. "They leaned forward, following every word with the most intense interest. Their faces often expressed amazement as well as conviction." "Col. Picquart is the real hero of the Dreyfus case," remarked the *Nation*, "and his testimony is easily the most important yet given at the trial. . . . His bold bearing, his quick sense of personal honor, and his love of justice, leading him to risk reputation and life in behalf of a man whom he never knew, have marked him out for admiration from the first."[15]

In the years that followed Rennes, Picquart grew bitter toward Dreyfus. He could not subscribe to the patently political gesture of amnesty. Convinced of his own guiltlessness, he insisted on being tried by a court-martial, acquitted by his peers, and restored to his position in the army. Dreyfus, he believed, by accepting a "pardon," had settled for less than justice, and he took to reading anti-Semitic literature and voicing anti-Semitic sentiments.[16] This side of his nature, however, was concealed from the American public, and to the very end his name was revered. A duel he fought with General Charles Gonse in July, 1906, was reported by the *New York World* as another act of Picquartian heroism: "Picquart, one of the best pistol shots in France, faced his old general, Gonse, received his fire in the face, and then lowering his weapon walked disdainfully away." In July of that year he was finally restored to the army rank which he would have achieved under normal circumstances— brigadier general. The *New York Times* remarked with elation: "There are two attributes which more than any others enlist human sympathy and enthusiasm for the hero." The first was the willingness to fight against fearful odds, and the second, the ability to master tragic situations. General Picquart, said the *Times*, "possesses these attributes in a fascinating degree."[17]

■ If Picquart exemplified the exception to French military behavior, as Americans saw it, the lawyer Fernand Labori represented an anomaly in French legal circles—a lonely voice crying out for justice in a corrupt world. Like his famous clients—Zola, Picquart, and Dreyfus—Labori was the object of a vicious public attack; like them, he attained the stature of a moral hero in the United States. It was his defense of Émile Zola that brought his name to the attention of Americans. Although American scorn for that event was reserved primarily for the prosecution, Labori was not immune from criticism. His courtroom orations, observed an American lawyer, though acknowledged to be eloquent, were nevertheless viewed as too verbose, a veritable "flood of statements and arguments that were perceptibly outside of the evidence." Labori, it seemed, failed to rise above the level of his opponents' tactics, succumbing to the temptation to make emotional statements and to engage in undignified exchanges with the attorney general and the presiding judge.[18]

Despite these criticisms, however, Labori's defense of Zola was highly acclaimed. Given the public prejudice which he faced, the insults and threats shouted at him from the gallery of spectators, and abuse flung at him from anti-Semites and haters of Zola, it was understandable that he might lose his composure. "I do not accept this insult that rises to me from your seat, Monsieur Attorney General, however high your position. From the viewpoint of talent you and I are equals. You have no lesson to give me," he thundered at one point during the trial. His summation to the jury was expressed in language most sympathetic to American ears: "You are the sovereign arbiters. You are higher than the army, higher than the judicial power. You are the justice of the people, which only the judgment of history will judge. If you have the courage, declare Zola guilty of having struggled against all hatreds in behalf of right, justice and liberty."[19] As an anonymous lawyer put it: "We ought in common decency to say that Maître Labori is one of the Frenchmen, one of the lots [sic] of France, who show us in the civil sphere, as Picquart has shown us in the military sphere, how sound a seed there is of Frenchmen in France, how justice and honor and duty are not the empty words we might suppose them to be if we attended only to the cavortings of the most conspicuous Frenchmen."[20] How many American lawyers would have accepted such an assignment, asked a New Orleans paper: "We confess that we do not know the leading lawyer of New York who would have undertaken so unpopular a course out of pure chivalry and human love of justice."[21]

Although only thirty-nine, Labori was acknowledged to be the most talented lawyer in France. His rise from modest beginnings through talent and effort appealed to Americans, who associated such success stories with their own leaders. Born in Rheims, the son of a minor official of the railway, he studied diligently in the local lycée and then was sent to Mainz and to England to acquire a mercantile education. He mastered what was required, including fluent English, but disliked bookkeeping and commercial arithmetic. Somehow along the way he developed a taste for the law and persuaded his parents to let him attend lectures at the Paris faculty of law.[22] In short order he attained the highest academic distinction, and in November, 1884, he was admitted to the bar as an advocate at the court of appeals. He was elected Secrétaire de la conférence des avocats, an honor accorded only to outstanding attorneys, and his fame increased with his success in defending clients whose cases were believed to be hopeless. At the same time, he acted as editor of the *Gazette du palais*, a daily law journal which, under his direction, quickly became a leading organ in the field, and assumed editorial direction of *La Grande revue*, a monthly politico-literary journal. For a more serious scholarly pursuit, he began to compile an encyclopedia of French law. At the time of the Rennes trial, twelve volumes of the encyclopedia had been issued; the thirteenth was ready to go to press when he was shot.[23]

Labori's reputation as a criminal lawyer and his courtroom skills commanded international attention. As one American admirer put it:

> It is not an exaggeration to say that *Maître* Labori is the most eloquent advocate in France today. His eloquence does not consist in uttering of flowery phrases and glittering generalities, but rather in welding together scraps of evidence which appear almost contradictory and having nothing in common, and in plain, simple, unvarnished language presenting them to the court. He does this with such thorough sincerity that all are astonished.
>
> Labori is one of the most powerful cross-examiners living. No witness can evade his questions; very few try to do so, for they usually unburden, as though pleased to tell all they know to this friendly and sympathetic lawyer. Therein lies his great power. What some can only elicit by brow-beating and bullying he can get by his magnetic manner. The witness will often tell the judge more than he has been asked, because he feels so sympathetic towards the counsel. . . .
>
> Fernand Labori is an artist. No great painter ever studied the light and shade necessary to produce a perfect work more thoroughly than does this masterly lawyer. He arranges his case artistically, his witnesses are called so that the proper light and shade may

be produced; in his speech he is dramatic, eloquent, but thoroughly artistic; like an accomplished chess player, he sees many moves ahead and never makes a mistake. The smallest detail becomes of immense importance if it aids his case, but the most convincing evidence loses its effect when once he attacks it.[24]

Labori's interest in the case of Alfred Dreyfus began early and, Americans were informed, was motivated by aspirations neither for personal fame nor for money but only from conviction.[25]

When he first assumed the defense of Dreyfus at Rennes, however, it was not his court activity which aroused American attention but the fact that on August 14, 1899, while walking to court, he was shot in the back. As he fell, his wife, a short distance behind him, rushed to his side, and stayed with him throughout the ordeal. The picture of Madame Labori sitting in the dirt, her husband's head in her lap, fanning him and whispering into his ear, captivated American readers. They wanted to know more about this devoted woman. As a heroine of the Dreyfus affair, she took second place only to Madame Dreyfus.[26]

Details of the tragedy were wired across the Atlantic and carried as front-page stories in major American newspapers. The shooting occurred at about six in the morning, not far from the lycée where the crowd had already assembled to await the beginning of the day's proceedings. The announcement of the crime caused the trial to be suspended, while the spectators rushed to the scene. New York reporter Harry J. Dam described it as follows:

> At the end of the bridge we stood speechless, gazing at the saddest picture the Dreyfus case has yet presented. And one of the saddest in all history. In the dust of the road lay Labori. The handsome, gifted young lawyer, whose steadfastness, courage and eloquence has made him known to the whole world. He lay upon his side, bleeding profusely from a large bullet wound in the back. His head was pillowed in the lap of his beautiful young wife, and his white face was brought into relief against the background of her black gown. She was dust-covered and blood-stained from his wound as she sat there in the road.[27]

A doctor was summoned; smelling salts were pressed to Labori's nose; the police converged on the scene. Two old men, road-menders working nearby and eyewitnesses to the crime, were interrogated. They said that a young man, whom they did not clearly see because it all happened so quickly, lunged behind the lawyer and fired point-blank at his back, then fled. Colonel Picquart and Edmund Gast, Labori's brother-in-law, who were walking with Labori, ran after the assassin but lost sight of him as he fled toward the woods and disappeared.[28]

There was speculation that the shooting might have been part of a conspiracy designed to eliminate the supporters of Dreyfus by fair means or foul. Labori, it was learned, had received a number of letters threatening his life, which he had discarded with indifference. To William Randolph Hearst the crime suggested a plot against the supporters of Dreyfus. It was clear, he editorialized, that "the Dreyfus crime includes the potentiality of all other crimes." The shooting was not an isolated event but "an incident of the war declared by the reactionary revolutionists against the existing institutions of France." The conspirators, he believed, "aimed first to destroy the republic and secondly to kill Dreyfus and his friends."[29] Compounding the tragedy was the fear that with Labori absent Dreyfus' defense would be irreparably damaged. General Mercier, one of Dreyfus' chief antagonists, had been scheduled for interrogation by Labori on the morning of the shooting. With Labori absent from court, Mercier's testimony, riddled with fabrications, would go unchallenged.[30]

It was not the trial, however, but Labori's physical condition that was the chief topic of interest at the moment. Medical bulletins were regularly wired from Rennes. At first they sounded ominous. Labori's "lung is endangered," screamed the *New York Herald*. "The spinal cord has been cut! He is growing weaker every minute. He is spitting blood!" The reports sounded worse on the following day: "His agony had increased and a fever had set in." Even if he recovered, Labori would have permanent paralysis of his legs.[31] By the third day the medical reports became more hopeful. Normal breathing was restored and the patient's fever had subsided. He would live, and paralysis of the legs was now doubtful. His spirits appeared to be excellent, in part, American newspapers suggested, because of his devoted wife's constant presence at his bedside.[32]

Labori's rapid recovery suggested to the American press a parallel with the assassination of President Garfield, eighteen years before: "The shooting in both instances occurred early in the morning. Both men were shot in the back to the right of the spine. President Garfield fell just as Labori did and rallied sufficient to turn himself over when the doctors reached him. With President Garfield, as with Labori, the surgeons resolved not to probe for the ball, hoping that it would encyst."[33] (Garfield eventually succumbed to an uncontrolled infection.)

Crimes of violence in Paris, as in American cities, were rising sharply.

However, the perpetrators of crimes in France, Americans were informed, represented a "new, modern criminal type." Appearing as young delinquents or neglected street urchins, they were collectively designated by the Paris police as "Camelots." They congregated in dingy cafés and were pale, anemic, and heartless. "They are ready for anything which will furnish money for their absinthe, their gambling and their women." The suspect, it was believed, might be one of these. The woods surrounding Rennes were thoroughly combed. All roads leading to Paris were blocked. Railroad stations were carefully watched. But as the days passed and the culprit still remained at large, Americans grew impatient. In an interview with the commandant of the Agence de la Sûreté Générale, or Criminal Investigation Department, Harry Dam, a prominent reporter for the *New York Evening Journal*, was assured that the organization was especially skilled in capturing anarchists. "My men," boasted the chief, "in addition to being distributed over all parts of Rennes, are supposed to protect all the prominent persons in the Dreyfus case." He refused to reveal the number of men stationed under his command, but he assured Dam that they were scattered throughout every town in France. "My men know every rat hole in Paris," he added; "They are hard at work, and in a day or so I shall know exactly what men answering the description are missing from their accustomed haunts."[34]

From early announcements it appeared that the French police were hot on the trail of Labori's assailant. They had a clear description—a young man, sporting a dark mustache, described as a "Spanish anarchist" type. "Anarchists" of any sort were far from popular in the United States, and American reporters followed the police investigation closely. At the same time, their attention was also focused on the nature of French crime and criminal procedure.[35]

As the days passed, however, it became increasingly evident that the culprit had eluded the French police. "Hope of finding Labori's assassin has vanished," announced the *New York Evening Journal* on August 24. Still, the French police insisted that no mismanagement could be attributed to them. "Our machinery . . . is as perfect as we can make it. . . . The French police system is the best in the world." Why, then, was Labori's attacker still at large, an American reporter inquired. "He will probably be caught through a woman," the French authority replied with a chuckle. "I don't know what we shall do without the women."[36] The criminal was never caught nor even properly identified, but at least Americans were treated to a glimpse of the ingenuous French system of criminal apprehension.

Once he had recovered somewhat, Labori was eager to return to court, "even if he has to be carried there in an ambulance," reported the *New York Evening Journal.* He was dissatisfied with the way Maître Edgar Demange, who was directing the defense in his absence, was conducting the case. Labori's intention was to put the generals back on the witness stand. In anticipation of his return, a special chair, which would allow him to conduct the cross-examination from a seated position, was improvised. His reappearance in court on August 22, earlier than expected, was compared to a royal procession by the United States press. He entered the courtroom with his entourage, surrounded by a contingent of bodyguards and police[37] ("in no country," remarked an observer, "do they lock the stable door after the horse is stolen more firmly than in France"). He was greeted tumultuously:

> All present, whatever their attitude toward Dreyfus, joined in a
> storm of handclapping, cheers, hurras and various outcries in which
> emotional French natures find vent. Many French journalists jumped
> on the desks. One picturesque poor devil who writes for a Socialist
> paper in Paris, waved his breakfast consisting of half a loaf of bread
> and a lump of chocolate, in his wild enthusiasm. The warmth of the
> reception quite unnerved the tall, brawny, handsome young lawyer.
> He stood still, much moved, waving his right hand in a cramped way,
> caused by bandages, as if in deprecation of such sensational proceed-
> ings.[38]

American journalists made no effort to conceal their satisfaction that Labori had resumed command of the defense of Dreyfus. His style and manner were clearly more effective than those of Demange, who was solemn, ponderous, and plodding. Like a good American lawyer, it was said, Labori knew the way of "putting a witness through a threshing machine." "The accusers of Dreyfus hate him, fear him more than they do the devil." American observers were captivated by his "swift thrusts" at the military witnesses, who "descended from the witness chair . . . passing, with bowed heads before the Generals whom they had tried to defend. . . . They looked like a lot of very small, very cowardly boys afraid of their school-master's punishment." The *Nation* agreed that "the assassin fired at the right man, for in disabling Labori he took out of the courtroom the one man whom the prosecution stands most in fear of, the one man who knows most about the case, the one upon whom the defense leans with the greatest confidence. If Labori's strength holds out, the tissue of perjury and forgery which the Court of Cassation partly exposed will be riddled to the satisfaction of the lovers of truth throughout the world."[39]

The most impressive tribute paid Labori, however, came from the lawyers in Buffalo convened for the annual meeting of the American Bar Association in August, in the form of a resolution of sympathy and support for Labori's "courage in defending the cause of justice." Some delegates questioned the appropriateness of a statement about the domestic affairs of another country. A Texas lawyer remarked, "If the trial of Dreyfus be a matter of military proceeding, then is it germane to the work of this Association? The American Bar Association should be slow in passing resolutions. Matters political should be eschewed. Labori, like all great lawyers, doubtless does not desire and certainly does not need public applause for his fearless advocacy in behalf of his client." Another delegate argued that "as individuals we may entertain profound convictions of the prisoner's innocence, and as individuals we may so express ourselves to *Maître* Labori, but as an association of American lawyers we cannot do that. What right have we," he asked, "who are neither members of that Court or citizens of that Republic, to interfere in the process of that trial?"[40]

Most members, however, were not troubled by such matters. E. T. Lovatt, a New York lawyer, believed that even a stronger statement on behalf of Labori would not have been inappropriate. Such a protest "is germane to this Association's objectives,—to stand by a brother lawyer, no matter to what country he belongs." It was important for the world to know, he said, that the American legal establishment did not shrink from doing "honor to the man of our profession who, in the teeth of such danger—danger that we in this country do not have to face, thank God, will stand up for his client without any reward excepting the approval of his conscience, and face that tribunal and plead the cause of his client without fear of man and asking no favor at the hands of anyone." "We are not only citizens of the United States," another delegate added, "we are also in a very important sense, citizens of the world." The resolution was amended to delete the words "in defending the cause of justice" and was adopted overwhelmingly by a vote of 130 to 60.[41] The lengthy debate evoked sentiments that would not often be heard from the American legal profession in later years, but which were typical of the American world view and sense of mission at the close of the nineteenth century.

The unsatisfactory conclusion of the Rennes courtmartial weakened but did not obliterate American interest in Labori. Rumors about his activities continued to circulate during the following months. He was engaged in writing a book about the famous case, it was said, and his career continued to interest legal-minded Americans.[42]

■ As in the case of Picquart, a breach developed between Labori and his former client Dreyfus. Like Picquart, Labori was angry that Dreyfus and his brother had accepted a "pardon" from the government; he was annoyed at their acquiescence in an "amnesty" which had been granted to the guilty generals as well as to the innocent. This bland dismissal of a momentous issue appeared to Labori a betrayal of the whole system of justice, and he came to believe that Dreyfus did not appreciate his own sacrifices for him. On the occasion of Dreyfus' final vindication, he was merely an embittered spectator.[43] "He washed his hands years ago of the Dreyfus Affair," an American writer noted in 1908, "which made him for a space, it is true, the most talked-of lawyer of two continents, but which brought him otherwise little but vexation, disenchantment and misfortune."[44]

VII

Depravity and
Dislocation in Gaul

There is but one love which a Frenchman places above his country,
and that is his love for another man's wife.

MARK TWAIN, 1899

the moral degeneracy which so many eminent Frenchmen are now
exhibiting in regard to Capt. Dreyfus is closely related to the sexual
immorality which widely prevails in the highest circles of French society, and which, from that source, poisons the soul of the entire
nation.

New York Sun, January 17, 1899

From the American standpoint, the events in France were manifestations of a general moral and social decline. The case against Dreyfus,
the persecution of Zola and Picquart, and the attempted assassination
of Labori were tragic pieces of a larger puzzle. The harsh language with
which these events were greeted in the United States represented a
revulsion from a civilization that seemed to be crumbling. "Dry rot per-
meates all of France"; France's "true malady is degeneracy"—these typical comments supported the conviction of Anglo-Saxon superiority.
French happenings were described as "shameful" and "grotesque";
French society was compared to a "cesspool . . . having its contents
turned out to stink in the nostrils of a disgusted world." On her return
from Paris in January, 1899, the wife of the senior senator from Maine,
William Pierce Frye, cautioned parents not to send their children there:
"I say it is better for our young people never to learn art or music than
to learn them under such terrible odds."[1] Did conditions in France indicate the shape of the world to come? If so, then there was much to fear
for the future, commented one Englishman: "If what is now springing

up rankly in France is germinating throughout the world, then the beginning of a new century may be a rude one, a terrible shaking, the end of which no human foresight can predict."[2] Such insights, however, were not common. Emphasis upon current French delinquency was a more popular pastime. France had reverted to the age of medievalism, to the Spanish Inquisition, or to the New England Puritans' witch-burning, it was said.[3]

Few Americans surpassed Samuel Clemens in open contempt for France. "Oh, the French! the unspeakables!" he cried on one occasion; "I don't think they have improved a jot since they were turned out of hell!" In his European travels, he carefully avoided France and advised his friends to do likewise. When he wrote in 1898 that he held no prejudice against any race "bar one," his readers needed no further elaboration.[4]

The American philosopher William James was in Europe at the height of the affair, and its social implications also left a deep impression on him. As his biographer writes, the Dreyfus event erupted during a difficult and transitional period in James's life. He viewed it as a "nightmare" hanging over civilization, and it prompted him to compare the moral decline of France with what he saw as the relatively minor failings of American society. "We must thank God for America," he wrote to an acquaintance,

> and hold fast to every advantage of our position. Talk about corruption! It is a mere flyspeck of superficiality compared with the rooted and permanent forces of corruption that exists in the European states. . . . Damn it, America doesn't know the meaning of the word corruption. . . . Corruption is so permanently organized [in France] that it isn't thought of as such—it is so transient and shifting in America as to make an outcry whenever it appears.[5]

■ As Americans reflected on the moral condition of France, they tended to conclude that it was rooted in a fundamental emotional instability, a national tendency toward capriciousness and confusion. The atmosphere of irrationality surrounding the affair was quite incomprehensible to Americans. Visitors to France were struck by the emotionally charged atmosphere. "Everyone, intelligent or not, seems to fling the rein to passion; and even with the intelligent . . . right reason seems to have very little to say," an American girl wrote from Paris. Another visitor remarked that "French opinion seems, to my Anglo-Saxon mind, blind and childish with prejudice. With most people it seems an affair of

the emotions; reason seems to have little to say." The entire experience
was too alien for Americans to understand.[6] In the fall of 1898 a Philadelphia correspondent pictured for his readers

> a howling mass of Parisians apparently playing at burning news-
> papers, but terribly in earnest and worked up about something. This
> "something" was the report of the Dreyfus proceedings. An Ameri-
> can who disagreed with an article he read in a newspaper might say,
> "Pshaw!" in a contemptuous tone, and then forget all about it. It
> scarcely seems possible to men of the Anglo-Saxon race that adults
> can vent this rage over a newspaper article by setting the journal on
> fire and dashing madly through the streets, waving the burning sheet
> in the air and gesticulating furiously. Yet this is what the Parisian
> did.[7]

That the character of the French press was both a manifestation of
and the cause of this public emotionalism was universally acknowledged. To be sure, this was an age of sensational journalism, but in
France, it seemed, the yellow press had risen to unprecedented heights
of irresponsibility. As Barbara Tuchman writes, the Parisian newspapers
were "variegated, virulent, turbulent, literary, inventive, personal, con-
scienceless and often vicious." In 1898 the *New York Times* accused the
"cheap papers" of France of "preaching destruction of the Jews until
they have filled the weak and ill-balanced brains of their hundreds of
thousands of readers with the most savage ideas." The *Nation* charged
the Parisian press with "keeping alive the myths and passions and prejudices which are the only real evidence of Dreyfus's crime." "What with
clerical organs of slander like the *Croix*," commented the *Times*, "furious
anti-Semite papers such as the *Libre parole*, and the shrieking army-wor-
shipping and foreign-hating *Petit Journal*, the difficulty of making the
truth known in France begins to be seen. It is these newspapers," the
Times was convinced, "which have fooled the majority of the nation."[8] In
contrast, said G. W. Steevens, the English journalist, "the cheapest rag
in New York would blush for the recklessness, gullibility and foul-
ness of the baser French press." Another Englishman, M. De Blowitz,
assured the readers of the *North American Review* that no country
"exposed to such an unbridled license of speech and expression" could
long survive.[9]

■ To a society which, from the point of view of later decades, placed an
inordinate emphasis on proper sexual comportment, the charge of con-

jugal laxity assumed a special importance, and French licentiousness, it was argued, offered a clue to an understanding of the Dreyfus affair. Mark Twain's view that "there is but one love which a Frenchman places above his country, and that is his love for another man's wife" was shared by many Americans.[10] With this thought in mind, a New York newspaper proposed in the fall of 1898 that the Dreyfus mystery might be unraveled if only "the women" in the case could be found—that Dreyfus was falsely charged with the crime Esterhazy had committed largely because of the influence of General Boisdeffre's mistress. Her charms were said to have been employed on behalf of Esterhazy, thus bringing about the false incrimination of Dreyfus:

> Had the event which we are considering occurred anywhere but in France, this explanation would be at once dismissed as too fantastic and far fetched to deserve serious attention, but unfortunately, the morality of Frenchmen in high stations is so notoriously perverse and debased, especially where women are concerned, that nothing in the way of sacrificing honor, justice and reputation to satisfy the demands of a dissolute woman, is too monstrous to be credible.[11]

The fact that almost without exception the popular novels of France employed the theme of the adultery of a respectable married woman was stressed. Reading these books, one American writer believed, led inevitably to the conclusion that "there is no married woman in France who is not ready, upon the slightest inducement, to betray her husband":

> Every heroine is an adultress, and every hero her accomplice in her crime. The physical relations of the sexes are described in thinly veiled but suggestive language, and the writers revel in descriptions of libidinous enjoyment, varied and heightened in a manner best calculated to excite a prurient imagination. Thus, French literature depicts a community in which what we regard as the foundations of the social fabric, the marriage relation, is flouted and despised, and that the consequence should be a general loosening of the bonds of morality in other respects is only natural.[12]

This was not to say that "the mass of Frenchmen and French women are not as pure in sexual relations as the people of any other country," wrote an American critic. Unfortunately, however, immorality was widespread in the most influential circles, among French political and social leaders. The writer concluded that the "moral degeneracy" which so many Frenchmen were exhibiting with regard to the Dreyfus case was closely related to the sexual immorality which he reported: "The fact that Gambetta died from a wound inflicted by his mistress, that Victor Hugo openly lived with a woman not his wife, and that even Zola has two families, one legitimate and the other illegitimate, besides many other illustrations of the same character which it is needless to recapitulate, prove that the upper stratum of French society is poisoned by a disregard of moral restraints, which makes any crime charged against it probable." [13] In this "upper stratum," charged the New York Sun, "are found the personages who direct . . . the policy and acts of the nation, and who, as we see, are able to pervert courts and legislatures into denying to a presumptively innocent citizen the simple justice of the retrial to which he is entitled. By submitting to their dictation the French people become their accomplices, and must share in their ignominy." The Sun concluded that if Frenchmen "have not sufficient moral strength to overthrow these unworthy leaders, they must sink into the abyss of the putrid moral deliquescence toward which they are being conducted." [14]

The questionable circumstances which surrounded the death of the president of France, Félix Faure, on February 16, 1899, strengthened this impression of immorality in high places. Rumor had it that Faure suffered a fatal stroke while in bed with a beautiful woman, either in his private study or in the lady's boudoir. It was common knowledge that Faure was in sympathy with the anti-Dreyfus forces and the French nationalists. Anti-Semites quickly spread the rumor that his death was engineered by the Jewish Syndicate so that revision of the Dreyfus decision would be hastened. Despite official efforts, rumors abounded. One story suggested that the belle juive in whose embrace he succumbed (her exact identity was unclear) had poisoned him; another claimed that Faure had committed suicide to prevent dreadful revelations about his personal life. The gossip had it that the lady was the wife of a Belgian painter, or an actress in a state theater. The president himself, it was said, had been in the habit of driving about Paris in disguises, seeking recreation. A New York newspaper revealed to its readers that Faure had had a private exit made leading from the Elysée Palace through the gardens to the Rue de l'Elysée in order to depart secretly for these adventures. [15]

Actually, despite his stand on Dreyfus, some Americans had learned to respect the French president. A few weeks before his death a Philadelphia paper had described him as a "sportsman, an athlete, an ardent yachtsman, a fearless horseman, . . . a fine fencer, a man of robust mind, quick and alert in conversation, with the quiet composure of the born leader." The incident, however, harmonized with their impression of French society and of the dark shadows within its political life.[16]

■ During the fall of 1898 American reports portrayed France as perched upon a volcano. "The whole country is plunged into moral perplexity and confusion," remarked the *Outlook*. It was clear that the injustice to Dreyfus had brought this condition about. Within it were contained the "seeds of issue that are shaking France to her foundations." The future of France seemed bleak and uncertain. Press reports hinted at a possible coup by a pretender or man on horseback. Early in 1899 there were indications that the Bonapartists, with a large fund at their disposal, had completed arrangements for a dramatic coup to re-establish the Napoleonic dynasty.[17] In an editorial entitled "Napoléon the Fifth?" *Puck* put it this way:

> France is still a puzzle, like a spoiled, and capricious unbalanced woman. The looker-on cannot tell why she did what she has done. Still harder would it be to calculate what she is going to do. . . . There can be little doubt that she is now listening for the gallop of the horse that shall have the man on his back, the only rescuer upon which she ever seems to rely with perfect faith.[18]

The funeral of Félix Faure provided Americans with an occasion to observe how a civil disorder could erupt even at the most solemn moments. Faure's successor, Émile Loubet, was not popular with the French Right. In favor of revision, he was believed by extremists and their sympathizers to be in the Dreyfusard camp, and he was hooted and shouted at as he drove through the streets.[19] The state funeral for Faure, scheduled to take place five days after Loubet took office, was seen as an opportunity to stage a dramatic coup and restore authoritarian rule to France. The mind behind this bold conspiracy was that of Paul Déroulède, an extremist who believed that he need only give the signal for the entire French army to rush to his support. Much to his dismay, however, when he gave the call at the appointed hour, the army declined to accept his invitation, and his plan was an embarrassing failure. Déroulède was arrested for disturbing the peace, tried, and acquitted, a humiliating turn of events for one who aspired at the very least to martyrdom.[20] Observing the acquittal, a New York newspaper editorialized with a note of satisfaction that "France has declined to be 'saved,' she has refused to accept M. Paul Déroulède for her nineteenth century

Joan of Arc. . . . M. Paul Déroulède will have to seek some new character in which to save his country and keep himself before the eyes of the boulevards."[21]

American observers could not predict what kind of government would appear in France should its republican institutions collapse. A number of pretenders to the throne, all living, in accordance with French law, in exile, were active in the wings: two brothers, Louis and Victor Napoleon, and the Duc d'Orléans. Their following actively agitated on their behalf, and all members of these factions opposed Dreyfus and the cause his name represented. Indeed, it was the affair that helped bring to the surface all these disruptive elements. Everything indicated, according to the *Times*, that "Caesarism was ever latent in the French nature, while its failure only showed that Caesar had not yet appeared."[22]

■ The unruly character of Frenchmen, their excitability, and the ease with which their public assemblies could disintegrate into small-scale riots offered opportunities for moralizing about the relative stability of France and the United States. Americans were no strangers to mob violence in the nineteenth century, but the disorders in France baffled them. Their ideological fervor and clash of social classes—Monarchists against Republicans, rich against poor, militarists against anti-militarists, Dreyfusards against anti-Dreyfusards—were strange to American sensibilities.[23] Reports of French duels, suicides, assassinations, and howling street crowds filled American newspapers.

It is "impossible for Americans to understand the outbursts of fury indulged in frivolous reasons by French mobs," remarked a Philadelphia newspaper. Furthermore, these lawbreakers "are not for a moment to be compared with the revolutionaries of 1789. . . . The founders of the French Republic attacked the Bastille, one of the best fortified and most dreaded places in Paris. But the crowd of stabbers and stone-throwers . . . did not venture to attack anything more dangerous than a church, a café and a few newspaper stands."[24]

The quotation describes the agitation that gripped the streets of Paris on the eve of Dreyfus' second courtmartial. Dreyfus' second trial was held in Rennes to remove it from the mobs of Paris. As anticipated, while it was in progress, violent disturbances erupted in the French capital, perpetrated first by fanatics on the Right and then by an unruly mob of anarchists. The anarchists, about a thousand men and women, sacked two Catholic churches, the Church of St. Ambrose and the Church of

St. Joseph. The attack on St. Ambrose, according to one account, was sudden. The column of anarchists rushed toward the church and smashed its windows and religious artifacts. According to the *New York Journal*, "A figure of the Savior hanging on a great cross above the altar was made the aim for all sorts of missiles, and was fractured in several places."[25] Such a disgrace could never have occurred in New York City, said the *New York Herald*. Unlike "the timid guardians of the peace in the French capital," the New York police "would have driven the anarchists off the streets and into police cells with a rush that would have made them dizzy for hours."[26]

The anarchist riots constituted a spontaneous response to the right-wing protests against revisionism and liberalism organized by Jules Guérin, founder of the Anti-Semitic League. Shortly before the Rennes trial Guérin purchased a house in Paris, at 51 Rue Chabral, which he fortified and turned into a central meeting place to house his printing press and his gang of toughs. He vowed that should the courtmartial deliver a verdict favorable to Dreyfus he and his men would march on the capital. This time, however, the French government acted swiftly. Before dawn one morning, without warning, the police descended on the extremists and arrested more than one hundred, many still in their nightclothes. However, Guérin and fourteen of his supporters eluded the raiders and fortified themselves in their Paris headquarters, which thenceforth was known as Fort Chabral.[27]

For a few weeks, from mid-August to mid-September, 1899, Fort Chabral provided a bit of comic relief, as well as additional evidence of French political decadence, for American observers. The satirist Finley Peter Dunne visualized Guérin, as he appeared at the window of his fortification, as a

> tur-rble sight. He was dhressed fr'm head to foot in Harveyized, bomb-proof steel, with an asbestos rose in his buttonhole. Round his waist was sthrapped four hundred rounds iv ca'tridges an' eight days' provisions. He carried a Mauser rifle on each shoulder, a machine gun undher another, an' he was smoking a cigareet. "Ladies an gin-tlemen" he says, "I'm proud an' pleased to see ye prisint in such lar-rge numbers at th' first rivolution iv th' prisint season," he says.[28]

To avoid making a martyr out of Guérin, the French police were ordered to stay back and to allow hunger and discomfort to take their toll. Guérin, however, was well stocked with provisions and arms, and his stronghold had thick walls and iron window blinds. His eventual dislodgement was vividly described in the United States newspapers. First the French authorities cut his telephone connections and shut off his supply of water. Anyone entering or leaving his headquarters was arrested.[29] Then Guérin's men, succumbing to hunger, began to desert him. When they surrendered, those few who remained in Guérin's house were described as "wild with excitement, their eyes starting from their heads . . . drinking alcohol to keep up their strength and courage."[30] The siege had lasted forty days.

This spectacle was seen as more than a comic opera in the United States:

> At Rennes, one man . . . was deliberately sacrificed to save a few conspirators of the general staff. . . . At Paris, another man—representing the same prejudices and passions which had immolated Dreyfus, and pledged to treason in his abominable pursuit—has successfully defied the law, as it is understood in France; laughed at the judicial and police machinery of Paris and for weeks maintained a scandal which would have caused any other people to weep with sorrow and humiliation. . . . What astounds the world today . . . is the fact that, while there was power enough in France to immolate an innocent victim like Dreyfus, and to do this in full view of a generation that knew him to be innocent, there was not power enough—or will enough—to arrest a common malefactor like Guérin.[31]

Even the style of Guérin's surrender made a mockery of French justice. What other choice but to capitulate did Guérin have, asked an American journalist, when poised before him were "a general of division, a prefect of police, 1200 mounted gendarmes, 600 policemen on foot, 150 firemen with fire engines belching steam and smoke, three hook and ladder companies."[32]

■ Americans did not participate in the Dreyfus tragedy, with one striking exception, one American whose life became deeply enmeshed in the turmoil of France—Anna Gould, daughter of the American millionaire. Through her exploits Americans caught yet another glimpse of French events, especially those of its aristocracy. That she should have contributed to the furor aroused by the Dreyfus affair seems almost fitting. Born in 1875, the fifth of six children of Jay Gould, wrecker of railroads and Wall Street manipulator, she could not have chosen a more unpopular rich family. Few American millionaires were more despised than Jay Gould, the richest of them all. As his biographer observes: "Wall

Street needed one villain on whom to blame all the ills of the business community." Gould fitted the role neatly, with his "secretive nature, his black beard, and his air of mystery." (American anti-Semites suggested that he was a Jew; in fact, he was a devout Episcopalian whose family could trace its roots to the *Mayflower*.) His death on December 2, 1892, was greeted with relief in the American business community, "the sort of relief the Hebrew warriors felt when Goliath fell." Prices on Wall Street rose a few points at the announcement of his death, while the newspapers continued to vilify his name.[33]

By American standards Anna Gould was not beautiful. Short and robust, she had a pleasant, outgoing personality, enjoyed the company of young men, and gave the impression of shyness, which, however, concealed a determined and stubborn will. One thing was certain: she was very rich, unmarried, and a prize catch. In 1894 she became engaged to Oliver Harriman, an eligible young bachelor related to the Wall Street financier Edward Harriman. Following the announcement of the engagement Anna decided to sail for France, to shop, she said, for her trousseau.[34]

Anna's stay in Paris transformed her life. Under the watchful custody of Fanny Reed, who operated a finishing school for wealthy American heiresses, she was introduced to a select group of marriageable young men, among them members of the French nobility. Two were especially taken with her, the Duc de Talleyrand-Périgord and his younger cousin, Count Ernest Paul Boniface de Castellane. The latter, titled but penniless, from the moment he set eyes upon Anna was determined to marry her and pursued her with a romantic intensity she found hard to resist. "Count Boni," as he was known in Parisian circles, was twenty-seven years old, fluent in English, tall and slender, with a pencil-thin mustache and a peaches and cream complexion; he was known widely for his promiscuity, dueling, and gambling. When Anna returned to New York in 1895, perhaps to test her suitors' true intentions, Boni borrowed the money to follow her.[35] He was successful, and the two were married in the spring.

The marriage of Anna Gould to Count Boni de Castellane in the spring of 1895 was not the first social event of the kind seen in New York City. Since the middle of the century such unions had been increasing in frequency. A growing appetite for European titles of nobility was gnawing at a select circle of newly enriched Americans. They stood ready to exchange their daughters and a substantial fortune for a proper arrangement. Americans grew accustomed to announcements of marriages of their country's heiresses to impecunious European nobility and accepted such unions with a measure of curiosity, envy, and disdain. "The millionaire who marries his daughter to a French . . . noble banishes her; this can no longer be her home," wrote William Dean Howells in 1897. The French also chuckled at such arrangements, according to Edwin Hoyt, the process being described by a boulevardier as "manurer les fraises," that is, the fertilization of "the strawberry leaves of the coronets."[36]

The newspapers reported the preparations for the wedding of Boni and Anna as if it were a major national event. To protect the interests of American society, their agents were dispatched to France to check on the authenticity of the groom's claims to nobility. The *New York Herald*'s man in Paris wired that as far as he could tell there was "nothing wrong with the Castellanes." Although the count's girlish complexion prompted some to call him a "powder puff," they quickly learned that such language could cost them dear. The count, their readers were told, was every bit a man, one who exacted immediate payment on the field of honor for any insult.

On March 6, 1895, the newlyweds boarded the *Oceanic* and sailed for France. The following years were stormy and extravagant for this odd pair. According to George Painter, the count was accepted in French social circles as brilliant and dashing, "with his golden hair . . . the cold lapislazuli eyes, the flying monocle and darting movements." He was a peculiar contrast to Anna, who appeared "short, . . . and sallow, with a line of black hair down her spine—'like an Iroquois chieftainess.'"[37]

Proud of his aristocratic ancestry, an admirer of the Duc d'Orléans, Boni looked forward to a royal restoration in France. Shortly after his marriage, he plunged into a political association with anti-Semites, nationalists, and anti-Dreyfusards. In his autobiography, he says that in 1898 "I put myself up for election at Castellane [his ancestral home] and I was nominated [and elected] on a frankly reactionary program." Hostile to Dreyfus, viewing all who supported the cause of revision as traitors to France and its army, Boni also believed that all who disagreed with his views were conspiring to destroy him. "A plot against me was hatched by the secret societies of the world," he wrote years later, comprised of "Jews . . . and foreigners who understood nothing of the point at issue. The Yellow press of America censured my actions—in short, the entire press was in favor of the man on Devil's Island. Fortunately, these bitter attacks did not ruffle my serenity or shake my belief in my star. I simply ignored my persecutors."[38]

Boni's money, or, rather, Anna's, flowed freely into the coffers of right-wing causes. To Paul Déroulède, the anti-Semitic nationalist leader, he said on one occasion: "If ever you need money, let me know, I have a million at your disposal." He also contributed heavily to the cause of the Duc d'Orléans, not to mention Guérin's Anti-Semitic League. Such generosity was not looked upon favorably in the United States: "In his zeal in helping the royalist cause, he has spent many of the good American dollars which came to him with his $5,000,000 bride," complained one newspaper, and his association with Déroulède, who was actively plotting the overthrow of the French Republic, was considered most un-American in view of the fact that he was employing United States currency in the attempt.[39]

It was Anna Gould de Castellane's militant involvement in French reaction, however, that proved most disconcerting to Americans. Her public combativeness began early in June, 1899, when it was announced on June 3 that the United Court of Appeal had declared Dreyfus' conviction by courtmartial null and void and ordered a new trial. The decision was a great blow to French nationalists and enemies of Dreyfus. On the following day, they incited an attack upon President Loubet while he was attending the annual Grand Prix d'Auteuil in the Boi de Boulogne. Loubet's appearance at the races was greeted by hoots, insults, and shouts of "Down with Loubet!" and "Resign!" In the midst of this display, he was struck on the head with a walking cane wielded by an ex-Bonapartist, Baron Chevreau de Christiani, and a pink parasol swung with determination by none other than Countess Anna Gould. Christiani was dragged away by the police before he could seriously injure Loubet, but in the confusion and for reasons not altogether clear, Anna escaped arrest.

The incident was of particular interest to Americans when they heard that one of the most active instigators and organizers of this disturbance was the daughter of the American millionaire. "The little Countess got into the thick of the excitement," ran one front-page account; "placing herself at the head of the Jeunesse Royaliste, she marched up and down shouting 'Vive l'Armée!' followed by a howling mob."[40] Curious readers wanted to know what had prompted her to become involved in a French royalist demonstration. The answer was clear, noted the *New York Journal*. The Duc d'Orléans, reportedly hiding in Paris, had promised the Castellanes that "in the event of his winning the throne he will load them with honors in return for the use of the Gould millions." The entire incident, according to the *Journal*, was calculated to be nothing less than "a logical sequence of the step she and her family took when they purchased the little Count of Castellane as a husband for her." "Should we expect a woman having married such a title to be content to minimize it? Should we expect an empty decoration?" With the success of the royalist schemes, Anna's husband would attain a dukedom, "the highest rank that was bestowed by the kings of France, and she would become a duchess." Furthermore,

> as the Count of Castellane takes his present title from a town in Provence, he would doubtless be pleased to become the Duke of Provence. With the dukedom would go several minor titles, including a marquisate and a countship. He might take the titles of Marquis of Roulon and Count of Toulouse. . . . Anna Gould would then be at the court of King Phillippe VII, Duchess of Provence, Marchioness of Castellane of Roulon, Countess of Toulouse . . . Grand Mistress of the Court of the Queen. In this capacity she would have a leading part in arranging all state functions and in seeing that every woman was kept in her place. It is not possible to conceive of an office more grateful to the soul of a society woman.[41]

Anna's spirited action caused something of a sensation. "Little else is talked of on the boulevard, at the Elysée [Palace] and in the lobbies of the Chamber and the Senate than the dramatic appearance of the rich young woman of American 'parvenue' birth . . . leading a mob of her own sex in a delirious parade in favor of the army." Yet the women of Paris viewed her actions with mixed emotions, not so much for their political as their social implications. The women of France were far from ready to accept the "comtesse américaine" as their representative. "Already today there are extravagant outbursts of admiration for her conduct, as there are also criticisms in every key of irony, satire and open denunciation." Nor was the American colony in Paris overly enthusiastic about Anna's exploits and possible intentions.[42]

The incident was taken by some as a comic interlude, but more thoughtful observers saw nothing humorous about Anna's adventures. "It unveiled the real enemies of the country, who, under the guise of attacking Dreyfus, made war on the republic," a New York newspaper quoted Émile Zola as saying. France's complacency in the face of its president's public humiliation shocked New York Senator Chauncy M. Depew: "If such an attack had been made upon the President of the United States, no matter how bitter were party passions, there would have been universal indignation at this insult to the office."[43] A citizen from New Jersey wondered whether the countess's behavior did not suggest the potential danger which American millionaires posed to democratic institutions:

this country has developed an aristocracy as clearly defined as ever existed in Europe—lacking titles. There are hundreds of women in this country who would do as Anna Gould has done if the opportunity offered itself. In their mad desire for titles and notoriety they would welcome the overthrow of our form of government and the establishment of a monarchy, and in proof of this statement many instances could be quoted of Americans who, having acquired an immense fortune in this country, have turned their backs on their native land; marrying into the aristocracy of Europe, and spending their time and income in trying to strengthen and uphold a class whose only claims to distinction are titles and degeneration. And what makes these facts seem illogical is that many of these sycophants came from ancestors who fled from Europe to escape the domination of the same aristocracy.[44]

A correspondent from Alabama wrote to his editor about "the foreign anarchists who came to this country with empty purses to overthrow our institutions. Is it possible that our rich anarchists are trying to offset the debt by seeking the overthrow of republican government in Europe?"[45] "It has taken a great number of American millions to send Anna Gould to Paris," wired one reporter from Paris, "and while we were sorry to lose the millions, we at least hoped our social representative among the upper circles of Parisian society would remember the land of her birth—and bonds—and instill in a decadent aristocracy an invigorating and rejuvenating spirit of Americanized democracy."[46] William Randolph Hearst questioned whether Anna was fully aware of the implications of her actions—whether she understood that by her gestures she was interfering with the "redress of the monstrous crime of the age." Clearly, as a representative of "America's financial elite she has shamed the country of her birth."[47]

Anna Gould's support of the anti-Dreyfus forces in France thus touched a sensitive chord in the United States. She was, after all, the product of a society whose moral and political sensibilities were presumed to rest on a set of standards above those of France. It was one thing to view from a distance the turbulence of a disordered and decadent society, one ill-equipped to understand American notions of democracy and public order; it was quite another to lend financial and personal backing to the exacerbation of that condition.

VIII

Return of the Martyr

He bore his punishment with the [stolidity] of an Indian, and the breaking of his sword and the tearing off of the insignia of his rank never evoked the trembling of an eyelash. This was incomprehensible to the Frenchmen. It was the *prima facie* evidence of his guilt.

MAX NORDAU
Washington Post, September 6, 1899

The story of the heroism of Mme Dreyfus is one of the brightest pages in the history of the century.

New York World, July 4, 1899

Before 1898 more was known of Dreyfus' tormentors and defenders than of the victim himself. During his imprisonment he remained a nebulous figure, representing a call for action rather than flesh and blood. Not until early 1898 did the shape of his life begin to be clear to the public. He was born in 1859 in upper Alsace, of a well-to-do Jewish family, and was provided with an education appropriate for an aspiring professional soldier. He went from the gymnasium to polytechnical school and on to the distinguished artillery school of Fontainebleau. By 1889, after two successful years at Fontainebleau, he had risen from artillery lieutenant to captain. When he was attached as a probationary officer to the General Staff in 1893, he took on an assignment accorded only to officers of talent and unusual promise and never before given to a Jew. He seems to have been happily married to Lucie Hadamard, daughter of a wealthy family; the couple had two small children. His career had proceeded in the prescribed manner until his sudden arrest and charge with treason on October 14, 1894.[1]

Five events connected with Dreyfus' personal tragedy commanded attention in American circles—his degradation, his confinement on Devil's Island, his wife's heroic exertions on his behalf, his return to France in the summer of 1899, and his second courtmartial at Rennes. After his conviction in closed courtmartial in 1895, suspicions were raised in the United States about the legitimacy of the proceedings. The anti-Semitic slurs flung about by the French press indicated that prejudice had clouded the entire issue.[2] Still, the possibility of his innocence had not yet been raised, and so long as he was presumed guilty, little attention was paid to his mistreatment.

By early 1897, however, when the French critic Bernard Lazare publicly challenged the courtmartial's verdict and the evidence upon which Dreyfus had been found guilty, interest in his fate began to mount, and Dreyfus began to take on the status of a martyr in the United States. Journalists, inspired by Lazare's revelations, retold the story of his public humiliation on the parade grounds of the École Militaire: the reading of the verdict, the snapping of the prisoner's sword upon an adjutant's knee, the rapid tearing of the buttons and gold lace from his uniform, his barely audible protestations of "Vive la France," smothered by a rolling crescendo of drums and angry, vindictive shouts from the surrounding multitude that came to enjoy the display—"À Mort le Traître!" "Down with Judas!"[3]

The memory of that day lingered in the United States. When Dreyfus himself described it in his autobiography in 1901, the popular *McClure's Magazine* printed the first translation of his recollections:

> my whole being racked by a fearful paroxysm, but with body erect and with my head high, I shouted again and again to the soldiers and to the assembled crowd the cry of my soul, "I am innocent!" The parade continued. I was compelled to make the whole round of the square. I heard the howls of the deluded mob; I felt the thrill which I knew must be running through the people, since they believed that before them was a convicted traitor to France.[4]

Even the name of Devil's Island, the French possession off the coast of Guiana, suggested an element of viciousness in French justice. Americans became curious about its precise location, why it was so named, and whether anyone could escape from it. To satisfy such inquisitiveness, American newspapers informed the curious that the Île du Diable, a five-acre piece of land in the Atlantic, was the smallest of a group known as the Îles du Salut, or Safety or Salvation Islands, which stretched seven miles off the coast of French Guiana. Dreyfus was condemned to spend his remaining years in solitary. "Seen on a fine day," remarked an observer, "the islands are gems in the ocean. . . . In reality, they are full of fever, alternately scorched by the sun and drenched by the rain, swarming with snakes, mosquitoes and noxious insects."[5]

Once the plight of Dreyfus became common knowledge, there was speculation about the possibility of his escape. The prisoner's brother, Mathieu, fearful that Alfred's name would be forgotten, calculated as early as 1896 that an announcement of an attempted escape from Devil's Island would revive interest in the case. Working with a journalist from the London *Daily Chronicle*, he arranged for such a report to be published on September 3, 1896. The story was picked up in the *Libre parole* a week later, and on the following day every newspaper in Paris carried it. It was said that Lucie Dreyfus had arranged for her husband to be snatched from Devil's Island and carried away on an American schooner. French newspapers, hostile to Dreyfus, embellished the tale of the daring adventure. Unfortunately for Dreyfus, though such stories were immediately proved false, anxiety about security on the island had been aroused. André Lebon, minister of the colonies, concluded that extreme precautions must be immediately instituted. Dreyfus, who knew nothing of the reports about his escape, was ordered closely watched by day and chained by both legs to his bed by night.[6]

The details of these events, unknown to Americans at the time, came to light as a result of Lebon's later testimony at the Rennes trial. Meanwhile, as the months passed and news of Dreyfus' fate was scant, the public interest in rumors of his escape was evident, and the yellow press detected in such stories an invaluable aid to circulation. It has been suggested that William Randolph Hearst, eager to strike a blow not only for his *Journal* but also for the American flag, gave serious thought to engineering Dreyfus' escape.[7] Hearst's interest was clear in the stories he featured. In December, 1898, his *Evening Journal* ran an interview with Dr. Léon Berthault, a French physician in the convict settlement of Île Royale who claimed to have talked with the prisoner. Asked by a reporter about the possibility of rescuing Dreyfus, Berthault responded that at one time it would have been easy, but not now: "A tower with a Hotchkiss gun commands Devil's Island and the surrounding ocean. The guards have orders to kill Dreyfus in case of an attempt at rescue." However, if the bribe were sufficient, he said, there were "many adventurers in Cayenne who would make the attempt," and he believed that they would probably succeed.[8]

Questioned about the condition of the prisoner, Berthault described him as

chained in his bed every night. . . . At the foot of the bed an iron rod
was fixed. To this Dreyfus's ankles were fastened every night by
means of chains. . . .

In his one living room is an iron cage in which the sentry sits perpetually and watches him. . . .

I took the opportunity to examine this cage. The bars are far
enough apart to allow the man inside to shoot through them. Inside
is a button connecting the electric bell by means of which the sentry
can alarm his companions in the guard home. The most curious feature of the cage is that the sentry is locked in from the outside, so
that he may not be tempted to come out and fraternize with the prisoner.[9]

Dreyfus was "condemned to perpetual silence," though surrounded by
six guards. His quarters had been removed to a part of the island which
could not be seen from the sea. Near his cabin was a guardhouse, sur-
mounted by a twenty-five-foot watchtower, constantly manned. Within
the sentinel's grasp was a Hotchkiss revolving cannon, "which has been
fired more than once in warning."[10]

Life was unbearable for Dreyfus. His letters to his wife were held
back by prison officials, who also censored and tampered with his wife's
mail to him, fearing that it might contain some hidden message. He was
informed that his family was convinced of his guilt, that his wife was
about to remarry. With a fierce light streaming nightly into his face,
attracting insects and mosquitoes, sleep became an ordeal. "Not since
the world began has any man suffered as this son of civilized France has
suffered," commented the *New York World*. "It is impossible to figure it by
analogy. For when in history or fiction, is there any approach to this
physical and mental vivisection?"[11] "The stage management was too
good, the situation was too dramatic, to be forgotten," commented an
English journalist in *Harper's Magazine*: "Dreyfus on his own island—the
very name of Devil's Island was a melodrama in itself—sitting in the sun
within his palisade, in irons, asking his guards for news and met always
with dead silence, informed—as we now know—that his wife had borne
a child two years after he last saw her: who could ever get the picture of
such a purgatory out of his head?"[12]

Another physician who claimed to have seen the prisoner confided
to a reporter that by 1897 Dreyfus was close to physical and mental
collapse; that he frequently spoke of suicide; that he complained of "dys-
pepsia, exhaustion, prolonged insomnia and headaches." The *Evening
Journal* indicated that everything was being done in the island prison to
"drive him to despair by restrictions and punishments of a character

that must break him down." When Dreyfus was sent to Devil's Island, "he was a very blonde man. Now his hair is as white as snow and sparse. His big blue eyes have become lustreless and are encircled with wrinkles. Though he was middle height, he now appears short and stooped. His exceptionally energetic manner has been replaced by an air of decrepitude." [13] Although American interest in Dreyfus was fed by a stream of rumors in the yellow press, the general account of the treatment of the prisoner was quite accurate and made frightening reading.

As his tribulations were unfolded, Dreyfus' reputation grew. "It would be difficult to point to an example, in any time, of sorrow and suffering more courageously borne," commented the *Brooklyn Citizen*. "Evidently there is in the man the strain of blood that flowed in the veins of Deborah and of Barak, of Gideon and Jeptha, and of that first hero of their line who was also the noblest of the Macabees. He has awakened the world's sympathy and has constrained the world's affection." The story of his plight was dramatized on stage, and poets composed verses in his honor. [14]

There was also intense interest in the prisoner's own writing. When his *Lettres d'un innocent* appeared in Paris in the summer of 1898, through his wife's efforts, the *New York Times* immediately printed a partial translation of them, but cautioned its readers that, despite their poignancy, because of French censorship only a fraction of the prisoner's true ordeal was revealed. In July, 1899, a complete translation, *Letters of Captain Dreyfus to His Wife*, was published in New York; newspapers offered the public a taste of them under the title "Letters of a Martyr," with an introduction by Émile Zola. "They have attained the sublime in sorrow," wrote Zola, and "will endure like an imperishable monument when our own writings, perhaps, shall have passed into oblivion. For they are the sob itself of all human suffering." [15] Perhaps it would have been better not to have published the letters at all, said the editorial page of the *New York World*: "Intelligent though the French people are . . . it is doubtful if they could withstand the impulses which that unparalleled story of pity and of horror would stir within them." "They make harrowing reading, every one of them and there are two hundred and twenty-four pages of their passionate despair, starved love, half-crazed impatience, and illusive hopes," commented a literary critic. [16] The theme of innocence which ran through his correspondence, declared Walter Littlefield, a prominent American observer of French affairs, "a declaration that is repeated with awful and tragic monotony until it smites the ear like the wail of an innocent soul in Dante's Inferno," moved him deeply. "The story of the indignities that he endured, the tortures that he suffered at the *Ile du Diable* . . . is like a chapter from the dark ages."[17]

Even more impressive was Dreyfus' personal memoir and selections from a diary which he kept for a while during his imprisonment. These writings appeared in an English translation in 1901 as *Five Years of My Life, 1894–1899*. Selections such as these were reprinted in American periodicals:

> (April 15) It is impossible for me to sleep. The cage, before which the guard walks up and down like a phantom haunted my dream. The plague of insects which run over my skin, the rage which is smothered in my heart . . . drives away sleep.

> (June 2) Nothing. Nothing. Neither letters nor instructions concerning them; always the silence of the grave.

> (October 26) . . . To say that I do not suffer beyond all expression, that often I do not aspire to eternal rest, that this struggle between my deep disgust for men and things and my duty is not terrible, would be a lie.

> (September 8, 1896) These nights in irons! I do not even speak of the physical suffering; but what moral ignominy, and without any explanation, without knowing why or for what cause! What an atrocious nightmare is this which I have lived nearly two years!

> (September 9) . . . I have only an immense pity for those who thus torture human beings! What remorse they are preparing for themselves when truth shall be known, for history has no secrets.

> (September 10) I am so utterly weary, so broken down in body and soul, that today I stop my diary, not being able to foresee how long my strength will hold out or what day my brain shall burst under the weight of so great a burden.

However, Dreyfus stubbornly refused to let go of life, as he recalls: "Whatever the torments they inflict on you, you must march forward until they throw you into the grave; you must stand up before your executioners so long as you have a shadow of strength—a living wreck to be kept before their eyes by the unassailable sovereignty of the soul which they cannot reach."[18]

By the time of the publication of *Five Years*, Dreyfus was launching his battle for total vindication. The *Nation* said that "anything which can keep so phenomenal a case fresh in memory may be regarded as a public service." *Current Literature* agreed that for moral reasons the Dreyfus event should linger in the public eye, for it remains the "colossal crime against liberty." The book "will take a permanent place among the great human documents of the world."[19]

■ Americans made little distinction between the cruelty inflicted on Dreyfus and the treatment of his wife. Her efforts to uncover the truth behind her husband's arrest and to obtain support for a new trial, endeavors which were carried out in the face of hysterical opposition, vicious public criticism and personal attacks, were enormously admired in the United States. "History contains few pictures more pathetic, more touching," commented the *New York World*. "If Dreyfus is a martyr, Mme Dreyfus is a heroine. The French nation shall yet be proud of her."[20]

Americans shared her despair when all communication from Devil's Island ceased in November, 1898. In Dreyfus' last letter to her, widely reprinted in the United States, he wrote: "Despair is beginning to seize me. Have all my friends forgotten me? . . . I shall no longer communicate with my family, as I have said all there is to be said, and I have nothing more to say."[21]

James Creelman, well known for his interviews with internationally known figures, was impressed by her lack of bitterness. She appeared, he said, serene, dignified, and as convinced as ever of her husband's total innocence. "Men of honor do not betray their country," she said. What is more, she told Creelman, there was "no motive to induce him to commit such an act of treason." Besides, "he was condemned upon evidence which was never shown to him nor to his counsel." Even more damaging to the prosecution was the fact that "the character of the men who are most bitterly opposed to my husband is such that it establishes a strong presumption in favor of his innocence." His enemies, she said, "have hesitated at no crime. Forgery, roguery, conspiracy, duplicity, lying, and perhaps murder, have been resorted to [to] keep my husband in chains."[22]

American reporters vied to obtain interviews with Lucie Dreyfus, especially in the few months preceding her husband's release. Her willingness to absolve her husband's tormentors they found most astounding: "I shall forgive everyone when my husband is liberated. Enough have suffered already." She persistently denied rumors that her husband would leave France for good after his release. He loved France, she told a reporter. Like many patriotic French Jews, she refused to acknowledge the prejudice that lay behind her husband's imprisonment. Asked by a correspondent whether she believed that her husband was the victim of a conspiracy, she denied it vigorously: "Why a conspiracy? Mistakes were committed in good faith, at first. Then arose the desire to hide these blunders from the public because of the attacks on the army that would surely rise out of them." To the question as to what she would do were Dreyfus again found guilty, she replied, "I would fight it for five years, for ten years, for all my life . . . for I know he is innocent."[23]

To millions of Americans, Lucie Dreyfus epitomized true womanhood. Her faith in her husband and her efforts to prove him innocent made her an exemplary wife. It mattered little that many of the dialogues between American correspondents and Lucie Dreyfus did not in fact occur but were little more than imaginative journalism. The popularity of such "interviews" attests to the universal interest in her plight. When her husband was finally released, she gratefully acknowledged the encouraging words she had received from the United States, especially from American women.[24]

■ Americans awaited Dreyfus' return to France with great anticipation. Speculations circulated about his preparations, his mode of travel,[25] the precise time and place of his arrival and his appearance and physical condition, for only a few had seen the chief character in this long drama. Most important, his return to France was seen as the first step in one of the great moral and legal victories of the century.

Dreyfus was reported to be in a state of bewilderment about the sudden change in his fortunes. Informed that his rank of captain in the army had been restored, wrote the foreign correspondent Leon Bassiers, Dreyfus looked like "a statue suddenly animated." The few words which he then uttered indicated total ignorance of the excitement that his celebrated case had inspired. "He seemed to believe that the revision of his trial was due to his former chiefs—Du Paty de Clam, to General Mercier and the rest."[26]

Early announcements indicated that Dreyfus would debark at Brest some time during the night of June 26. "Thousands of eyes are straining seaward to catch a glimpse of the war ship carrying Dreyfus," reported James Creelman. A mass of reporters awaited him, but his family was not allowed to meet him:

> Heart hungry as his wife and family are for sight of him after all these terrible years, they do not dare to go where they expect him to land, lest their presence might attract a mob of pitiless persecutors and he might die on the very threshold of his vindication.

> There is something appalling in the thought that this man, whom the whole Court of Cassation have declared to be unjustly condemned, must be taken in secrecy to the seat of justice.[27]

The *New York Journal* solicited salutations from selected individuals in honor of the famous prisoner. "Will you join with the prominent Americans throughout the country in a testimonial of congratulation . . . to Captain Dreyfus to be presented to him on his landing in France?" wired the *Journal's* editor to the United States secretary of state, John Hay, on June 8. Americans showered him with congratulatory messages. William Jennings Bryan forwarded his best wishes, as did the governor of Illinois, John P. Altgeld. John Henry Barrows, president of Oberlin College, James B. Angell, president of the University of Michigan, and E. R. A. Seligman of Columbia University saw in his return a turning point in French civilization. The evangelist Dwight L. Moody wrote Dreyfus: "America hails the victory of justice, and millions of countrymen rejoice in your vindication." The feminist Elizabeth Cady Stanton declared: "Heroic Dreyfus! I rejoice for the honor of France that she does justice at last."[28]

Dreyfus actually landed in France on June 30. Reporters hovering in Brest were caught off guard. To elude curious crowds and potential assassins, the ship carrying Dreyfus discharged him in the peninsula town of Quiberon, late at night, in the midst of a summer storm. The *New York Evening Journal* told its readers:

> Upon his arrival, Dreyfus was described as "silent and grim." As he stepped ashore he walked erect with his head thrown back, and his whole bearing that of a trained military man. He bowed to the officials, but uttered not a word. There was nothing defiant nor theatrical in his manner, but his silence was extraordinary. . . . In the uncertain light it could be seen that his face was thin, but his complexion was bronzed and ruddy. His mouth was straight and firm, his lips were tightly compressed. . . . His strong soldierly bearing presented a strange contrast to the pictures that have been drawn of the imagined invalid. . . . From a French point of view he was disappointing. There was no emotion betrayed in his face, no *"Vive la France"* declarations, no posing attitudes, nothing to say to the public.[29]

Not far from the landing, in the darkness, a special train awaited the prisoner and his military escort. When it arrived at Rennes, it was met by hundreds of reporters and curious bystanders who had streamed into the ordinarily placid town throughout the night. A series of subterfuges were arranged. Moments before Dreyfus' arrival a carriage raced through the streets, accompanied by wild shouts of "here he comes!" A short distance behind, Dreyfus rode in an unguarded carriage, followed by a closed carriage with drawn blinds, heavily guarded; James Creelman reported that "the suddenness of the movement stupefied everybody as, apparently it did the prisoner, whose face showed from the quickly passing carriage." He noted how difficult it was "to realize in faraway America the thrilling, fearsome nature of that scene. Every one of us who waited in the streets that night felt that the knife or the bullet of an assassin might rob the poor, lonely victim of life on the very threshold of justice. . . . The fate of the French Ministry, perhaps of the republic itself, depended on the getting of Dreyfus into the military prison alive." [30]

Accounts of Dreyfus' first day in France varied. Americans preferred to believe, and were assured, that one of his first acts was to read the numerous sympathetic messages which awaited him: "this written welcome from distinguished men and women thousands of miles away was the happiest incident of his return to his own country." [31]

His wife was permitted to visit his cell shortly after his arrival, and their first encounter also generated considerable journalistic gossip. The *New York World* correspondent gave an account of the meeting:

> When the cell door opened Mme Dreyfus . . . flew to her husband with a single piercing, "Alfred!" She clasped him in her arms.
>
> Dreyfus made no answer; no step forward. He remained passive in her embrace, looking down on the head of his wife sobbing against his breast. There was still between them the barrier of four years of exile and agony such as, perhaps, no other living man has endured.
>
> While pushing his wife back gently to look at her face, Dreyfus said: "Well, yes, I am here. I am not much better than a corpse, but here I am." He then walked away without kissing her. He began to pace up and down the cell, his hands behind his back. . . .
>
> Surprised by his strange, cold attitude his poor wife stood where she was abandoned, in the middle of the room, absolutely dumbfounded. . . .
>
> "Alfred, look at me! Don't you know me?" she cried. . . .
>
> Dreyfus answered: "Of course, I recognize you . . . I am sick, not insane."
>
> There was little conversation for some time. Four years of absolute silence had made connected speech little more than a memory to him. He seemed to have forgotten how to utter his thoughts or to realize the necessity of uttering them. . . . Mme Dreyfus issued from the prison in a state of collapse. [32]

The public wondered whether Dreyfus could withstand the stress of another trial. It was obvious that he had little comprehension of the complexity of his case, of the sacrifices that many had made on his behalf, and of the passions that had been let loose in France since his conviction. Like his wife, he persisted in the belief that his suffering was the result of an honest error, which, now that it had been discovered, was bound to be rectified by his military superiors. Americans were somewhat disappointed at the reports from France that "Dreyfus is no Dreyfusite." His attachment to the army was either praised as an admirable quality or pitied as product of his long isolation. The second view was expressed by Creelman: "There is something infinitely touching in his childlike loyalty to the organization from which he was driven like a leper into shameful exile."[33]

Accounts of his general health differed also. "The story that he is a physical wreck is a preposterous invention," wrote one reporter. "Dreyfus looks strong and healty. He moves quickly and with decision. His eye is clear, his head erect. I can vouch for this, for I saw him on his arrival at Rennes." Another asserted that the prisoner was "bent and grey from his mental suffering, barely able, after his long silence, to form an intelligible sentence." His inability to show signs of emotion, to emit "a flow of feeling," caused concern. The *New York World* featured a front-page story on the subject early in July. A psychologist in Paris told an American reporter that "Dreyfus was rescued in the nick of time," that "insanity was already clutching his brain." An eminent American psychiatrist, Dr. Jackson R. Campbell, after reading the reports of Dreyfus' mental state, assured Americans that he had an excellent chance for a complete recovery: "I have absolutely no fear for the future. Capt. Dreyfus will soon learn that he is surrounded by friends. . . . He will recover."[34] The French intellectual Max Nordau believed that it was Dreyfus' lack of "temperament" which enabled him to survive: "He uttered no apostrophes to justice and heaped no anathemas on the heads of his tormentors. He bore his punishment with the [stolidity] of an Indian. . . . This was incomprehensible to the Frenchmen. It was the *prima facie* evidence of his guilt. They could not tolerate that phlegmatic self-control which enabled one to receive insults with . . . manifest dignity." His salvation stemmed from this "psychic anaesthesia," said Nordau, which kept him from going mad.[35] "Here is an illustration of the marvelous strength and power of endurance of the human brain," said the *New York World*: "A severer strain is inconceivable than those nearly two thousand days of solitary confinement of a man who knew he was innocent. . . . The human brain is delicate beyond description. Yet here is an instance of its having survived a strain that would have burst to atoms a mechanism infinitely more powerful but not so finely balanced."[36]

Dreyfus was admired in the United States for his refusal to succumb to despair or death.

> He drew together all the forces of his mind and soul. He would not die; he would live in spite of the iron manacles, the racking fever and the torturing silence—live to see his wife and children, live to wear the beloved uniform of France again. It was the supreme psychological hour of his long ordeal. The love of life and liberty and the hope of a perfect vindication and rehabilitation filled his nights and days. He beat down death with a resolute will.[37]

■ The courtmartial at Rennes, which opened on August 7, stands as a striking example of how law can be grotesquely twisted in the hands of patriotic but mediocre men. For five hot summer weeks, Dreyfus was once again subjected to a bizarre legal exercise. This time it was performed in public, before an audience of six hundred congregated in the local *lycée*. Most had never set eyes on the prisoner. When he appeared, almost everyone stood, and "some mounted on benches to obtain a better view. There were subdued cries of 'Sit down.'" One reporter described him as "stiff as his uniform. He held his head high, as if on purpose, but his shoulders stooped. The step was that of a man not used to freedom, and extremely measured and mechanical. One might think that he marked time as he walked. . . . His mode of saluting the court was jerky and very composed, but his fingers betrayed febrile nervousness."[38] The reporter Julian Ralph saw the sweat pour from the prisoner's brow, though the courtroom was cool. "When he has the chance," said Ralph, "I hear him talk faster than even Phillips Brooks or Gladstone could utter words. Then I know he is trying to say, in the few moments allowed to him, all that he has been thinking of in his self-defense for more than four years."[39]

The testimony of André Lebon, minister of the colonies and the architect of Dreyfus' tortured existence on Devil's Island, elicited the first sign of real emotion from the defendant. "The scene in the courtroom was positively painful as the record of horrors was read amid the most intense silence. . . . For the first time Dreyfus's own iron nerve gave way as he was compelled to revive those awful memories." Asked, at the conclusion of Lebon's apologia for his own actions, whether he had anything to say, Dreyfus replied: "I am not here to describe the horrors I suffered for five years. . . . I am not here to complain, and I bear no malice." "It was a splendid rebuff," said the *New York Times*; "even the seven judges looked ashamed. The audience wanted to applaud, but did not dare to."[40]

When the guilty verdict was pronounced, Dreyfus appeared little moved. According to Julian Ralph, not a sign of bitterness was evident on the prisoner's face: "A smile I caught as he threw it toward Labori gave me a wholly new view of him. Thank Heaven, he goes to comfortable quarters; he knows now of the immense human brotherhood that weeps and fights for him." The *New York Times* reported that "Dreyfus has borne the terrible shock of his reconviction with marvelous fortitude—one might almost say, with unnatural calm."[41]

Some Americans, worried about Dreyfus' ability to sustain this second blow, sent his wife advice on how to care for his health. Mark Twain wrote to an acquaintance in England asking him to suggest to Madame Dreyfus that a Mr. Kellgreu be consulted. Kellgreu, Twain believed, "can cure any disease that any physician can cure, and . . . in many desperate cases he can restore health where no physician can do it."[42] This gesture mirrored a universal concern. Never had France sunk lower in the American estimation than during these bleak days following the second courtmartial.

■ The American outrage over Dreyfus' second conviction was somewhat alleviated with the announcement of his pardon on September 19. Why the guiltless should require forgiveness was a puzzle. The sudden death of the courageous Senator Sheurer-Kestner, one of the first to support the cause of Dreyfus, at great personal political sacrifice, on the very day of the presidential announcement, also dampened enthusiasm for an event that might have been greeted with greater festivity even if it were only a partial victory. The judgment was understood to be one of "expediency" rather than justice. If the court that condemned him was stamped as "guilty of a crime more odious than was charged on Dreyfus," the pardon was viewed as possessing some merit. "Pardon will enable him to live quietly and gain health enough to go on in the work of complete vindication," one magazine said.[43]

There was hope that Dreyfus might visit the United States. Rumors that he would undertake a lecture tour in America began circulating even before the conclusion of the trial. In the belief that he would first rest in London, an American agent went there to make the necessary arrangements for a tour.[44] Others, more solicitous of Dreyfus' welfare, hoped that he would at least convalesce in the United States. At Otsego, a little Michigan village, there was a move to buy him a house and invite him to make his home there. Charles F. Jones invited him to move to Louisville, Kentucky, where a "quiet residence" would be provided him and his family until he regained his health. The house offered was a "well-built, three story and basement family residence on Walnut Street. . . . If he cares to reside there, I will present him with the place."[45] But Dreyfus had no intention of leaving France.

For a while after the pardon Dreyfus almost vanished from public view. He did attend the funeral of Émile Zola in October, 1902, and, out of gratitude, kept watch by Zola's coffin throughout the night preceding the funeral. The intricate legal maneuvers which led to his full vindication in July, 1906, failed to catch the public interest in the United States, although the French High Court's final, historic decision clearing Dreyfus of all charges brought against him did create a momentary stir, and the announcement that he would rejoin the French army as a major was greeted with satisfaction. "After eleven years the most notorious error of justice of the age has been righted," said the *New York Times*. "The disgrace of his broken sword, his stripped uniform, the deprivation of family and society, the hideous tortures of Devil's Island have not been in vain."[46]

It did not go unnoticed by the *Times* that a number of key conspirators, some officers of major rank, went unpunished, "incapable even of regret, and . . . still mumbling their senseless calumnies . . . or drawing their grimy swords in defense of a long lost 'honor.'"[47] But there was agreement that France had righted the great wrong. On July 22, 1906, a small military ceremony took place outside the École Militaire, on the very spot where Dreyfus had been publicly disgraced. There were few people present, but for Dreyfus and his American friends it was a ceremony of supreme significance. Dreyfus was given a medal and made a knight of the Legion of Honor. "Historical records, criminal annals, romance and the drama, furnish no stranger tale of human life and destiny, than that which has reached its culmination in the final and complete exoneration of Dreyfus," commented a Cincinnati newspaper. The *Outlook* was convinced that

> in the history of fiction there is nothing bolder in invention or more
> dramatically striking in incident than this famous trial. . . . A man of
> fortune and of unusual promise, publicly degraded as the result of
> one of the vilest plots in the history of a jurisprudence, surrounded
> by scoundrels who heaped lie upon lie and forgery upon forgery . . .
> restored at last, after the complete crushing of all his enemies. . . .[48]

The *Independent* concurred: the affair afforded "the best possible material for the study of the workings of modern democracy in many of its characteristic manifestations." In this particular instance the conclusion was a satisfactory one.

IX

America and the Dimensions of French Anti-Semitism

Taking advantage of the circumstances that Dreyfus is a Jew . . . they called to their aid the antisemitic feeling, that meanest and most hideous remnant of medieval barbarism, which never appears on the surface without an exhibition of the basest impulses of human nature, casting a dark shadow of disgrace on our boasted Christian civilization.

CARL SCHURZ, 1898

The whole business . . . undoubtedly soothes our sense of self-satisfaction, so that we thank heaven that we are not as Frenchmen are. We ought also, however, to thank heaven that we are not subject to the same conditions which embarrass the French. If all the Jews of Continental Europe were suddenly to be transported to this continent, we might find the national digestion, powerful as it is, badly nauseated.

JOHN T. MORSE, JR., 1898

It was the Jewishness of Dreyfus that transformed the Dreyfus case into the Dreyfus "affair." It made it possible for the simple and the evil-minded alike to magnify the victim's purported treachery. Hatred of Dreyfus the Jew triggered the forces of reaction—militarism, monarchism, clericalism—and gave them a common target and an audience. For a while the Dreyfus affair made hatred of Jews fashionable in France, with those who declined to participate seen as unpatriotic, even villainous. Its violent expression, as Hannah Arendt observes, foreshadowed the fate of Europe's Jews; it seemed to be "a huge dress rehearsal for a performance that had to be put off for more than three decades."[1]

This is not to say that modern anti-Semitism was born in France during the age of Dreyfus. The hatred was deeply rooted in ancient Christological fantasies, but it was nourished by the ideas of the Enlightenment and the French Revolution. Jews were accused by one side of perpetuating the religious superstition of antiquity and by the other of financing the Revolution. In nineteenth-century France the left made little effort to conceal its disdain for Jews, whom it frequently associated with the decadent forces of capitalism. In literature and legends the Jew was a convenient chief villain; on the stage he was portrayed as a grotesque and hateful figure.

One might debate the degree of intensity of anti-Jewish feeling in France, but not its existence. Before the 1880s it was less noticeable than in other countries of Europe, but by the middle of that decade it had become marked.[2] The failure of the Panama Canal Company in 1889 was partially responsible. Its collapse proved financially disastrous to thousands of hard-working, middle-class, mostly Catholic investors whose loans to the venture had nationalistic as well as economic motivations. For years the shaky structure of the company had been hidden from the people of France. Bribes to key parliamentary officials guaranteed a continuous flow of government subsidies and loans for the enterprise. The discovery that a few Jewish businessmen were indirectly implicated in the scandal provided a scapegoat. Upon his return to the United States from France ten years after the failure, James B. Eustis reported that the people of France "believe that the Jews are responsible for the corruption that is said to prevail in governmental circles. They claim that before the Panama scandals, corruption of officials was unknown in France. . . . they attribute this lamentable decadence and downfall of public morality to the corrupting practices of the Jews."[3]

Edouard Drumont's Jew-baiting daily *Libre parole* converted the Panama scandal into both an anti-Semitic crusade and an attack upon France's republican and parliamentary institutions. With the appearance in 1886 of his two-volume polemic *La France juive*, Drumont became the principal anti-Semitic theoretician of late nineteenth-century France. His audience was drawn largely from the discontented middle classes, merchants, petty bourgeoisie, and dissatisfied professionals, especially lawyers, journalists, and clergy. Riddled with modern racial and medieval Christian mythology, *La France juive* blamed the Jews for all the economic, social, and political misfortunes of France. Together with Freemasonry and Protestantism, which, according to Drumont, had also succumbed to Jewish manipulation, France had capitulated to such Judaic notions as parliamentary democracy and the decline of Christian values, thereby paving the way for an ultimate Jewish conquest and destruction of France. To counteract this threat, Drumont's *Libre parole* urged Frenchmen to take matters into their hands and drive the Jews out of France.[4]

Given this mood, resentment over the presence of Jews in the officer corps of the army increased, and Jewish officers were subjected to harassment and humiliation. The *Croix*, a Jew-baiting tabloid especially popular in Catholic and army circles, and the *Libre parole* mounted a strenuous protest against Alfred Dreyfus' appointment to the General Staff in 1893.

This hatred was not expressed only in words, however. These years were marked by brutality and bloodshed, with the Jews residing in France's North African provinces suffering the most. With Drumont as Algeria's representative to the French Parliament and Max Régis, an anti-Semite, as the mayor of Algiers, one might have expected little else. At the height of the Dreyfus affair Jews were beaten to death in the streets of Algiers, their synagogues were defiled, and their businesses boycotted, while French political leaders and statesmen looked on with relative indifference.[5]

This eruption did not escape notice in the United States. Through a consular dispatch President McKinley was informed in November, 1898, of the precarious nature of Jewish existence in France. Few Frenchmen would have objected to their wholesale massacre, wrote Albion Tourgée to McKinley, and he equated their condition with that of blacks in the American South. American newspapers frequently carried descriptions of French crowds yelling "Death to the Jews," the stoning of Jewish shops, and anti-Semitic ravings even in the Chamber of Deputies. In Algeria, Americans were informed, government authorities themselves urged the pillage of Jewish shops. The names of Jules Guérin and Max Régis were well known in the United States, though their activities were difficult for ordinary Americans to understand. They wondered "how human beings could descend to such savagery."[6]

A handful of Frenchmen did not share these passions. In June, 1897, an anonymous French contributor to the *Forum*, "Vindex," wrote that Dreyfus was being persecuted because he was a Jew, and blamed the "diatribes" of such newspapers as the *Croix* and *Libre parole* for launching the campaign against the Jews. "The Jew Dreyfus was helpless against the will of the anti-Semitic mob. . . . Anti-Semitic papers and clerical publications, lying without scruple, had built up a great conspiracy." Even those who believed Dreyfus to be guiltless "submitted to anti-Semitic terrorism, not wanting to resist it; or rather, by adding to it, they took advantage of the patriotic excitement." The *Forum* piece concluded with a warning to Americans to be vigilant against oppression and invited "those in every country who believe that nothing is indifferent to them which affects humanity . . . right and justice—may they labor with me to hasten that day!"[7]

The names of Émile Zola, Max Nordau, and Bernard Lazare were of course familiar in the United States. Interviewed by Robert H. Sherard, an American reporter, in March, 1898, Zola at first hesitated to acknowledge that "France, the great, generous, enlightened nation, will tolerate a movement which . . . throws us back into the dark of the Middle Ages." The wave of anti-Semitism, he asserted, is "an idiotic one, fostered by certain men who wish to derive from their connections with it a notoriety which they could not obtain in any other way." Zola was convinced that they would be unsuccessful, but he was surprised at the intensity of the anti-Jewish feeling around him:

> The very initiation of the movement stupefied me—that there should
> be a return to fanaticism, an attempt to light up a religious war in
> this epoch of ours, one hundred years after the revolution, in the
> heart of our great Paris, in the days of democracy, of universal tolera-
> tion, at the very time when there is an immense movement being
> made everywhere toward equality, justice, and fraternity. A handful
> of madmen, cunning or idiotic, come and shout in our ears every
> morning, "Let us kill the Jews. Let us devour the Jews. Let us massa-
> cre them. Let us exterminate them." . . . Is it not inconceivable?
> Could anything be more foolish? Could anything be more abomi-
> nable?[8]

Max Nordau, more worldly in such matters, was less sanguine about the future security of France's Jews. Born in Hungary, Nordau had lived in Paris for twenty years and had become famous for his commentaries on the condition of European civilization. A non-practicing Jew, like Theodor Herzl, he had been greatly alarmed by the Dreyfus affair, and he had become an ardent supporter of the new Zionist movement. When interviewed by a reporter from the *American Monthly Review of Reviews* in March, 1898, Nordau was blunt: "We are quite simply marching in France toward a new St. Bartholomew's Eve, to a massacre which will be limited by the number of Jews the Catholics can find to knock on the head." He firmly rejected the popular notion that Jews had been more favored in France than elsewhere in Europe and believed that, although the Revolution had planted the seeds of Jewish emancipation, the Catholic Church had stood in its way.[9] In a moving address in Basel to the Zionist Congress some months later, which was widely reprinted in the United States, Nordau again stressed the ominous changes in France with respect to the Jewish population: "France, the France of the Great Revolution, and of the Declaration of Human Rights," he declared, "is today marching at the head of the anti-Semitic movement."[10]

One of the most outspoken critics of French anti-Semitism and one of the first to join in the defense of Alfred Dreyfus was the Jewish literary critic Bernard Lazare. The case altered his views about the future place of the Jew in France and also brought him to the Zionist movement. His *Anti-Semitism, Its History and Causes*, published in 1894, was the first major response to Drumont's *La France juive*.[11] He was even more convinced than Nordau that the Catholic Church was responsible for the irrationality and prejudice that had spread throughout France. He told the *North American Review*:

> It is a clerical principle that a confession is better than proof. All inquisitorial jurisprudence . . . is founded upon obtaining a confession and not on founding proofs. The Church has always opposed the latter; it will not admit scientific demonstration, but prefers an authoritative and hierarchical affirmation, which does not permit the development of rational examination and free criticism. . . . It demands not proofs of guilt . . . but a dogma of culpability. It is in this way that the treason of Dreyfus became a dogma for the great majority of Frenchmen.[12]

Such French voices, primarily Jewish, were neither typical nor numerous, and it is not surprising that their most sympathetic audience was not at home but in the United States.

■ The condition of Jews in France and the pivotal role that anti-Semitism played in the Dreyfus affair were well known to the American reading public, as we have seen, but what is less certain is the meaning of such knowledge to Americans. Social discrimination against Jews was not uncommon in the United States in the 1890s, and the Dreyfus affair coincided with an influx into American cities of hundreds of thousands of Jews fleeing Russian persecution and economic deprivation in eastern Europe. They arrived at a time of sinking farm prices, a shaky national economy, and flight from farms to urban communities, events which in themselves generated a variety of social problems. Furthermore, the American intellectual climate was dominated by Darwinian and racial notions which relegated East Europeans, including Jews, to an inferior social and biological status and by a religious view which equated virtue and salvation with Protestant Christianity. It would seem that the conditions were ripe for anti-Semitism to flourish in the New World as it did in the Old.[13]

Yet one could argue that the degree of American anti-Semitism was minor compared to that which existed in the countries of Europe. The nineteenth-century American Jewish historian Peter Wiernik asserted with patriotic pride that "we . . . have no Jewish problem here, in the sense in which the term is understood in the backward countries of the Old World." The prominent biblical scholar and historian Max L. Margolis noted with considerable satisfaction, while teaching at Berkeley in 1898, the congenial relations between Christians and Jews. More recently, the historian Oscar Handlin has asserted that "the ten years after 1890 were not only free of anti-Semitism; they were actually marked by distinct philo-Semitism."[14]

Indeed, increasing attention was paid to the Jewish Question in the United States at this time, quite possibly because of the Dreyfus case. A number of writers began to observe with greater astuteness the Jew's contribution to civilization and the treatment accorded to Jews in ancient and modern societies. Mark Twain, for example, was quite taken with these issues and, in his characteristic style, remarked to a friend in 1897: "The difference between the brain of the average Jew" and that of a Gentile "is about the difference between an Archbishop's and a tadpole's. It's a marvelous race—by long odds the most marvelous that the world has produced, I suppose." He chronicled the achievements of the Jews in order to underscore France's miscalculation of the value of its Jewish subjects. "His contributions to the world's list of great names in literature, science, art, music, finance, medicine . . . are also away out of proportion to the weakness of his numbers," he remarked in a widely read essay: "He has made a marvelous fight in this world, in all the ages; and has done it with his hands tied behind him. He could be vain of himself, and be excused for it."[15]

The anti-Semitic crusade in France and elsewhere in Europe observed a writer in the *Arena*, was a virus easily spread, not only across geographic boundaries but to future generations. In a thoughtful article James Eustis described France's perception of her Jewish citizens:

> In France the Jew is considered an enemy of *la patrie*; the prejudice against him does not arise from causes which are alleged to exist in other countries, such as the successful competition of that remarkable race in the struggle for individual success and supremacy in the

various departments of trade and industry. This deep-seated and
dangerous prejudice against the Jew in France springs from an
apprehension that he is attempting, by the secret use of power or his
wealth, to dominate and control the Government of France to the
detriment of the State. . . . It is a common accusation against the Jew
in France that he is plotting to overthrow her institutions and to
bring about her ruin.[16]

The eruption of violence against the Jews of Paris, Marseille, and
Lyons during the Zola trial was treated in the American press as a form
of French fanaticism and as a convenient tool employed by demagogues. Fabian Franklin, a well-known Baltimore newspaper editor,
explained that anti-Semitism could start as "a convenient and simple
rallying-cry for those who want to break up something" because "it is so
much easier to get a rabble excited over Jews, who can be imagined to
be supplied by nature with something peculiarly diabolical, than over a
class defined simply by wealth, or by opinion, and whom the masses
know to be all of the same blood as themselves." He warned that "wherever anti-Semitism has become rampant, governments, however much
they might have seemed disposed to coquette with it at first, have found
it necessary to do all in their power to curb it, for it contains within itself
the germs of some of the most serious dangers which threaten modern
civilization."[17] The elder statesman Carl Schurz, writing in *Harper's
Weekly* in March, 1898, described the anti-Semitic movement in France
as "that meanest and most hideous remnant of medieval barbarism,
which never appears on the surface without an exhibition of the basest
impulses of human nature, casting a dark shadow of disgrace on our
boasted Christian civilization. . . . In all her internal commotions France
has hardly ever beheld a spectacle more grotesque and alarming than
this."[18]

Outside of France, the sight of howling, undisciplined mobs pillag-
ing the Jewish quarter of Algiers made even more vivid the precariousness of Jewish life. The *Outlook* referred to the mayor of Algiers, Max
Régis, as a "fanatical anti-Semite" who saddled the Jewish residents of
his city with countless burdens:

He has lately crowned the device of his small-minded and mean-
spirited persecution by a bit of childish malice which would seem incredible if it were not reported from trustworthy sources. He has had
photographers sent to the Jewish shops to take snapshot portraits of
the ladies who visit these shops as customers, and these portraits are
to be hung in a public place! What has become of the French devo-

tion to women, or of that courtesy with which the French have so
long been credited, even by those who have not respected their political character? The world has outgrown the age when one race can
entertain itself by sticking pins into another race. Such exhibitions
are offensive to all right-minded people.[19]

The *New York Sun* remarked that the violence of these attacks seemed
incomprehensible to Americans. It quoted the mayor of Algiers: "the
tree of liberty must be watered with the blood of Jews," and reported
that officials in Paris did nothing while "Spanish viragos with whips
seized female Jewish children and scourged them naked through the
streets," "sick Jews were cast naked out of the hospitals," and women
were "dragged by their hair through the city and their husbands . . .
clubbed to death before their eyes."[20]

As the Dreyfus affair neared its climax in the summer of 1899,
American reporters were struck by the mounting hatred even in the
heart of France. Grumblings about the "Jewish Syndicate" were over-
heard daily along the boulevards and in the cafés. "How often I have
trudged about . . . waiting for 'the Jew' to return from his five years'
ordeal of silence and hear the voice of Christian France shrieking for a
sacrifice," wrote James Creelman. "Dreyfus is a Jew," commented
another observer at this time, "and to the people who have never been
able to rid themselves of the impression that the Jews of today are
responsible for the crime of Calvary that is sufficient to justify his conviction." Even the arrival of Lucie Dreyfus in Rennes was greeted by
hoots and howls. Shopkeepers, Americans were informed, refused to
serve her, and she was compelled to make her purchases under an
assumed name.[21] A correspondent wired that there were rumors of a
pogrom against the Jewish community of France, possibly aroused
because St. Bartholomew's Day was imminent. "All night long," wrote
Harry J. W. Dam from Rennes, "the cry has echoed from thousands of
throats under our windows, 'Death to the Jews! Death to the Jews!'" The
St. Louis Post-Dispatch predicted that there would be a Jewish exodus
from France, just as centuries earlier in Spain. "As I sat at the desk on
the evening of the verdict," wrote Julian Ralph from France, "Rennes
went into rejoicing, the air quivered with the voices of the people sing-
ing the *Marseillaise*." Below his window he could hear the mobs chanting
"Conspuez les Juifs!" ("Spit upon the Jews"). "Remember when you weigh
the act of the courtmartial," Ralph urged his American readers, "that
the best elements in France supported the verdict."[22]

Although an official protest of the verdict by the American government was never issued, on the ground that it would be construed as meddling in the internal affairs of France, such a nicety, explained the *Washington Post*, should not discourage American citizens. It urged a boycott of French goods to punish France. The *St. Louis Post-Dispatch* encouraged Americans to boycott the Paris Exposition, scheduled to open in a few months.[23] Such open recommendations from respectable and relatively conservative sources suggest an unusual degree of dissatisfaction with France.

■ Among the critics of French anti-Semitism were leading American clergymen from a variety of Protestant denominations. American Protestant spokesmen became critics of France during the age of Dreyfus for as many reasons as those that propelled many other Americans. No doubt, an element of anti-Roman Catholicism was involved in the pattern: the fact that the outbreak of Jew hatred had occurred in Catholic France and was supported by popular Catholic journals and numerous parish priests made the American Protestant protest not only convenient but palatable. To say this, however, is not to take away from the seriousness of the moral crusade which American Protestantism saw itself waging on behalf of Dreyfus, justice, and social order.

The years of Dreyfus corresponded in the United States with a movement in Protestantism which deemed it incumbent upon Christians to strive for social improvement. This age of the "social gospel" was rooted in the earlier years of American Christianity, in Protestant revivalism and perfectionism, but at the end of the nineteenth century, more than ever, salvation was linked to moral and social involvement. For this reason Richard Hofstadter described the Progressive Era in American history as "a phase in the history of the Protestant conscience, a latter-day Protestant revival."[24]

Although its primary consideration was the improvement of domestic conditions and the eradication of poverty, political and corporate corruption, illiteracy, and crime, the Protestant conscience also concerned itself with discords abroad. Heber Newton, a leading liberal religious spokesman, urged his congregants in 1898 not to take too strictly George Washington's warning about foreign entanglements. That warning, he explained, was directed to an infant country. For Americans of today to close their eyes to wrongs committed abroad, according to Newton, was equivalent to moral cowardice.[25]

Among such wrongs the plight of the Jews of Europe often figured. The Jew as an historical figure had assumed a renewed significance in

Protestant thought: the Protestant emphasis on a theology of social reform compelled many of its leaders to take a more serious look at the Jewish sources of Christianity. The books of the Prophets took on a special meaning. "They are an integral part of the thought life of Christianity," observed Walter Rauschenbusch, the acknowledged theologian of the social gospel. "What other nation" but that of the Jews, he remarked, "has a library of classics in which the spokesmen of the common people have the dominant voice. It would be hard to find a parallel to it anywhere."[26] Prominent ministers often spoke of the debt Christianity owed to Judaism. "Nearly everything we have that dignifies us and sweetens us and refines us and makes us significant . . . has come to us from them," wrote George E. Merriam. Edward C. Baldwin, author of *Our Modern Debt to Israel*, was convinced that the social gospel movement was but the rediscovery of Judaism by the Christian world. Unlike those historians of his day who sought the germ of constitutional government in the midst of Germanic forests, Lyman Abbott, whose popular magazine, the *Outlook*, was prominent in liberal Protestant circles, attributed even the origins of modern democratic behavior to Jewish biblical thought. "Every legislative hall, every courthouse . . . to say nothing of less visible and tangible manifestations of our national life and temper are monuments of our indebtedness to this ancient people," he wrote early in the century. The political activist and social gospeler Washington Gladden periodically reminded his congregants in Columbus, Ohio, that the religious insight of the early Jews "entitles the race to the distinction of religious leadership."[27]

In this context, it is understandable that the news from France should be displeasing. "No public movement of late years has been more odious in spirit or more contemptible in method," wrote Lyman Abbott when he heard of the Algerian pogroms. "The leaders of that movement have shown a lack of humanity and an indifference to the decencies of civilized life which seem like survival of barbarism." French behavior became a popular target in Sunday sermons. "It is not true Christianity, but rather the spirit of Satanism" which dominates France, remarked a prominent Baptist in New York: "If we believe the antagonism was the legitimate result of Christianity, many of us would repudiate the name of Christian." "Why the cry in Paris, 'Down with the Jews?'" asked the Reverend D. B. Greig, a Michigan Presbyterian: "are not these Semites human beings? . . . Is it because they differ from us in their religion? Is it because they crucified Jesus? The truth is, we owe to these Hebrew tribes the religion of today."[28]

At the height of the Rennes trial, Christian leaders in Boston organized a Committee of Fifty to erect a monument in memory of the French-Jewish philanthropist Baron de Hirsch and invited John Hay, the United States secretary of state, to support their endeavors. The purpose, they explained to Hay, was not only to honor Hirsch's generosity but also to "break down the deplorable prejudice that exists against the Hebrews as a race, and which the progressive Christian thought of our time is striving so hard to allay."[29] Dreyfus' struggle against a miscarriage of justice, a deceived public, an irresponsible press, and a misplaced emphasis upon the honor of the French General Staff now seemed a contest waged for the highest moral stakes. Washington Gladden saw in its outcome the proof that truth, regardless of the odds, would eventually prevail. The sight of an "entire French nation humbling itself before this upright man and confess[ing] the wrong that it had done to him" was evidence that even one man, "fettered and speechless," can "put forty million to flight."[30] In its own way the happy conclusion of the Dreyfus affair reinforced the optimism of the age of the social gospel.

American Protestant support for Dreyfus and criticism of France's mistreatment of Jews should not, however, be equated with deep understanding of the causes that underlay the plight of French Jewry. Christian sympathy for France's Jews was, in fact, occasionally touched by a note of ambivalence, an uncertainty about the true character of French anti-Semitism. The editor of the *Outlook*, for example, the "Christian evolutionist" Lyman Abbott, wavered peculiarly in his analysis of the roots of Jew hatred in France. The magazine admitted on one occasion that "passion instead of reason" lay at its base but in the same breath said that Jews must share in the responsibility for their rejection. The trouble with the Jew, said an editorial during the height of the Zola event, "is that, in a sense, he detaches himself from the society in which he is; and the pathos of his position lies in the fact that the more he strives to identify himself with a society, the more completely he brings out his own isolation. This is partly the result of tradition, partly the result of his own temperament, and partly the result of the prejudices of modern society."[31] Jewish commercial practices, the writer went on, have alienated the Jews from the peasants and workers of France. Furthermore, the widespread belief that the Jews control more and more of the European economy and diplomacy cannot be dismissed as a myth. The suspicion that "a comparatively small group of men . . . without public responsibility, have practically taken Europe by the throat" has aroused fury in France, and "that there is a certain amount of truth in this belief that the Jews control Euorpe is beyond question." As might be expected from a Social Darwinist, Abbott advised that to wail against the growing power of the Jew was a futile exercise: rather, Gentiles must fortify themselves with the skills and education to better compete with Jews on their own terms. "Education and ability must be pitted against education and ability. It is not only base but idle to attempt to neutralize education and ability by race prejudice."[32]

Alvin F. Sanborn, a contributor to Abbott's periodical, also believed that French anti-Semitism, although unjustified, was based on a broad popular foundation. The Jews of France, he observed,

> powerful out of proportion to their numbers—there are very few laborers among them—are hated and feared by the working people on economic grounds, as capitalists and userers, not by reason of crass racial and religious prejudice, as is often charged. The working people believe, wrongly it may be but none the less sincerely, that the attempt to secure a new trial for Dreyfus would not have had the ghost of a chance of success if the Jewish bank had not been back of it. The much-talked-of "Syndicate" is, to them, a reality. . . . Because Dreyfus has had the solid support of the Jews rather than because he happens himself to be a Jew, his cause is seriously compromised in their eyes.[33]

Similarly, the pro-Dreyfus sermons of Minister Gladden were mixed with those which attacked "traditional Judaism" and its rejection of the message of Christ. Gladden enjoyed contrasting the popular Christian notions of Hebrew justice—"life for life, eye for eye, tooth for tooth, hand for hand, foot for foot"—with the more compassionate attitudes of the early Christian church. The Jewish form of justice "is pure vengeance, nothing more," he told his Ohio congregants on one occasion.[34]

This ambivalence is seen among other American champions of Dreyfus as well. John T. Morse, a Bostonian well known for his legal evaluations of the case, was in some respects a sharp critic of French anti-Semitism. In 1898 he called it "a vastly more significant, more expressive feature of this age than a whole budget of Venezuelan episodes or Cuban questions." "No one on this side of the water," he told Americans, "unless he has read the French daily newspapers most industriously, can form an idea of the savage, merciless onslaught which [Frenchmen] have combined to make upon the unfortunate race. . . . In France today it is perilous to be a Jew." Yet, almost in the same breath, he suggested that the Jewish exodus from eastern Europe had intensified hatred of the Jews, and that, given the proper conditions, anti-Semitism could also erupt in the United States. "If all the Jews of Continental Europe were suddenly to be transported to this continent, we might find the national digestion, powerful as it is, badly nauseated." [35]

■ Although organized anti-Semitism had not yet intruded itself into American institutional life, the United States did not lack its anti-Jewish voices, which increased markedly during the years of Dreyfus, when xenophobic souls were emboldened to articulate their thoughts. One such was Henry James. Unlike his brother William, he showed neither sympathy for the victim of the affair nor concern about the anti-Semitic feelings that it engendered. Like William, observes a student of the two,

> Henry James was an outspoken foe of imperialism and militarism. . . . But the brothers part company with the Dreyfus Affair. The novelist's celebrated declaration, "Thank God, I've no *opinions* . . . not even on the Dreyfus case," is disingenuous, and his exclamation, "I'm more and more aware of things as a more or less mad panorama, phantasmagoria and dime museum," though expressive of his growing disgust with the public scene, reflects not reticence but embarrassment before a Jewish problem of world-wide notoriety. He did not see, as William did, the need for an organized defense of the victims of the racial intolerance that the Dreyfus case provoked. [36]

When Henry Adams heard that Émile Zola had been condemned to the maximum penalty of a year's imprisonment and a fine of three thousand francs, he expressed a similar judgment. "He should have been sent 'to join his friend Dreyfus on Devil's Island. . . . with as much more French rot as the Island would hold, including most of the press, the greater part of the theatre, all the stockbrokers and a Rothschild or two for example.'" [37] Indeed, Brahmin writers, as Michael N. Dobkowski observes, saw the Jew as "the despoiler of all values, the agent of destruction . . . the symbol of all they disliked about the new industrial America." [38]

If these were the sentiments of some of the most distinguished American intellectuals, one could hardly expect the readers of the yellow press to be more restrained. They even attacked the papers themselves:

> Don't you worry. There will come a day when even you will be liberated from Hebrew influence.
>
> There will be a day when truth will dawn in the editorial brows that mislead the journal today.

Kindly state in your paper amount of money contributed by the Jews of Germany, England, France and America for the defense of Captain Dreyfus.

I am glad to read in your paper today an admission by your grotesque correspondent that Judas Iscariot is to be convicted, which was the conclusion reached at long ago by all lovers of justice.

whenever Dreyfus gets ready to take off his coat and get down to good hard work he will be offered a salary of 475,000,000 a year, with free board, to do nothing but write love-sick poems.[39]

The popular and widely circulated literature of late nineteenth-century America—dime novels, plays, humor sheets, and magazines—tended to reinforce the stereotype of the clannish, unscrupulous, grasping Hebrew.[40] Yet such sentiments did not represent the preponderant opinion. The majority of the country's newspapers spoke up for the cause of Dreyfus. As the editor of the *Atlanta Constitution* put it, "If there is any section of the American . . . press—and this term in the present connection is synonymous with the American people, which has insisted on the guilt of Dreyfus, or even hinted of its possibility, such demonstrations are not on record."[41]

That the wave of anti-Semitism which had swept across France might wash across the Atlantic was a thought which many found disconcerting, and, in fact, any sign of anti-Semitism in America was typically attributed to European influence.[42] The *Independent* warned against the danger of replicating European excesses: "Anti-Semitism, which was the mainspring of the Dreyfus persecution, has not yet reached in the United States the pitch of intensity that it has in Russia, Austria, Germany and France. But it exists as a subconscious feeling, and shows itself in many petty, spiteful ways in large cities, where the Jews form a distinct class."[43] The story of Dreyfus ought to be "told for many generations as a warning to republics," advised the *Outlook*, "for he was not the victim of an autocracy or of a monarchy, but of a free people; and his case is a terrible illustration of the tyranny which can be employed under the forms of law, by people who have substituted passion for reason."[44]

In their own way, many Americans understood that hatred of the Jews was the key to the national calamity in France in which democratic practices were driven out and reaction reigned. Many took the experience as a clear warning: "We, too, are becoming infected with the virus of anti-Semitism" which may "bring national disgrace upon us, as the Dreyfus Affair has upon France."[45] If the affair had one central effect

on Americans, then, it was to shed some light upon their own suscepti-
bilities to the forces that were about to engulf a large segment of Western civilization.

X

Perspectives
of the American
Jewish Community

It is, in my opinion, neither accurate nor wise nor just to speak of anti-Semitism in the United States.

MORRIS JASTROW, JR., 1898

Dreyfus is not being tried as a Jew, but as a man. His case is not for the Jews to protest against, but for the whole civilized world. He is not a test for Judaism, but of justice. It is the American people which should speak, not the American Jews.

RABBI EMILE H. HIRSCH, 1899

The arrest and conviction of an obscure captain in France at first excited little commotion among assimilated American Jews. Even after 1898 they tended to follow rather than lead in the outcry against France, although their reticence was not as marked as it was among the Jews of France. There, as Hannah Arendt observes, "the Jews were more deluded" by the placid and peaceful years of the close of the nineteenth century than were other Europeans. Not only did the arrest of Dreyfus excite little alarm, but, as Bernard Lazare lamented, thousands were "ready to stand guard over Devil's Island, alongside the most rabid patriots of the country." At best, French Jewry was ready to blame the whole fiasco on a judicial error, said Arendt, "the victim of which just happened by chance to be a Jew." [1]

Recently emancipated and yearning for social acceptance, French Jews chose, as a strategy for survival, to ignore any signs of anti-Semitism. They closed their eyes and ears to the hateful chants of Drumont and his clan. When the grand rabbi of France, Zadoc Kahn, threatened to sue the author of *La France juive* for his insulting rhetoric, Franco-Jewish leaders persuaded him not to do so. As the Dreyfus affair thickened, Zadoc himself became convinced that any vigorous response would prove counterproductive. In a letter to a New York newspaper following the attempt on Labori's life, Zadoc assured Americans that all would turn out well for the Jews of France—that the tragic event would only "stir the conscience of France to the moral courage necessary for the acknowledgement of Dreyfus's innocence" and "help to kill anti-Semitism."[2]

American Jews spoke their minds with less hesitancy, especially after the facts of the case became public knowledge. Yet here also a degree of caution was evident. A conservative segment of American Jewry, mainly German Jews and spokesmen for the reform movement, urged their co-religionists to refrain from petitioning the government and participating in concerted protests and actions against France. The persecution of Dreyfus was the fault of France's misguided leadership.[3]

Within this conservative group were a few prominent rabbis. A petition from the Jews of Memphis to the German emperor in September, 1899, requesting that he speak out on behalf of Dreyfus angered Rabbi Emile Hirsch of Chicago, a leading spokesman for the reform movement. Hirsch had recently returned from a visit to France convinced that any public agitation would intensify anti-Jewish feeling. "It is a great mistake to send such a message from a community of Jews," he warned his congregation.[4] Rabbi Isaac M. Wise, perhaps the most prominent voice in liberal Judaism, hesitated to draw any ominous conclusions from the Dreyfus affair. His biographer writes that to Wise "it did not appear . . . a world-shattering event, or one having much to do with the essential status of democracy or liberalism in France." Wise preferred to look at the Dreyfus event as a retrogressive but temporary deviation from the universal and inevitable progression toward human brotherhood.

Many of Wise's followers from German-speaking Europe, now comfortably integrated into American society, had little hesitation in stating that America was their Zion. Although sympathetic to the trials of their French brethren, they refused to admit that a political gesture on their part would alter or alleviate the misfortunes of their fellow Jews in France, whose difficulties, they believed, were at worst transient.[5] "Dr. Nordau," wrote Wise in February, 1898, "is the sarcastic pessimist, that discerns everywhere the black side of the picture. . . . So he saw in Paris two or three weeks ago the approaching bloody massacre . . . where other eye-witnesses saw a Parisian comedy." Nordau's vision of pogroms

inspired by the Roman Catholics was severely castigated in more affluent, better assimilated Jewish circles. The *American Hebrew* exclaimed:
"The Catholics have been among the best friends of the Jews." The *Jewish Messenger* linked his faulty prognostications to an "ill-balanced mind."
A spokesman for the expanding Jewish community of San Francisco
asserted: "The one thing American Jews cannot and will not believe is
that the Roman Catholic hierarchy assists or approves of an organized
conspiracy to persecute the Jews of Europe."[6] For the *Jewish Voice* of St.
Louis, Nordau's opinion was of no importance because, it explained,
somewhat ambiguously, "to us he is naught but a *race* Jew, who clings to
Judaism for interior motives." Said the *Voice*, "there will be no massacre
in France, because France, after all, is not Russia. The leaders of 'Zionism,' particularly those of the religious standing of Nordau, have not
participated in the history of our people in the past half century. . . .
Hence we do not accept Nordau as a prophet. . . . This is, at any rate,
no time to attack the Roman Catholic or any other Church."[7]

If the Dreyfus event moved this coterie at all, it was less for the sake
of their fellow Jews than for the sake of humanity in general. To view
events in France only from a Jewish perspective, they believed, was to
minimize their significance. The Dreyfus affair was commanding international attention. Even Czarist Russian newspaper editorials were sup-
portive of Dreyfus' cause—indeed, few events in the annals of anti-Semitism have evoked a comparable universal response. When these Jewish
spokesmen, therefore, talked about the affair as being primarily a threat
to the rule of law and to democratic principles and claimed that a victory
for Dreyfus would constitute the triumph of right over madness and
that his death would mean death to all good people, they were employ-
ing the language common to enlightened mankind in general at the
close of the last century.[8]

In an address to a national gathering of reform rabbis, Henry Berkowitz reflected such notions:

> Let us not forget that from Macaulay to Beaconsfield and Gladstone,
> England has been on our side. . . . Let us remember that the era of
> emancipation is hardly a hundred years old. What is a hundred years
> in our history! Sad as is still the fate of the myriads of Israel, it is
> today not as hopeless as at any time in the last nineteen hundred
> years. . . . Never before was the evidence so strong that mankind has
> set its face resolutely towards a future of justice. This is not theory,
> but history.[9]

Unlike Theodor Herzl and Max Nordau, who interpreted events

about them in a different light, Berkowitz and others refused to lose their faith in the triumph of justice. When the Court of Cassation agreed to a new trial in June, 1899, they saw in the judgment "a most marvelous proof of the grandeur of our century. Let an act of wrong be committed in any corner of the globe, and thanks to the press, the greatest champion of right, it becomes known today to the entire world, and all humanity, irrespective of creed, and so long and so loud that the wrong is righted and justice is done." [10]

The insistence that Dreyfus was a problem for civilization rather than for the Jewish people was reiterated in the American Jewish press even after his second conviction. "It requires a striking affair like the Dreyfus conspiracy," proposed the *American Hebrew*,

> full of dramatic incident and exposed to the public gaze in all its horrid nakedness, to arouse men's souls to the impending danger to human liberty which besets the individual in the French republic. . . . so that all may know that human happiness is in peril on French soil.
> Such a disclosure can only be regarded as a distinct gain for civilization. . . . It will . . . serve as a valuable object lesson of the sacredness of individual liberty, the importance of jealously safeguarding it, the necessity for eternal vigilance upholding it. [11]

Its editors were not displeased that the Dreyfus affair had stimulated a discussion of the broader issue of anti-Semitism, but took issue with a minister from Binghamton, who had recently said in a sermon that "all the world is watching the second trial of Captain Dreyfus, because Dreyfus is a Jew." The *American Hebrew* believed that "outside of anti-Semites, who would like to see Dreyfus shot simply because he is a Jew, the world at large is interested in the case purely in the cause of justice." [12] While supporting this point of view, Chicago's Rabbi Hirsch did show a keener historic appreciation than some of his contemporaries when he admitted at the same time that Dreyfus exemplified an "old, old story. When a country wants a scapegoat on which to unload its shortcomings it selects a Jew." [13]

Still, Hirsch and his colleagues were convinced that the ancient aberration of anti-Semitism was being eradicated, as seen by its almost complete disappearance in the United States. Although they acknowledged the presence of social prejudice against the Jews of the United States, they hesitated to call such behavior "anti-Semitism." Indeed, as one of this group put it, Jews did not "have the right to speak of the existence of anti-Semitism in America when we remember what the word means in Europe." Such prominent Jewish scholars as Cyrus Adler of the

Smithsonian Institution and Morris Jastrow of the University of Pennsylvania even insisted that there was no anti-Semitism in the United States and that it could never take root in their adopted country. Kaufman Kohler, spiritual leader of Temple Beth El in New York, agreed: "It is antagonistic to the spirit of both the American people and American institutions." His evidence for this claim was American support for Dreyfus.[14]

Such reluctance to see the issue of Dreyfus exclusively in Jewish terms was evident among the small group of Jewish socialists and radicals as well. However, here the conviction stemmed not from an optimistic view of the future course of human behavior but from a cynical assessment of contemporary society, a belief that anti-Semitism was nothing more or less than the poisonous and inevitable result of a capitalist social order, which would disappear with the demise of the capitalist system. Besides, Dreyfus' ties with the military and with the affluent were unappealing to those who dreamed of the proletarian revolution. These Jewish radicals were imbued with a cosmopolitan ideal which, in its most grotesque form, was manifested as Jewish self-denigration. Daniel De Leon, a Jew, mirrored this attitude during the Zola trial: "We cannot join the trumpeting of almost all Jewish newspapers who think that since Dreyfus is a Jew, that they must shout that he is innocent. . . . Dreyfus's heritage as a grandson of Jacob is for us no witness for his innocence."[15]

■ This style of thinking was not typical of that of the masses of recent arrivals from eastern Europe, many of whom were nurtured within the traditional or orthodox wing of Judaism. To them, events in France seemed to signify the re-enactment of the terrors which they had just escaped. Dreyfus' lack of commitment to his Jewish heritage, his social and familial background, and his wealth and military career were irrelevant, as they knew from experience that anti-Semites drew little distinction between one Jew and another. The daily reports also made it quite clear that the alleged guilt of Dreyfus had become a rallying cry for the French mob. The *Jewish Daily Forward*, widely read in eastern European immigrant circles, awarded both Czar Nicholas and President Faure first prize for anti-Semitism for the year 1897.[16] Readers of the Yiddish press were familiar with the villainous activities of Edouard Drumont and his *Libre parole*. This segment of American Jewry could not effectively differentiate between the attack upon Dreyfus and an assault on all the Jews of France. "His case seems justly a matter of interest to all

Jews, and is thus effectively distinguished from an ordinary charge against a criminal, or suspected person, who happens merely to be a Jew," commented the *Yiddishes Tageblatt*.[17] Throughout the winter months of 1898 the *Tageblatt*'s, *Abend Blatt*'s, and *Forward*'s headlines and front-page stories trumpeted the news: "Jewish Blood Flows through France," "France Wants To Ingratiate Itself with Russia with Jewish Blood," "A Small Pogrom in Marseilles," "A Pogrom in Lyon," "Pogroms in Algiers." Max Nordau's forebodings found echoes among these recent immigrants.[18]

The accounts of Dreyfus' martyrdom on Devil's Island were frequently recalled in Jewish ghettos. Translations of his letters to his wife were read hungrily. The vaguest rumors about his condition, his health, or his future plans were treated as events of public importance, and his return from captivity was awaited with an intensity unparalleled elsewhere in the country.[19]

For his selfless sacrifices on behalf of the victim, the name of Émile Zola was embraced in the Jewish ghettos. The charges brought against him and the court proceedings which followed filled the front pages of the Yiddish-language dailies. The crowds that gathered to abuse him were characterized as "wild animals" and "cannibals," and the *Tageblatt* announced his conviction thus: "The lie wins!"[20] Equal homage, if not adulation, was paid to Picquart and Labori. Quoting from the journal *Christian Work*, the *Tageblatt* praised the untypical soldier: "all along, outside of his family, Dreyfus had a friend, not a Jew, whose belief in him, whose love for him, never faltered—who even went to prison for him. History will write that the true hero of the Dreyfus case is not Dreyfus at all, but Picquart." When Labori was struck down in the assassination attempt, the trauma experienced in the Jewish ghetto was equal in emotional intensity to news of a pogrom.[21]

The Jews of the ghetto were quicker than their more Americanized brethren to vilify the Vatican and Roman Catholic establishment. "Is the Pope anti-Semitic?" asked the *Yiddishes Tageblatt*. An affirmative response was hard to avoid when its readers were told that *Osservatore Romano*, the Vatican's leading organ of opinion, had justified outbreaks of violence against the Jews of France as "the will of destiny," the revengeful act of a righteous God exacting a penalty upon God-killers and plunderers of humanity. They were stunned at the assertions from Rome that "the present universal outbreak of anti-Semitism is due to the fact that the Jews misuse their civil freedom to which they have no right and which only nations who are religiously and politically organized could rightly demand. The Jewish people do not possess such an organization because they remain under the curse of God!"[22] The *Tage-blatt* concluded, logically enough, that the notion that the Vatican or the pope opposed anti-Semitism was but a myth.[23]

Déroulède's ugly escapades, Henry's suicide, Esterhazy's hysterical ravings, the caning of Loubet, the shooting of Labori, Guérin's defiance of French authority—these new immigrants wondered what consequences these events held for the fate of Jews in France.[24] They were less inclined than other Americans to make legal, social, and racial distinctions between Anglo-American and Latin societies and, in general, could not view matters with detachment. The Yiddish press scrutinized and dramatized the tedious legal proceedings of 1898 and 1899 with great meticulousness and earnestness, for its readers saw in these events more than momentous juridic exercises. Perhaps nowhere else but in the prisoner's own family circle did a group of people yearn more intensely for an acquittal. Perhaps nowhere else did the terrible verdict of September 9, 1899, "guilty with extenuating circumstances," produce a more stunning disappointment. But the ghetto's reaction was stoic. "Anti-Semites win the battle but not the war," was the *Forward's* response, as it showered praise on the two minority members of the courtmartial who voted for acquittal.[25] They organized mass meetings, signed petitions, and cabled influential officials. They vowed not to purchase goods from France nor to visit that country and urged others to do the same. They asked Americans to boycott the forthcoming Paris Exposition. Both Émile Zola and Colonel Picquart became their heroes; in one city thousands of small offerings were collected to purchase testimonials—an engraved gold pen for Zola and a gold loving cup for Picquart.[26]

■ That the pivotal events in the Dreyfus drama coincided with important Jewish festivals and holy days intensified the emotional impact of the affair upon the Jewish community as a whole. For example, the French cabinet decided to support a revision of the Dreyfus case on the Day of Atonement, September 26, 1898, a decision announced from the pulpits of numerous synagogues. In a Boston house of worship, "the news was followed by a demonstration . . . such as never has been seen in a Jewish synagogue in the city."[27] Almost precisely one year later, the verdict of guilty with extenuating circumstances was handed down by the Rennes court during the holy week preceding the Day of Atonement in September, 1899. The judgment became the theme of numerous sermons delivered during the Yom Kippur services.[28]

The Rennes affair did not escape the notice of the journalist and novelist Abraham Cahan. In New York's Jewish immigrant neighborhoods, which Cahan knew so well, he sensed that the normal solemnity of the "days of awe" was intensified. Dreyfus was pictured as a scapegoat of the Gentiles, said Cahan, and "every child of the ghetto saw in his emaciated body a harrowed lump of his own flesh. . . . For two years the face of the unhappy man had never been absent from their minds." Now, during the Atonement exercises, as the cantor chanted the doleful words "Who shall be at rest, and who shall be wandering; who to remain tranquil," "the worshipers beheld the innocent man in irons over his bleeding wounds, and in the outburst of prayer which followed, their voices spoke as much of the pain of a martyr in Israel as of the accumulated anguish of their own hearts." [29]

News of President Loubet's "pardon" arrived at a most propitious moment, while Jews were assembled in prayer for the Festival of Booths, on September 19, 1899. It was a most appropriate religious symmetry, for the Festival of Booths is one of the most joyful on the Jewish calendar. Even in the stately Temple Emanu-El in New York City, services were interrupted so that the worshipers could be informed of the news. When they were, the *Times* reported, "the congregation was on its feet cheering wildly. Women wept and strong men wondered what it was that had suddenly dimmed their vision. Cheer followed cheer, and though the clergymen looked suprised, they did nothing to restrain the feelings of the worshipers." Immediately following the services, the temple's president, James Seligman, dispatched a cable to Dreyfus in the name of his congregation rejoicing in his victory and praying for his complete vindication. [30]

■ To the small and dedicated group of American Zionists, the Dreyfus affair indicated the truth of their warnings that Jewish assimilation into Western society would not resolve ancient hatreds. It was, indeed, during the years of Dreyfus that Zionism took on international scope. Theodor Herzl's prophetic *Jewish State* was directly inspired by his observation of the brutality meted out to Dreyfus and the anti-Semitism in France. The sight of Dreyfus' public degradation, which Herzl witnessed as a reporter for the Vienna *Neue Freie Presse*, haunted him; the shouts of "death to the Jews" that rose from the multitude as Dreyfus was paraded about the military field rang in his ears. "The Dreyfus case," he wrote in 1899, "embodies more than a judicial error; it embodies the desire of the vast majority of the French to condemn a Jew, and to condemn all Jews in this one Jew!" [31]

The first three international Zionist congresses, which met in Basel, Switzerland, were thus as much an outgrowth of French anti-Semitism as they were of the Russian pogroms. The American Federation of Zionists sent delegations to these meetings, and, when he returned from Basel in June, 1899, Richard Gottheil, a leading delegate, outlined for a Baltimore gathering the lesson of the Dreyfus affair:

> the position of the Jews in France is as uncertain as it is in most countries where our brethren dwell. One hundred years of loyal devotion to civic France, to their country, was not enough to save them from violent attacks of the press and the insults of the populace.
>
> Think of it. Suppose the present anti-Jewish rage subsides and a spirit of calmness prevails. What is there in that to argue or prove that it will not break out again? . . . Where or in what way have we improved our conditions? What has served to raise the hope of the Jew? For the last twenty-five years we have been advancing backward, and if this is true of a country where a century ago the emancipation of the Jew was proclaimed, what right have we to suppose that we will advance in countries where no such proclamations were ever issued, and where no such conditions ever existed?[32]

When the Zionist federation met in New York that year, a message of gratitude from Lucie Dreyfus to the people of America and, in particular, to the Jews of New York, was read to the gathering. Anxiety about the future security of the Jew was often expressed. "If France wants to suppress the Jews," declared one speaker, "there is Germany for us to go to; if Germany seeks our suppression there is Austria; if Austria, then there are other countries—and, above all, where we are certain to be free, there is the United States." Despite statements such as these, however, events in France made the idea of a Jewish state more compelling. Harris G. Altshul, an American delegate to the Basel congress, observed upon his return that "the Dreyfus trial in France and the Congress of Zionists at Basle, Switzerland, mark the turning point in the history of the Hebrews as a scattered nation, and the two events will have a greater political bearing than most statesmen imagine. . . . the Dreyfus persecution has helped to forward the Zionist movement as nothing else could . . . to the extent that the resettlement of the Jews in Palestine as an independent nation is an assured success."[33] Altshul, although prophetic, was somewhat in advance of the vision of the majority of American Jews.

■ American Jews were neither politically nor psychologically prepared to wage an energetic campaign against anti-Semitism at the end of the nineteenth century, and they were happy to see the end of the affair. Notwithstanding the voices of a handful of Zionists and a larger number of intense eastern Europeans, the general Jewish reaction to the episode had been restrained. Until the very end, American Jews were determined, said the *American Hebrew*, that "the personal element should be entirely absent in our declaration about this '*cause célèbre*'"; Dreyfus' Jewishness was not to influence their judgment of the case.[34]

Despite these efforts to avoid being drawn into the controversy, however, the moral support that the cause of Dreyfus received from non-Jews was most encouraging to many. The *American Hebrew* singled out, among them, Major Ferdinand Forzinetti, governor of the Cherche Midi prison; Senator Scheurer-Kestner; Zola; Picquart; Georges Clemenceau; and those whose names were unknown, like Dreyfus' surgeon and the jailers who eased his misery. The *Hebrew's* highest acclamation was reserved for M. Auguste Scheurer-Kestner, who did not live to see Dreyfus finally free: "Younger and stronger champions than he bore the heat and burden of the fray later on, but to him is due the undying credit that he was the first of the strong men who came forward to battle for the oppressed."[35]

Gottard Deutsch, of the Hebrew Union College, although compelled to admit that the number of French Roman Catholics who disapproved the actions of their government were infinitesimal in number and influence, still declared: "I do not endorse retaliation. I hope no Jew will join the A.P.A. [the American Protective Association, an anti-Catholic organization]. I will not do it myself." Joseph Jacob, a leading observer of contemporary Jewish affairs, was satisfied that the Dreyfus case was not employed as an

> excuse for an attack upon clericalism, or even Jesuitry. . . . The Jesuits may have made use of the *affair* to increase their influence in the army; some of them may even have had something to do with the underhand methods by which Dreyfus was originally condemned and by which the revision was impeded so long; but that is no reason why Jews should allow themselves to be made [into] a beating-stick [to punish the] Jesuits or . . . the clergy in general.[36]

Even the Zionist Henrietta Szold appeared hopeful. "France is a striking illustration of the sporadic character of anti-Jewish demonstration," she wrote in 1900. "Last year the very hearth of anti-Semitism, it is by no means an unhappy home to Jews this year." Because of its ordeal, France had once more emerged a healthier and more democratic community. It did not matter that Dreyfus had not identified himself with his people, for his place in the history of the Jews was assured. "Without any initiative on his part," said Julius H. Greenstone, an insightful critic, Dreyfus "has helped to drive home to the world's conscience not only the perverseness and obstinancy of Jew-hatred, but the blood poisoning effect of race prejudice on the very vitals of a nation's truthfulness and honor."[37]

XI

Dilemma of
the American Catholic
Community

It is as absurd to suppose that a group of honor-loving officers would
conspire to tell a falsehood for any cause as it would be to imagine a
similar act of infamy on the part of as many American officers.
Pittsburgh Catholic, March 23, 1898

It requires only some crime of the Dreyfus character in one of the
unhappy lands where English is not spoken to call forth an exhibition
of that complacent self-righteousness, Pharisaism and cant, which
seem to be all of the inheritance of Puritanism.
Pilot, September 2, 1899

Like Jews and Protestants, American Catholics did not express a unified
point of view about France. A variety of events, historic as well as contemporary, molded a distinct Catholic position. In some respects the
Dreyfus affair proved embarrassing to American Roman Catholics.
Even if their sympathies lay with the victim and his supporters, they
hesitated to express them publicly lest they be seen as bolstering a movement viewed as anti-Catholic. As was suggested earlier, spokesmen for
American Protestantism not infrequently read into the events in France
a confirmation of their deepest suspicions about the Catholic establishment.[1] What is more, a wave of anti-Catholic bigotry in America coincided with the emergence of the Dreyfus affair. The French events
strengthened Protestant phobias, which had been present for some time
beneath the surface.

The primary reason for this ill will toward Catholics was the influx
of millions of Catholics from eastern Europe to the United States at the
end of the century. As a group they formed the bulk of what has been

dubbed by historians the "new immigration." This event, coupled with American acquisitions of Spanish colonies, which further swelled the Catholic population, aroused Protestant concern about the future religious character of the United States.[2] The spiritual and social threats that these events were alleged to hold for the American people were proclaimed from the pulpits of the most prominent churches in America, conservative as well as liberal. Conservative preachers warned of the decadence, immorality, and unimaginable evils of Catholicism; liberal preachers railed against the danger of a reactionary, medieval religious organization to a democratic society. "The question of religious freedom in our land is largely a question of the Roman Catholic Church," announced Heber Newton, a liberal Protestant, to his flock.[3]

Events in France did little to mitigate such anxieties. Non-Catholic periodicals frequently suggested that Romanism and Americanism were incompatible; as one student cautioned, "the policies and attitudes that had made possible the Inquisition and the Massacre of St. Bartholomew had not been fully abandoned by the Catholic Church." The president of Harvard, Charles W. Eliot, told a gathering of clergymen in 1894 that civil liberty was a doctrine alien to Catholic thinking. Theodore Roosevelt held certain Catholics, such as, for example, Archbishop John Ireland, in high regard and was opposed to Catholic-baiting, but still he believed that the Roman Church was unsuited for America. "Its thought," as he put it, "is Latin and entirely at variance with the dominant thought of our country and institutions." Roosevelt urged those Americans who "wavered from the doctrine of separation of Church and State" to "ponder what has happened in France."[4] Anti-Catholic circles frequently debated the question of whether Catholics were capable of loyalty to the constitutional principles of the United States. William Croswell Doane, Episcopal bishop of Albany, told a gathering of ministers in 1894 that if American Catholics were ever forced to choose between obedience to republican principles and the authority of Rome, "large numbers of them would be almost compelled to surrender political loyalty to what they thought the higher law." What irked this clergyman was Catholic allegiance to papal authority, to "a foreigner . . . claiming an absolute and infallible authority and control over everybody and everything everywhere."[5]

Opposition to Catholicism was reflected also in an American reluctance to side with Catholic powers in foreign controversies. America's neutral stand during the Franco-Prussian War was justified on this basis, for the event was seen by some as a contest between two branches of

Christianity. Charles B. Boynton, a Presbyterian spokesman from Washington, D.C., interpreted the conflict as "an attempt on a giant scale to arrest the progress of civil and religious freedom and to bring first Europe and then the world under the control of the Romish Church by the military power of France."[6] Not surprisingly, Frenchmen who had hoped for American support in their struggle believed that it was denied partly because of religious antagonism.

The Spanish-American conflict was likewise seen as a clash between the two Christian faiths and the American victory as a victory for Protestantism. "We applaud the triumph of a republican and Protestant nation representing liberty and modern civilization over the old monarchical and Catholic despotism which certainly fully deserved the catastrophe into which it is finally sinking," wrote Theodore Flournoy to his good friend William James in December, 1898.[7]

The American Protective Association, one of the most outspoken anti-Catholic hate groups which had appeared in the United States since the Civil War, was a product of this environment. It came into existence early in 1887, and its raison d'être was clear in the language of its oath of initiation: "I hereby denounce Roman Catholicism. I hereby denounce the Pope, sitting at Rome or elsewhere. I denounce his priests and emmissaries, and the diabolical work of the Roman Catholic Church, and hereby pledge myself to the cause of Protestantism." In a few years this "patriotic order" attained a membership of nearly two and one-half million, with active chapters in almost every state, and its Catholic-baiting program received the support of numerous churchmen. Madison C. Peters, a social gospeler and an American Dreyfusard, was a member, as was Richard Salter Storrs, paster of the respected Church of the Pilgrims in Brooklyn. Storrs was an early president of the American Historical Association and the author of an essay whose title speaks for itself: "Romanism, Illiteracy, Illegitimacy and Crime." Even the *Encyclopedia of Social Reform*, edited by the clergyman and social and religious reformer D. P. Bliss, classified the A.P.A. with scientific detachment as a reform movement.[8]

This is not to say that all or even most Protestant ministers supported or approved of the work of the A.P.A. Washington Gladden spoke strongly against it, as did many of his liberal colleagues. Not all non-Catholic Americans were eager to transform the French crusade against Dreyfus into an attack on the Catholic Church. Fred C. Conybeare, an Englishman who staunchly supported the cause of Dreyfus and whose comments on the case were widely read in the United States, was sharply castigated for his anti-Catholic bias, although his essays on the case, signed "Huguenot," were among the best-documented of contemporary writings about France. His book *The Dreyfus Case*, published in New York in 1899, was attacked by American reviewers because of the author's impassioned criticism of the Catholic Church, especially French Jesuits.[9]

Still, some widely read Protestant journals like the *Outlook*, the *Independent*, and the *American Monthly Review of Reviews* received the "Huguenot"'s writings more graciously and did not conceal their view of the Roman Catholic Church and its dogma. Much to the annoyance of American Catholics, they characterized the Church as "unchangeable . . . immobile, unalterable."[10] Their editorials strongly supported the belief that the Dreyfus tragedy could have occurred only in a society permeated with Catholic values. Its real significance they saw as a conflict between order and justice, between authority and free inquiry, and between faith and science:

> Dreyfus was merely an instrument for condensing the great invisible struggle into concrete form. . . . France has remained till now a country on the side of authority, inheriting from its Latin civilization a superstitious respect for all who hold the smallest share of power, for every functionary, in a word, civil, ecclesiastical, or military. It is well known that Catholicism supports this idolatry. It exacts from the faithful absolute submission, complete surrender of the rights of reason, unqualified acquiescence not only in the word of God, but also, and especially, in that of his accredited representatives.[11]

■ Pope Leo XIII's ostensible indifference to the fate of Dreyfus and to the pleas of his friends disturbed many Americans. The pope's declared devotion to social amelioration, it was observed, did not extend to any attempt to stem the mounting tide of Jew hatred in France. His silence provided a source of comfort, even inspiration, to anti-Semites, who interpreted Vatican neutrality as a tacit endorsement. "The Pope will never interfere in a French domestic question of this kind," boasted Drumont in 1898.[12]

In general, non-Catholics did not believe that the pope was directly involved in a campaign against French Jewry, but serious questions were raised about the role of the Vatican officials who surrounded him. Articles in *L'Osservatore Romano* not only condoned but inspired French fury against the Jewish population. Because of their inbred sinfulness, said one writer, "Jews must always be outcasts—a scattered and homeless race." They must perpetually bear the blame for the Crucifixion. "Jews have no right to complain of the outburst of hatred and violence," declared the Vatican newspaper, "for they have earned it," not only by their past offenses but by their current activities. They spread hateful doctrines of liberalism and "the pestilential paradoxes of free thought," undermining Western spiritual values.[13]

It is debatable whether Pope Leo XIII, one of the most revered pontiffs of the modern era, gave his approval to such thinking. In an interview with the *New York Journal* a French priest asserted that, on the contrary, "Pope Leo, who is always just and who is believed to be a Dreyfusard . . . cannot control the fanatical part of the French clergy." The *New York Sun* also reported that "his Holiness expressed his astonishment at the passions which had been aroused in France over the Dreyfus question" and "deprecated the attempt to transform the Affair into a war of race or religion."[14]

The pope's inability to control the rise of Catholic anti-Semitism in France, although not excusable, is understandable. National pride in that country had rendered papal authority relatively impotent. What is less clear is why he was unable or reluctant to censure anti-Jewish comments and suggestive remarks in the columns of such organs as *L'Osservatore Romano* and the Jesuit *Civiltà Cattolica*. The latter publication, which calmly advised its readers that "it is better not to kill or expel Jews" but rather to deny them political rights or public position, had its editorial offices at the pope's very doorstep. He must have read such pieces, and it was difficult for some Americans to avoid the conclusion that the eradication of anti-Semitism did not receive the highest priority at the Vatican. The indifference with which Dreyfus' second conviction was greeted in Rome was also noted in the United States. Vatican newspapers gave the matter scant attention, in sharp contrast to the press in other countries. The *Congregationalist* remarked with surprise that "amid the universal chorus of execration with which the condemnation of Dreyfus has been received in all civilized countries of the world outside of France, there has been one significant silence. From the palace of the head of that Church which calls itself Catholic and universal, claiming for its chief priest infallibility in declaring the truth of God, there has come no word of condemnation—only a declaration of neutrality."[15] "Under the crucifix at Rennes and in the name of Christ, the most unjust judgment was pronounced that history has recorded," an English Catholic complained, "yet, as far as I know, neither pope, nor bishop, nor priest of the Roman church has uttered a word against it." Another Catholic cried, "A single word could have put an end to this conspiracy of the leaders of the Church of Jesus in France against this man of the race of Jesus, on trial for his honor and his life. . . . The diplomatic silence of the Vatican will not pass unnoticed. . . . In the thought of the world, this large section of the Church, by the action of its accredited leaders, has deliberately separated itself from the ground of truth, justice, and pity, and must suffer accordingly." [16] The *Outlook* challenged the notion that the affair was only a matter of state and of military interests. In its view, "the Dreyfus affair has been utilized by the church to make an onslaught upon the liberal institutions and ideas, and to influence Frenchmen toward a clerico-military government." It recalled that when Madame Dreyfus wrote to the pope begging for help she received no answer, yet, at the same time, the pope warmly received the editor-in-chief of the widely circulated, anti-Semitic, Roman Catholic penny paper *La Croix*: "So scandalous a circumstance all Catholics must deeply deplore."

Quoting an English writer and an accomplished scientist, St. George Mivart, the *Outlook* went on to accuse Pope Leo of the "crime of silence":

> To keep silence may often be to participate in the evil left unde-nounced. . . . How eminently, how above all, must this apply to him who stands as the supreme ruler of the Christian conduct and the direct and immediate representative on earth of the God of truth, goodness, and justice!
> . . . To the excuse made by Leo XIII's apologists that the silence was due to a fear of offending France . . . Offend France! God's vicar to refrain from telling men what their duty is for fear of consequences! As if God could not be trusted with the consequences of any acts done in fulfillment of his behests! . . .
> To those who believe that Dreyfus is the victim of injustice—and nearly the whole world evidently so thinks—the Pope's silence does seem a lost opportunity." [17]

More than non-Catholics, American Catholics preferred to minimize their criticism of France. Justifications of French behavior, generally absent in non-Catholic circles, were common in the Catholic community. Even the liberal voices of what was a predominantly conservative institution preferred to withhold judgment about the matter. Until the end of the affair, Bishop John J. Keane, Cardinal James Gibbons, and Archbishop John Ireland, who were far more ecumenically minded than their European and American counterparts and who were eager to participate in a dialogue with Jews and Protestants, hesitated to condemn the behavior of French Catholics. The "Jewish Question" in Europe did not preoccupy their attention.[18] The ravings of Drumont, the editorials of *La Croix*, the Algerian pogroms, the escapades of Guérin—these were matters the Catholic leadership discussed in passing or not at all. This is not to say that American Catholics refused to acknowledge injustices committed in France. Liberal voices did express their annoyance: the *Pittsburgh Catholic* in the winter of 1898 called the attack on the Jews of Paris "a repetition of a blackened page in the world's history." The attack on Dreyfus it viewed as a "vicarious offering for the guilt of others." The *Iowa Catholic Messenger* joined other Americans in denouncing French legal procedures. Upon learning of the confession and suicide of Colonel Henry, the *Pilot*, a liberal Catholic weekly in Boston, called for an immediate revision: "Justice demands a reopening of the case and there is every indication that it will be granted and that Dreyfus will be vindicated."[19]

Those Catholic voices which did comment on the Rennes trial matched the general national mood in disillusionment. Labori's attempted assassination, a subject generally unmentioned by Catholic newspapers, showed "the utter perversity of the enemies of Dreyfus," according to the *Pilot*. If Labori should die, it said, France would have achieved as much as the Confederacy did by the shot Booth fired at Lincoln.[20] The *Pilot* found the verdict of Rennes—guilty with "extenuating circumstances"—unacceptable. "What the extenuating circumstances are the court did not state. For the good reason that there are none. . . . The verdict was cowardly as well as cruel." "The French army has triumphed," said the *Iowa Catholic Messenger*, and the people of France are disgraced.[21] Such anger, however, was not typical of American Catholic utterances.

It was the military subversion of justice in France which moved American Catholics most. The dominant voices of the American Church were Irish, a group haunted by memories of English military authoritarianism. Such feelings were easily transferred to French military arbitrariness, or, for that matter, to the American military ambitions of the day. Liberal Catholics in America took little satisfaction in American overseas adventures in Cuba, Puerto Rico, and the Philippines. Invited to contribute an article for a popular magazine on the topic "The Inspiration of the Flag" while war with Spain was in progress, Archbishop John Ireland declined: "just for the moment the flag does not inspire me much, and I must be silent until this war is over." American expansionism smacked too strongly of British imperialism.[22]

Political and judicial chaos in France was held up as an example of what an inflated military machine might do to America as well. "The integrity of the French Republic is today threatened by its Army. Do we want a great standing army in America?" said the *Pilot*. The *Irish World* evinced little concern for Dreyfus as a man—"He was what the American college student calls 'a grease grind,' and had all the unpopularity which attaches to that character"—but was moved by his plight because it illustrated the dangers of militarism: "In a monarchical country, where either the monarch is a strong man himself, or the monarch is strong in the affections of the people, there is a standing check to such excesses of military self-assertion. It is just in a republic like France or the United States that they are a social peril." America, the *Irish World* hoped, might learn from France what can happen when a republic decides to become a military power.[23]

At the same time, however, the Catholic disdain for England made it difficult to criticize France openly. Antipathy for things English among American Catholics exceeded their irritability over events in France, and Anglo-Americanism, as manifested in the united front in the Dreyfus case, was characterized as a conspiracy hatched by leading Protestant ministers and politicians.[24] The anti-French sentiment in Anglo-American circles became reason enough for American Catholics to take an opposing stand. The *Irish World* warned of English deception: "A part of the plan of campaign adopted by England and her allies in this country is to try and convince us that France is our bitter enemy. . . . Let us not forget that France helped us win our independence. Ingratitude in a nation is no less a crime than in an individual." As tension mounted between England and France over Fashoda, American Catholics of Irish ancestry rallied to the support of France. Rumors of friction between France and the United States were quickly refuted in the Catholic press. "There are no strained relations," observed the *Iowa Catholic Messenger*; "Our people will never show the . . . ingratitude of preferring our enemy to our friend, and turning our back on our old time ally to embrace the alluring hypocrisy of a common enemy."[25]

As the Rennes trial drew to a close, American Catholics hestitated to criticize the judicial process. "There is every evidence on the part of the tribunal before which the accused officer is tried to do him perfect and exact justice," asserted the Baltimore *Catholic Mirror*, an organ which frequently reflected the opinions of Cardinal Gibbons. The *Pilot* was also confident that although "French judicial methods are different from ours [and] there may be more noise and hysterics . . . in the end the criminal will get his deserts with more certainty in France than he will in America."[26] Anglo-American ridicule of French legal practices was resented. "The repulsive idea of Satan reproving sin," said the *Irish World*, "is never more disgustingly illustrated than in British press comments on alleged 'failures of justice' in countries outside the British Empire." In keeping with the rhetoric of populist anti-Semitism, even liberal Catholics tended to attribute the blocking of news favorable to France and the current enthusiasm for Anglo-American unity to Jewish influence. "Through the English and Jewish agencies and journalists England is trying to create the feeling in America that she is the only European nation that is friendly to America," the *Pilot* argued.[27]

Even in the months that followed the trial, editorials in the American Catholic press continued to minimize the importance of the decision. "Before jumping at the rash conclusion that it was as some call it, 'the monumental crime of the century,' let us see if France is alone in her ignominy." As world condemnation engulfed France, Catholics drew upon the Christian injunction to let him who is without sin cast the first stone. Similarly, American Protestants were blamed for singling out France for criticism:

> It requires only some crime of the Dreyfus character in one of the unhappy lands where English is not spoken to call forth an exhibition of that complacent self-righteousness, Pharisaism and cant, which seem to be all of the inheritance of Puritanism. . . .
> The fact that France, in the teeth of dangers that threaten her political existence, is striving hard to correct a judicial military crime appears to have no weight whatever with the British and American Pharisee. That saintly personage turns up the white of his eyes, lays his hands upon his fat paunch, assumes an air of meek sanctity, and announces to a mocking world: "the crime against Dreyfus would be impossible in Anglo-Saxon countries; such things occur only where other inferior races exist. . . ."
> Under the cover of that affair the enemies of France . . . are seeking to do all the mischief they can to the republic.[28]

"We are a very spontaneous people and on the slightest provocation go off half-cocked," said the *Pittsburgh Catholic*. American press reports had leaned too far toward the Dreyfusards; "every line published in the American press . . . was written to the one end, that Dreyfus was a victim, and that the entire French nation . . . were against him." "We participate in no such wholesale denunciation of France and her institutions as certain preferred newspaper haranguers have found occasion to utter in the present case," editorialized the *Catholic Citizen*. Archbishop Ireland, according to the *Iowa Catholic Messenger*, was displeased at the numerous public protest meetings which followed the second guilty verdict, reminding Americans that "France was our friend when we had no others" and that the affair was an internal matter from which Americans ought to remain aloof.[29]

■ American Catholics may have differed in their views of Alfred Dreyfus, but they were united in their antipathy toward Émile Zola. The announcement of Zola's indictment of French high officials and the judicial proceedings against him which followed, were, in most instances, ignored in the American Catholic press. There he was not perceived as hero, martyr, or victim. His attacks on French leaders, asserted one Catholic writer, his "vehement appeals, harangues and reproaches are . . . inviting anarchy." To Catholics, the significance of his trial was that it impugned the reputation of the Church. "The lamentable part of the whole matter is the interjecting religious feeling into the case, and the endeavor to saddle the Catholics of France as being instrumental in the conviction of Dreyfus on account of his nationality and religion."[30]

Most important, many Catholics believed that both Zola and his social opinions were decadent. The *Pittsburgh Catholic* was outraged that

> this leprous character, who has done his share to debauch the youth and morality not only of France, but of the world at large, is held up as a martyr. With an infamy peculiarly his own he dares to blaspheme and compare himself as a counter-part of the crucified Christ. . . . But Zola is no champion of innocence; he is the aider and abettor of revolution; and he would inaugurate the reign of the red and deep down in his heart he has the destruction of the reigning government.[31]

As for the almost universal praise showered upon Zola, the *Pilot* said: "M. Zola is exalted as a martyr; the man who used his talent to debauch humanity and pull it down to a level as low as in the time of Nero. This corrupter of youth, this deflowerer of chastity, gangrened and ulcerous apostate of bestiality, is now exalted even by a portion of the so-called religious press. In entering his prison house he fittingly graces his true home."[32] It was inconceivable to some that the word of this unsavory character would carry more weight than that of France's chief military officials. "Against the testimony of such a man there was the solemn affirmation of seven of the highest officers in the French army—men whose word we could take before that of any sensational novelist or journalist on earth. . . . It is absurd to suppose that a group of honor-loving French officers would conspire to tell a falsehood for any cause as it would be to imagine a similar act of infamy on the part of as many American officers."[33]

Such attacks on Zola continued unabated until the final hours of the affair. For his exertions on behalf of Dreyfus and justice he was to receive no credit from even liberal Catholics in America. His motives were seen only in the most sinister terms: "He has no desire for justice for the man Dreyfus, the Jew. He cares not a whit for him in this respect, but through him as the Jew, he would drag in the virtuous religious of France, and the great Catholic body of that country."[34]

The hostility toward Zola reflects the tendency among American Catholics described above, that of singling out particular issues for attention and disregarding or minimizing others. The choice of issue hinged largely on its relevance to American Catholic life. As the Rennes proceedings were almost ignored in Catholic newspapers, so the Labori shooting was minimized. "As to the attempt to assassinate Maître Labori," declared a Pittsburgh Catholic journal, "too much importance must not be attached to it. The dastardly deed was probably the act of one whose mental balance was seriously disturbed by the prevailing excitement." The Cincinnati *Catholic Telegraph* simply denied that the event had ever happened, citing the *Croix* to the effect that it "was all a game for arousing sympathy for Dreyfus."[35]

Those who demanded a boycott of the forthcoming World Exposition in Paris found little support among American Catholics, who viewed the festivity as what the *Catholic World* called a grand opportunity to display "the wonderful advancement made by the church during the nineteenth century." While masses of Americans were condemning France and her institutions, American Catholics were heaping praise upon the priests of France, of whom the *Ave Maria* remarked, "there is not a more exemplary body of men in any land." They constituted, it was said, the real force of the nation.[36]

To turn to another issue of the day, the castigation of the French nobility was not a popular pastime among American Catholics, and for good reason: as a class it was the most loyal to the Church. It is not surprising, therefore, that Anna Gould's marital and political adventures received but scant attention in the Catholic press and her involvement in the anti-Semitic movement was ignored, while she did attract some favorable notice as a recipient of the "Blessing of the Cardinal Archbishop of Paris." A charitable bazaar held in her honor in 1900 was described in a Catholic periodical as "an event of great magnificence. . . . the Countess de Castellane was surrounded on all sides by men and women whose names were notable in the old regime."[37]

With the exception of Colonel Picquart, the supporters of justice and order in France were rarely commended in the Catholic press. Guérin's anti-Semitic ravings and defiance of the Paris authorities were skimmed over, but the anarchist riots which grew out of the latter event received an inordinate measure of attention. The sacking of St. Joseph Church in Paris was seen as "the most serious outcome of the Dreyfus scandal" and shocked the Catholic community more than did any other incident of the affair: "It is almost impossible to believe that [it has] occurred in Catholic France," declared the *Catholic Mirror*.[38] The destruction of Catholic property, more than anything else, touched a raw nerve, and one might even conclude that to many American Catholics the Dreyfus affair took on life only after it was perceived as a threat to French religious institutions.

■ American Catholics, as we have seen, not only displayed less sympathy for the cause of Dreyfus than did any other identifiable group of Americans but were even perturbed at the degree of support shown for the victim in other quarters. Of course, as Thomas T. McAvoy observes, neither the hierarchy or the laity expressed itself in an identical fashion on this or any other public issue. James Cardinal Gibbons of Baltimore, Archbishop John Ireland of St. Paul, and Bishop John J. Keane of the Catholic University of America were viewed as the liberal spokesmen of the American Catholic community, while Archbishop Michael A. Corrigan of New York spoke for the Ultramontane or conservative faction.[39] French Catholic anti-Dreyfusards accused Ireland, Gibbons, and Keane, the "liberal triumvirate," of being too tolerant of Jews and too sympathetic to the cause of Dreyfus. They were even called "allies of the universal Jewish Alliance against Christianity." Conservative American Catholics applauded these rebukes.[40]

Except for minor differences, however, the Dreyfus case did not create a serious rift in the American Catholic community. The *Pittsburgh Catholic* observed that the agitation over Dreyfus had been inflated, that the aspersions cast upon his military judges had been uncalled for, and that accounts of French events circulating in the United States had been distorted. Even if Dreyfus were innocent, it was argued, he probably deserved some measure of punishment because of the liberal and radical elements that had been attracted to his defense. His cause had become a rallying point for all the enemies of France, the Church, and the army. "He is supported and encouraged by the worst class, the canaille from the slums of Paris," complained the *Catholic Mirror*. The *Pitts-*

burgh Catholic, liberal on most public issues, agreed that "Dreyfus is certainly unfortunate in his friends and supporters in France."[41]

There was also a tendency to deflate the prisoner's heroic image and minimize his martyrdom, even to attack his moral character. Perhaps Dreyfus was innocent of treason, argued one editorialist, but his admission that "he was an habitué and a companion of dissolute females" deprived him of any claims as a family man. "One's sympathy does not go out to a man who shrieks the honor of his family, and in the same breath admits himself a rogue and libertine."[42]

Catholics were among the first to accept the notion of a Jewish Syndicate, that phantom group of rich men who had dedicated their fortunes to the cause of the prisoner. "Captain Dreyfus is related to the Rothschilds," wrote Joseph A. Marmon in the *Catholic Citizen.* "M. Zadoc Kahn, Grand Rabbi of France, is said positively to be at the head of the great force called the 'Dreyfus Syndicate.'" The "Syndicate"'s relentless and powerful "silent campaign" even had Colonel Picquart in its pay. For his willingness to act as a "scapegoat for the Jews," Picquart was reported to have received a large sum of money. "The very contemplation of such a noiseless, daring power demands a certain admiration, not unmixed with fear," said the *Citizen.* Israel was "arrayed against Christianity," with the forces of agnosticism and socialism on its side.[43]

The *Catholic Telegraph* warned also of the ominous forces of Freemasonry arrayed on the side of the Dreyfusards. Dreyfus himself, it was claimed, had been admitted to the secret organization in 1893; it was rumored that he was a thirty-second-degree Mason. It was not surprising, then, that "super-human efforts are being put forth to clear Dreyfus. Organized Christianity seems to be determined to free its adept. The fact is noteworthy that the Masonic press throughout the world acts the part of advocate and judge for Dreyfus."[44]

American Catholics were also annoyed at Jewish attempts to boycott France. While some tried to belittle its possible impact ("the only persons who will boycott the Paris Exposition on account of the Dreyfus affair are those who never had any intention . . . of going," the *Catholic Mirror* noted), a Milwaukee Catholic offered Jews an ominous hint of a "final solution":

> The Christian world has burned Jews. It has hanged them, tortured them, but it has never stopped trading with them and the Jews have prospered and grown rich. The boycott is something the Christians have never tried and when they try it, that is the end of the Jews. . . . The boycott is a very ill-advised suggestion for the Jews

to make. It is the one appropriate measure the Christians have never
tried, the one measure that would be successful, the one measure
that would end the days of that [memorable] race as a separate
entity.[45]

Even the *Catholic World*, a leading voice of liberal Catholicism in
America, evinced little concern about the threat to the Jews of France
and lent its support to the chorus of French anti-Dreyfusards and anti-
Semites. Count Albert de Mun, an anti-Dreyfusard, was described in the
pages of this respected and widely read journal as "a man of extraordinary power. Identified with the *ancien régime*, he cut away from the past
and followed the guiding star of Leo. He rose rapidly in popular favor
by his remarkable power of eloquence, until today he is perhaps the
very pillar of strength of the new policy in France."[46] It opened its pages
to the staunch anti-Dreyfusard and Jew-baiter Father George McDermot,
a Catholic priest who was a strong opponent of the growing friendship
between England and the United States. McDermot cautioned against
supporting the cause of Dreyfus because it was an English trick to
estrange the United States and France. He was quick to assume that any
writer critical of France's treatment of its Jews was Jewish; he believed
that French animosity toward the Jews was not unjustified, as the Jews
had long been attempting to undermine France's moral and political
life. Together with the Freemasons, he argued, they had sapped the
vitality of France's last stabilizing element, the Catholic aristocracy.

Dreyfus' purported treachery came as no surprise to McDermot, for
to him Dreyfus was a grasping "German Jew," and, like others of his
kind, would stoop to anything if only the price were right. McDermot's
views were fully endorsed by the editors of the *Catholic World*, who went
so far as to say that his diatribe was the most lucid discussion of the
Dreyfus affair to appear in recent months and the best in English.[47]

American Catholics also shared with the French right a deep hostility
toward Léon Gambetta, a founder of the Third Republic. Within Gambetta's coterie were a number of prominent French Jews: his efforts to
liberalize and democratize French political life, his intense faith in the
republican and revolutionary ideals of France, appealed to Jewish journalists and politicians. He died in 1882, but his memory was kept alive
in part by such anti-Semites as Drumont, who identified Gambetta with
all that he found hateful in the Third Republic.[48] The *Catholic World*
supported Drumont in this and other views:

Many of the troubles of France today are an inheritance of the days

of Gambetta. In spite of his Italian name, Gambetta was partly of
Jewish extraction and, as was afterwards demonstrated, he was
wholly of Jewish persuasion. Before his death, at a banquet given by
the Rothschilds, when heated by wine, it was reported that he said
that "the priest is the past, the Jew is the future." At his death it was
found that the prefectures of forty-seven out of eighty departments
were in the hands of Jews. . . . It does not take a very acute observer
to see the long fingers of the money-changers tightening about the
throat of the body politic.[49]

It is difficult to find in American Catholic periodicals of the late nineteenth century a wholehearted endorsement of liberal trends in Europe.
Jewish and socialist influences were suspected behind every threat to the
ancient monarchies and their strong Catholic traditions. At the same
time the rising wave of anti-Semitism in eastern and western Europe
was virtually ignored, and one might almost conclude that the assaults
upon the Jews of Algeria and Paris had never occurred.[50] When Dreyfus
was convicted for a second time, the majority of American newspapers
were indignant, but Catholic periodicals such as the *Sacred Heart Review*
viewed the result and the subsequent "pardon" coolly. The *Catholic World*
regretted that so much time and money had been expended upon the
case. Many Catholics appeared irritated at American reports of the case:
"Every little fact or sentiment that was calculated to stir up a feeling of
pity for an injured man was made much of. Of course we were not
prepared to prove that there was a moneyed conspiracy in all this. But
it is well not to allow ourselves to be carried away by an enthusiasm
which may after all be founded on what is not so."[51]
   In the wake of the embarrassment that the affair caused the Church,
there was a tendency in some conservative circles to accuse the Jewish
people of collective treachery toward France. The *Catholic Columbian and
Record* characterized the Jews as the historic enemies of France, who had
been paid by Germany to engineer the downfall of the French empire
in 1870. Behind the advancing armies of France's enemies, explained
the popular Catholic journalist James R. Randall in 1900, "was a procession of men with long beards and gabardines representing Hebrew
money lenders, who were about to settle the financial affairs of the
fallen French Empire after the two Christian nations had ceased killing
each other in battle."[52] When American Jews objected to these infamous
suggestions, Randall assured them that his intention was not to impugn
the Jewish race or religion but only its commercial methods. It was common knowledge, he explained, that Jews hold "most of the coined gold
in the world. . . . I have not attacked the Jew on his spiritual or religious

side or his race issue. . . . I regret that the Israelite . . . cannot make proper distinctions on this subject." Randolph added the warning that Jews maintained a potent and insidious grasp upon the American economy as well.[53]

■ It is difficult to measure precisely the intensity of anti-Semitism in the American Catholic community, although its presence was unmistakable. It varied from city to city, from editor to editor, even from week to week in the same periodical. Although the Church did not endorse the ancient aberration, there is little evidence that its leaders, not even the most popular and venerated prelate of his time, Archbishop John Ireland, tried to curb it. Of Irish parentage, Ireland was a seminarian for eight years at Belley, France, where he became fluent in the language. In Rome he was considered an authoritative spokesman on French domestic issues. Both within the American Catholic Church and outside it, he had a reputation for tolerance, liberalism, and patriotism.[54]

Ireland was in Paris on a visit in the summer of 1899, when the Dreyfus case had reached a climactic and explosive stage. He was alarmed more by the rift between France and the United States which the affair had caused than by the prejudice and injustice associated with it. He had a deep affection for French Catholicism; he said on one occasion that to him it illustrated "the faith in a manner unequalled in any other country. . . . who can believe in the essential rottenness of a nation that can produce such an incomparable fruit?"[55] He admitted his irritation with the Jews of France and his belief that Jewish support for Dreyfus had unnecessarily injured the pride of the French army. French Jews' control of capital and of the press, he declared, had also made them unpopular. The American Jewish crusade for Dreyfus' cause and public gatherings critical of France annoyed him:

> It is my belief that public meetings in America such as it is proposed to hold for the purpose of protesting against the sentence of the Rennes Court-martial are untimely, unfair to France, and likely to breed regrettable ill-feeling between that country and our own. . . .
> This whole matter belongs to the internal life and to the internal administration of France and international courtesy as well as justice, bids us talk about it very carefully and very slowly. France is a proud, sensitive nation. She will deeply resent, as it is her right, undue criticism and hasty judgment of her acts by foreign people, and especially will she resent, as is surely her right, any uncalled for interference

with her internal administration or any imprudent challenging of her national honor.[56]

Not surprisingly, the few French sympathizers in the United States found these views refreshingly untypical of the general American attitude:

> It is indeed a relief from the scandalous abuse of the pulpit and vituperations from lesser divines who lately have thundered down a species of crusade against Frenchmen, their justice, fair name, renown, genius and morality, to read the soothing, Christian-like and charitable admonition of Bishop Ireland, one of the most learned, wise, independent and thoroughbred Americans, when he appeals to the common sense and sensible, unprejudiced good hearts of his countrymen.[57]

On the other hand, James Cardinal Gibbons of Baltimore, who shared with Archbishop Ireland many views and was an equally prominent cleric, was more outspoken in attacking anti-Semitism. His condemnation of Russian pogroms was the strongest which came from an American prelate. "For my part," Gibbons wrote, "I cannot well conceive how Christians can entertain other than kind sentiments toward the Hebrew race when I consider how much we are indebted to them. We have from them the inspired volume of the Old Testament, which has been the constitution in all ages to devout souls; Christ our Lord, the founder of our religion; His Blessed Mother, as well as the Apostles. These facts attach me strongly to the Jewish race."[58] For such views Gibbons was condemned in France, where his ecumenical tendencies were little appreciated. The French priest Father Henry Delassus accused the American prelate of working with the Jews to "hasten the overthrow of the Catholic Church and the triumph of 'anti-Christ.'" Even the *Catholic Mirror* of Baltimore, which supported the cardinal's position on many public and religious issues, offered little support to the cause of Dreyfus or sympathy for the plight of French Jewry.[59]

■ The dramatic growth of American Catholicism during the final quarter of the nineteenth century was one of the great religious achievements of the age. Between 1880 and 1900 the American Catholic population doubled in size, increasing from six to twelve million, primarily as a result of a huge influx of European Catholics. Adjusting comfortably to an environment institutionally dominated by a Protestant life style, Catholics could boast by the end of the century over ten thousand churches and chapels and priests and seminary students, about a hundred colleges, and four thousand parochial schools and academies.[60]

The ability of the American Catholic Church to fit into and thrive in the democratic atmosphere of the New World raised questions in Latin Catholic clerical circles. Old World, Ultramontane clerics found it disconcerting to see such spectacular strides made largely at the expense of Europe's population. The fact that this achievement was taking place at a time of American military and imperial successes, which were enveloped in Anglo-American and stridently Protestant slogans, was not overlooked.

Notwithstanding Ireland's abortive attempts to alleviate the prevailing belligerent mood, both his and Gibbons' patriotic postures when actual war with Spain began in 1898 were observed with dismay in Catholic Europe. The Vatican, France, and other Catholic powers in Europe maintained a position of benevolent neutrality toward Spain, but Ireland told a Chicago audience in March, 1898, that, "no true American Catholic will talk of espousing the cause of Spain against that of his country because the former is a Catholic nation . . . To do that is to set oneself down as traitorously inclined to the teaching of this religion, as well as to the country which it is his bounden duty to defend against all enemies." Theodore Roosevelt was impressed with Ireland's patriotism, and most American Catholics resented even a hint that they lacked enthusiasm for the war.[61]

Viewed in this context, it is understandable why a charge of heresy was flung at the American Church by French priests, "conjured up," as a contemporary put it, "by men who detest every form of free government, and who dreamt that they could ruin the leaders of Catholicism in the United States, by fastening on them an imputation of unsound and heretical teaching." The charge was viewed by American Catholic leaders as an insult, particularly when it resulted in a mild but significant papal rebuke of American religious tendencies in the form of a letter, *Testem Benevolentiae*.[62] The controversy engineered by conservative French Catholic prelates coincided with the Dreyfus affair; it divided the French and American clergy; and it marked the American Church in French eyes as permissive and susceptible to liberalism and modernism. French ultraconservatives saw their American co-religionists, as Robert D. Cross observes, as "pro-Semitic, just as they were pro-Masonic and Protestant."[63]

Any measure of American Catholic anti-Semitism, therefore, must take into consideration the fact that from the perspective of European Catholicism, anti-Semitism did not exist in the United States—indeed, the American Church had simply adopted Jewish and Protestant values. Its mild criticism of Dreyfus did not go far enough to satisfy Ultramontane appetites. In the United States, however, even a genteel variety of anti-Semitism was open to public criticism, not only from Jews but from liberal Gentiles as well. Even those who gave moderate support to French anti-Dreyfusards were seen as prejudiced observers of an open-and-shut case, a case with momentous implications for justice and the maintenance of civil and legal morality.

American Catholics were thus eager to divest their church from any charge that it was involved in the encouragement of anti-Semitism. Repeated questions about the pope's significant silence on the Dreyfus matter disturbed American Catholics, though they tried to dismiss the issue as a fantasy of the yellow press, typical of its irresponsible and sensational reporting. They accused their critics of demanding a higher standard of moral behavior from Catholics than from other religious groups:

> How about the other Princes and Potentates? We have not observed that the Czar of Russia, Head of the Greek Church; the Queen of England, Head of the Episcopal Church; the President of the United States, the Sultan of Zanzibar, or any other of the great ones of earth took pains to interfere in a matter which did not concern them directly. The Pope, with the generous spirit which governs all his acts, interceded for clemency—politely, because he is a gentleman; but knowing his place, as a gentleman does, he demanded nothing."[64]

Efforts were made to disassociate the actions of the Holy Office from anti-Semitism. The popes were pictured as the lone protectors of the European Jew throughout the centuries. Jewish survival itself was attributed to papal tolerance. Writing in the *Catholic World*, Elizabeth Raymond-Barker acknowledged that "it is true that at Rome as elsewhere the Jews were despised, obliged to live in their quarter of the city, and as a rule, compelled to wear a distinctive badge or color." "Still," she argued, "to the student of history, there is no doubt that amidst the intolerance and barbarities of the Middle Ages and the times succeeding them, Rome set a great example of moderation."[65]

It was equally important to disassociate anti-Semitism from the Dreyfus affair and to insist that French Catholics were interested in justice, not Jew-baiting: "France was the first country in Europe to give civil rights to the Jews." "It would be very easy to prove that Jews are better treated in Catholic France today than they sometimes are in this country," declared the *Sacred Heart Review*. "There are no French hotels, for instance, which slam the doors in the face of Hebrews in the way certain American ones have done and still do. . . . The Jewish religion stands on the same footing in France as the national church. It is recognized and supported by the State."[66]

Particularly objectionable to American Catholics were the frequent castigations of the Jesuit order, which, it was popularly believed, had monopolized the education of French generals. The friends of Dreyfus increasingly turned their wrath upon the Catholic order in the summer of 1899. The Catholic response was to portray the Jesuits as the innocent prey of Catholic-haters and as the victims of public ignorance and prejudice. A typical rebuttal was that of the *Pittsburgh Catholic*:

> Many of those journalists who are ever ready to discover that a Jesuit is at the bottom of every plot and agitation have raised the cry that Captain Dreyfus is a victim of the designs of the Jesuits. The truth is, of course, that the authorities that condemned Dreyfus were not in the slightest degree affected by Jesuit influence. In this, as in other debatable matters, the Jesuits, like other large bodies of men, take different views, and it will interest, if it will not please, the Jesuit-phobes to learn that some of the strongest advocates of a public trial for the prisoner . . . are to be found amongst the Jesuit fathers.[67]

Sydney F. Smith, a Catholic writer, pointed out that few of the officers involved in the prosecution of Dreyfus were practicing Catholics. Joseph Smith, a commentator on anti-Catholicism, noted that to many Anglo-Americans "the Jesuit did cover a multitude of sins, from eating raw babies to editing newspapers surreptitiously." In his view, anti-Semitism had little to do with the Jesuit order: "The Jesuit will hardly account for the Lutheran Jew-baiters of Prussia, nor the Greek Church . . . who torture and plunder the Hebrews of Russia." The *Catholic Citizen* also argued that the misbehavior of French clerics was the result of "their reactionary politics, not their religion." "There are gullible religionists in France just as there are gullible Protestants the world over. . . . But the Church is not responsible for human error."[68] From the Catholic point of view, the Jesuits were the innocents who suffered in the Dreyfus fiasco, and in the months following Rennes, the Society of Jesus and other religious orders did indeed become the targets of anti-clerical legislation and mounting public hostility. With pro-Dreyfus forces now politically respectable, Catholics in France braced themselves for a "war against religion." "That the aim of the present government is ultimately to wipe out all religion is scarcely beyond doubt," an American writer warned in 1903.[69]

The annulment of the Concordat by the French government in 1905 was a deep disappointment. Because of it, an amicable dependence of church on state had existed in France since the days of Napoleon I. French Catholic institutions were now set adrift on an uncertain voyage. Catholic leaders in the United States were aware that separation of church and state in France was seen as a threat to the very existence of religious life. "If the French government were a liberal, unmeddlesome power, like our own," wrote one American, "then the separation would be something that everyone would desire," but Frenchmen "have not been trained to support the priests" and "it would be doubtful if they could be relied upon to do so."

Americans heaped criticism upon the Briand bill, which legislated the annulment. It reduced churchmen to "the position of *peons*," said Manuel de Moreira. It denied clergymen freedom of expression, for it provided that "no cross or any religious emblem can be erected, or stay erected, in a public place."[70] It also severely limited the Church's right to possess or acquire property. "The injustice of this law is obvious," said the *Catholic World* in an editorial. "An ordinary association can increase its property indefinitely without being under the control of the state; the society which will supervise the celebration of worship is not allowed the same privilege."[71]

Other American observers did not deny the grievous pressures imposed upon the Church of France but believed that the crisis might invigorate France's religious life. One such, Thomas J. Shahan, a professor of church history at the Catholic University of America, thought that French Catholics "would be blind indeed, if their own trials . . . did not teach them prudence and humility for many centuries to come." He advised Frenchmen to take a leaf from the American experience and welcome rather than resist the separation. After all, he pointed out, under the Concordat French Catholicism had left much to be desired: "It is a common saying, humiliating enough if it be true, that forty thousand atheists and Jews govern France."[72]

It is interesting to note that the cause-and-effect relationship between the declining fortunes of the French Church and the Dreyfus affair became apparent only when Dreyfus was finally exonerated. As one writer put it in 1906:

> When Dreyfus was condemned, with every accompaniment of ignominy, to his living death, in a tropical hell, aggravated by man's inhu-

manity to man, there were in France about 30,000 men [and]
128,000 women, belonging to religious congregations. Their
possessions were estimated at four hundred and ninety-three million
francs. The Catholic Church was the religion of the State, established
by law. Military guards of honor stood at the entrance to the residence of every bishop, a papal nuncio resided in Paris, surrounded
with all the pomp and dignity that attends the representative of a
sovereign power; and, in turn, an ambassador of France represented
the eldest daughter of the Church at the Papal Court, as in the days
of his most Christian Majesty. On the day when Dreyfus was declared
an innocent man no religious order existed in France; their members
in thousands had taken the road to exile; the Church was reduced to
the same footing as the most petty and obscure sect; and France, as a
nation, had ceased to recognize the existence of the tiara. Between
this rapid change in the status of Catholicism and the fortunes of a
mere subaltern officer of the army, however improbable it may seem
on any *a priori* grounds, there is an intimate connection.[73]

A few American Catholics, and even they reluctantly, admitted that
their French counterparts had been their own worst enemies—that the
Church in France had been wrong to shut its eyes to the reality of
republican life or to dismiss it contemptuously as an "immoral usurpa-
tion" of a more glorious age. These Catholics saw in the French misfortunes a warning for themselves:

> We must beware of separating ourselves into a class apart. . . . we
> must assimilate the best spirit of America and be assimilated by it. . . .
> French Catholics have been brought to their present plight by dis-
> trusting democracy, and by remaining in their country somewhat as a
> foreign substance remains in the eye. They have been in the Republic
> as foreigners who refuse to become citizens. We shall avoid their mis-
> fortunes if we love democracy, heart and soul, cherishing and practic-
> ing the independence on which it rests.[74]

One further caveat was faintly audible: Catholics were urged to take
great pains to avoid being drawn into the insidious quicksands of anti-
Semitism. James J. Fox, an isolated voice among American Catholics,
reminded his readers that hatred of the Jews had been aided and abet-
ted by the French religious press and that it had had "the consent or the
approbation of responsible ecclesiastics. . . . the small number of clergy
that dissented . . . did not dare to express its opinion; for to do so rendered any one man an object of suspicion and reprobation." He admitted that it was not easy for his readers to accept the fact that "pru-

dent, learned, pious ecclesiastics, absolutely devoted to truth and justice," could be so led astray, but such was the case, as he saw it.[75]

Fox's warning was a thoughtful one, but it came somewhat late. Along with the secularization of the French state, the assault on Alfred Dreyfus and the Jews of France was to become an event with great meaning for the future course of Catholicism in the United States.

XII

Coda

Nothing but the story of Esther and the *Book of Job* can equal the
Dreyfus case in the symmetry of its ending.

Independent, July, 1906

Except for American Catholics, there was general support in the United
States for Captain Alfred Dreyfus and those Frenchmen who fought for
justice on his behalf. However, not all Americans supported Dreyfus or
were disturbed by events in France for the same reasons, nor did they
draw the same practical lessons from the case. The Dreyfus affair had
something of significance to say to most Americans, lawyers and laymen,
militarists and anti-militarists, reformers and reactionaries, ministers
and agnostics, Protestants, Catholics, and Jews.

To those inclined to the dramatic and the spectacular, the case
offered a rich panorama of exciting interludes and acts of heroism. The
chief participants had battled stubbornly against difficult odds. Dreyfus'
disgrace, his incarceration on Devil's Island, and his tragic correspondence with his wife contained all the elements from which folk heroes
are created. Zola's challenge to the generals and leaders of France and
the penalties inflicted upon him because of his determination to expose
the treachery of France's highest officials made him famous and much
admired in the United States. Similarly, the exploits of the soldier Picquart and the lawyer Labori captivated the attention of countless Americans. Although the French military and the French bar were little
admired in the United States, these men, because of their willingness to
risk their professional and personal reputations for the cause of truth
and justice, were seen, with Zola, as just men within a society in moral
decline.

To those who shared the sense of moral mission and the superiority
of "Anglo-Saxonism," the Dreyfus affair served as a convenient catalyst.

Diplomatic issues of the day also tended to cement Anglo-American relations. English support of the United States in its war with Spain was a sharp contrast to the cool reception of that conflict in France. The Anglo-French crisis over Fashoda, coinciding with the Dreyfus trials, also tended to underline the differences between the English-speaking peoples and the "Latins."

To those Americans who were especially concerned about the relationship of law to society, it was particularly difficult to view the Dreyfus case without a measure of suspicion. As has been noted, even the American Bar Association took time in its annual meeting in 1898 to denounce French legal practices; in the 1899 meeting a resolution was offered honoring Labori. Americans enjoyed contrasting their own practices with those of France; they believed that because of the safeguards guaranteed under the common law a Dreyfus case could not occur in the United States. They ridiculed France's courtroom behavior, its handling of witnesses, and the absence of cross-examination and of a comprehensible law of evidence in its criminal trials. They complained about the brutality and arbitrariness of French judges, the unruly behavior of spectators in court, the admission into the court record of hearsay observations and gossip, the mistreatment of witnesses prior to trial, and the absence of the guarantee of habeas corpus. The editor of the *American Law Review* advised lawyers not to attend a law conference in France in 1900, and a few respectable voices even demanded extraterritorial court privileges in France for Americans who fell afoul of the legal system.

Not all Americans, however, were caught up in the flood of Anglo-American sentiment. Because of its militaristic and imperialistic implications, it was rejected by some as a form of American and English jingoism. The conquest of Caribbean and Pacific territories was not welcomed by many thoughtful Americans, and the Dreyfus affair provided an example of what could happen to a democratic, civil polity which placed an inordinate trust in its military establishment. Such critics supported the cause of Dreyfus and Zola because their cases had challenged the corruption of the French military. They needed no convincing that the French army was primarily responsible for the monumental fiasco. The affair offered them a platform from which they could warn their own government about military domination of civil affairs.

To another group of Americans, who adhered to Victorian standards of behavior, the affair confirmed what they had long suspected— France's moral depravity, a nation in social and political decline because of loose conduct. With marital infidelity dominating the highest levels of French society, and violence and political instability sending periodic tremors through its political institutions, Americans sighed with relief that their political structure had more stable moral foundations.

Americans were also conscious of the anti-Semitic undercurrents of the Dreyfus affair. Although social discrimination against Jews existed in the United States as well, as the French were fond of pointing out, the violence perpetrated against the Jews of France, and unpunished by its highest authorities, was viewed as an additional symptom of French decadence. Although many leading American Protestants were ambivalent on the issue of anti-Semitism, as we have seen, Christians driven by a desire to hasten God's kingdom through social reform took some satisfaction in observing the spectacle of corruption in Roman Catholic institutions in France. Protestant spokesmen were quicker than others to criticize the silence of the pope on the Dreyfus matter and to blame the Roman Catholic Church and its clergy for the plight of Dreyfus and for fostering violence against the Jews. Though it would be a mistake to equate this position with any profound understanding of the nature of French anti-Semitism, the American Protestant community was at least made sensitive to the dangerous and insidious consequences of an anti-Semitic movement.

American Jews, more than any other group, felt the Dreyfus affair personally and deeply, yet even their perspective reflected cultural, economic, and ideological differences. Whereas the more Americanized German Jews tended to universalize the issues, more recent East European immigrants tended to personalize them. Zionists and non-Zionists each saw French events and the world response to these events as a confirmation of their respective ideological positions. Despite these varied reactions, however, when Americans overwhelmingly supported the cause of Dreyfus, and when he was finally vindicated and France publicly admitted its judicial error, all American Jews appeared to have been reassured about their future position and security in their new home.

Like Jews, American Roman Catholics had also a highly personal stake in French events. Faced by anti-Catholic bigotry at home and charges of doctrinal laxity from abroad, they preferred to say as little as possible. Irish Catholic hostility toward England also confused the issue. The majority of Catholic spokesmen were reluctant to criticize French judicial procedure, and, when they did speak out on the matter, they condemned America's concern for the prisoner, objected to public criticism of France, minimized the existence of French anti-Semitism, and denied that the Catholic Church had encouraged Jew-baiting. From the Catholic perspective, the most significant result of the calamity was the debilitating effect that it had on the French Church's relationship with the state. The full impact of French events did not make themselves felt until after Rennes. By that time some believed that the annullment of the Concordat and corresponding weakening of the position of the French Church was the result of Catholic reluctance to offer full cooperation to the republic and of its sympathetic stance toward the anti-Dreyfusards.

All in all, American Catholic observers could feel that their own pluralistic environment contained strengths yet to be appreciated by European Catholics. Most Americans of other religious and political persuasions would have endorsed this view. American fears of the dangers inherent in the Dreyfus affair have proved generally well justified in the years since the trials. Whether these cautionary instincts have become a part of the American psyche, only time will tell.

Notes

Notes to Chapter I

1. The story of the Dreyfus affair is most accessible in English in the following works, all of which I have relied upon: Hannah Arendt, "The Dreyfus Affair," *The Origins of Totalitarianism* (New York: World, 1958), pp. 89–120; Guy Chapman, *The Dreyfus Case: A Reassessment* (New York: Reynal & Company, 1955); Nicholas Halasz, *Captain Dreyfus: The Story of a Mass Hysteria* (New York: Simon and Schuster, 1955); Wilhelm Herzog, "Six Phases of the Dreyfus Affair," in *From Dreyfus to Pétain: The Struggle of a Republic*, trans. Walter Sorell (New York: Creative Age Press, 1947), pp. 4–17; Douglas Johnson, *France and the Dreyfus Affair* (London: Blandford Press, 1966); Alfred and Pierre Dreyfus, *The Dreyfus Case*, trans. and ed. Donald C. McKay (New Haven: Yale University Press, 1937); David Lewis, *Prisoners of Honor* (New York: William Morrow, 1973). Still very helpful is "The Dreyfus Case," in *The Jewish Encyclopedia* (Philadelphia: Jewish Publication Society, 1903), Vol. IV, pp. 660–88. In French the bibliography is extensive, but Joseph Reinach, *Histoire de l'affaire Dreyfus*, 7 vols. (Paris: Librairie Charpentier et Fasquelle, 1901–5), especially the first four volumes, is still the most comprehensive survey of the subject.

2. Samuel E. Morison et al., *The Growth of the American Republic*, Vol. II (New York: Oxford University Press, 1969), pp. 218–19; see also Robert W. Desmond, *The Press and World Affairs* (New York: D. Appleton-Century, 1937), pp. 38, 100–103.

3. James Creelman, *On the Great Highway: The Wanderings and Adventures of a Special Correspondent* (Boston: Lothrop, 1901), pp. 174–75. See also Charles H. Brown, *The Correspondents' War: Journalists in the Spanish-American War* (New York: Charles Scribner's Sons, 1967), pp. 10–38.

4. James B. Eustis, "Dreyfus and the Jewish Question in France: French and American Democracy," *Conservative Review* 2 (August, 1899):18; "Is a Dreyfus Case Possible in America?" *Independent* 61 (July 19, 1906):166–68.

Notes to Chapter II

1. Of these, Henry Adams was the most notable. See Henry Adams to Elizabeth Cameron, February 14, 1898, in *Letters of Henry Adams, 1892–1918*, ed. Washington C. Ford (Boston: Houghton Mifflin, 1938), pp. 145–57 (the case of Roman Catholics in the United States will be discussed later); *A Catalog of Books Represented by Library of Congress Printing Cards* (Paterson, N.J.: Rowman and Littlefield, 1963), pp. 590–601; Robert E. Spiller et al., *Literary History of the United States* (New York: Macmillan, 1953), pp. 1016–17, 1022, 1028; Emily Crawford, "Emile Zola," *Contemporary Review* 55 (January, 1889):94; Henry Blumenthal, *American and French Culture, 1800–1900* (Baton Rouge: Louisiana State University Press, 1975), pp. 190–92.

2. Guy Chapman, *The Dreyfus Case: A Reassessment* (New York: Reynal & Company, 1955),

pp. 178–79; Lee M. Friedman, *Zola and the Dreyfus Case: His Defense of Liberty and Its Enduring Significance* (Boston: Beacon Press, 1937), pp. 38–39; Joseph Reinach, *Histoire de l'affaire Dreyfus*, Vol. III: *La Crise* (Paris: Librairie Charpentier et Fasquelle, 1905), p. 314.

3. *New York Times*, December 5, 1897, January 13, 1898; "Zola and the Dreyfus Case," *ibid.*, January 14, 1898. See also *Boston Evening Transcript*, January 13, 1898; *New Orleans Daily Picayune*, January 11, 1898; *Philadelphia Public Ledger*, January 14, January 20, 1898.

4. "The 'Down with Zola' Stillness," *Boston Evening Transcript*, January 18, 1898; Robert H. Sherard, "M. Zola on French Anti-Semitism," *American Monthly Review of Reviews* 17 (March, 1898):320; *New York Times*, January 15, January 20, 1898; *New Orleans Daily Picayune*, January 15, January 16, January 18, 1898; *Kansas City Star*, January 18, January 24, 1898.

5. *New York Times*, February 6, February 8, 1898. These proceedings were soon published in an English translation in the United States; see Benjamin R. Tucker, ed., *The Trial of Émile Zola Containing M. Zola's Letter to President Fauré Relating to the Dreyfus Case and a Full Report of the Fifteen Days' Proceedings in the Assize Court of the Seine, Including Testimony of Witnesses and Speeches of Counsel* (New York: Benjamin R. Tucker, 1898). See also *New Orleans Daily Picayune*, February 8, 1898; *Chicago Tribune*, February 11, 1898; *Boston Evening Transcript*, February 7, February 8, February 21, 1898; *New Orleans Daily Picayune*, February 8, February 9, 1898; *Philadelphia Public Ledger*, February 8, 1898; *Atlanta Constitution*, February 7, February 8, February 9, 1898.

6. "The Trials of Dreyfus and Zola," *American Law Review* 32 (May–June, 1898):442–44; *Boston Evening Transcript*, February 21, 1898; "The Recent Zola Trial," *Green Bag* 10 (May, 1898):187, 190–91; *New Orleans Daily Picayune*, February 19, 1898; *Kansas City Star*, February 15, February 19, 1898; *Philadelphia Public Ledger*, February 9, 1898.

7. Quoted in "The Recent Zola Trial," p. 193.

8. *Ibid.* Even Mr. Dooley, a supporter of Dreyfus' cause, threw some darts at Zola; see Finley Peter Dunne, *Mr. Dooley in Peace and War* (Boston: Small, Maynard, 1898), pp. 235–37.

9. "Dreyfus and the Jewish Question in France: French and American Democracy," *Conservative Review* 2 (August, 1899):10.

10. Carl Schurz, "France after the Zola Trial," *Harper's Weekly* 42 (March 12, 1898):243; *Boston Evening Transcript*, February 23, April 30, 1898; *New Orleans Daily Picayune*, February 23, 1898; *Philadelphia Public Ledger*, February 24, 1898; *Atlanta Constitution*, February 24, February 25, 1898. There were, of course, exceptions, but they were not typical of the responses of most Americans. Henry Adams, for example, was one of the few prominent Americans who did not conceal his contempt of Émile Zola; see Ford, ed., *Letters of Henry Adams*, p. 249.

11. *Boston Evening Transcript*, March 31, 1898.

12. *New York Times*, May 22, 1898.

13. *Ibid.*, May 22, 1898. See also John Durand to Charles Hart, April 9, 1898, John Durand Papers, New York Public Library.

14. "Zola, Dreyfus and the French Republic," *Political Science Quarterly* 13 (June, 1898):259–60, 264–65, 271–72.

15. Joseph H. Choate, "The Annual Address," *Report of the Twenty-First Annual Meeting of the American Bar Association, Held at Saratoga Springs, New York, August 17, 18, 19, 1898* (New York: n.p., 1898), pp. 288–89; Joel Benton, "French Law and Law Courts," *Green Bag* 10 (September, 1898):417–20.

16. *St. Louis Post-Dispatch*, January 15, 1899; Ernest Alfred Vizetelly, *Émile Zola, Novelist and Reformer: An Account of His Life and Work* (London: John Lane–The Bodley Head, 1904), pp. 465–66, 477; *New York Times*, March 2, March 28, May 1, May 28, May 30, May 31, 1899; *New York Journal*, June 5, 1899; *Washington Post*, June 3, June 4, 1899; *Kansas City Star*, June 3, 1899; *St. Louis Post-Dispatch*, June 3, June 4, 1899.
17. "The Dreyfus Dénouement," *Nation* 68 (June 8, 1899):432–33. See also "Justice and Retribution," *Outlook* 62 (June 10, 1899):330.
18. "Justice at Last," *St. Louis Post-Dispatch*, May 30, 1899.
19. *Boston Evening Transcript*, June 8, 1899; Sherard, "French Anti-Semitism," pp. 318–19.
20. Quotations are from newspaper clippings in the Friedman collection at the Houghton Library.
21. *New York World*, July 10, 1899; *St. Louis Post-Dispatch*, July 10, 1899.
22. *Ibid.*
23. *New York Sun*, June 25, 1899. Reported also in *St. Louis Post-Dispatch*, June 24, 1899.
24. *New York Journal*, August 5, August 9, August 20, 1899.
25. *Ibid.*, August 20, 1899.
26. *New York Times*, September 23, 1899; *Atlanta Constitution*, September 22, 1899; *St. Louis Post-Dispatch*, September 22, 1899.
27. Émile Zola, "The Fifth Act," *New York Herald*, September 13, 1899; *Washington Post*, September 12, 1899; *St. Louis Post-Dispatch*, September 20, 1899.
28. "Émile Zola, His Literary and Social Position," *International Quarterly* 6 (December–March, 1902):366, 381–82.
29. Quoted in Vizetelly, *Émile Zola*, pp. 524–25; I am indebted to Patricia Harpole, assistant chief librarian of the Minnesota Historical Society, for information about James Carleton Young. See also *St. Paul Pioneer*, January 8, 1918. I have been unable to discover why the project was aborted.
30. "Zola and Dreyfus," *New York Times*, July 15, 1906.
31. Quoted in the *New York Herald*, January 14, 1898.

Notes to Chapter III

1. In the United States, one of the most widely read English observers of the Dreyfus affair was George W. Steevens. See his *The Tragedy of Dreyfus* (New York: Harper & Brothers, 1899) and "Scenes and Actors in the Dreyfus Trial," *McClure's Magazine* 13 (September, 1899):515–23.
2. *Boston Evening Transcript*, March 11, 1898; *St. Louis Post-Dispatch*, December 25, 1898; Arthur C. Turner, *The Unique Partnership: Britain and the United States* (New York: Pegasus, 1971), pp. 50–52; Charles S. Campbell, Jr., *Anglo-American Understanding, 1898–1903* (Baltimore: Johns Hopkins University Press, 1957), p. 1; Bertha A. Reuter, *Anglo-American Relations during the Spanish American War* (New York: Macmillan, 1924), pp. 157–59; John R. Dos Passos, *The Anglo-Saxon Century and the Unification of the English-Speaking People* (New York: G. P. Putnam's Sons, 1903), pp. 48, 213–15, 233–35.
3. Richard Hofstadter, *Social Darwinism in American Thought* (Boston: Beacon Press, 1955), pp. 179–81; Thomas Barclay, *Thirty Years: Anglo-French Reminiscences (1876–1906)* (Boston: Houghton Mifflin, 1914), p. 139; Dos Passos, *Anglo-Saxon Century*, pp. 64–65. See, for example, the resolution of the Illinois Grand Army of the Republic, "Why We Stand by the Flag," May 18, 1899, William McKinley Papers, Library of Congress.
4. Quoted in Sidney E. Mead, "American Protestantism since the Civil War, I. From Denominationalism to Americanism," *Journal of Religion* 36 (January, 1956):15. For similar sentiments, see Charles Davis to Chauncey M. Depew, February 7, 1898, and

S. Chamberlain to Chauncey M. Depew, October 26, 1898, Chauncey M. Depew Papers, Yale University Library; Edward N. Saveth, "Race and Nationalism in American Historiography in the Late Nineteenth Century," *Political Science Quarterly* 64 (1939):421–41.

5. *Washington Post*, November 27, 1898; Mead, "American Protestantism," p. 13. See also William Lawrence, "Fiftieth Annual Address, Diocese of Massachusetts," *Journal of the 113th Annual Meeting of the Convention, 1898*, in William Lawrence Papers, Massachusetts Diocesan Library, Boston, courtesy of Catherine Higgins, the librarian of the Diocesan Library.

6. See Harvey Wish, *Society and Thought in Modern America* (New York: David McKay, 1962), p. 389; E. T. Peters to Edward A. Ross, May 31, 1900, Box 2, Edward A. Ross Papers, Wisconsin State Historical Society, Madison. For further examples of such rhetoric, see Henry Demarest Lloyd to F. Brocklehurst, January 5, 1899, Box 10, Henry Demarest Lloyd Papers, State Historical Society of Wisconsin, Madison; Washington Gladden, "War Impending" (sermon), April 3, 1898, microfilm edition, Roll 29, Washington Gladden Papers, Ohio Historical Society, Columbus; R. Heber Newton, "After the War—Our Dangers and Duties" (sermon), 1898, R. Heber Newton Papers, New York Public Library.

7. H. Wayne Morgan, ed., *Making Peace with Spain. The Diary of Whitelaw Reid: September–December, 1898* (Austin: University of Texas Press, 1965), pp. 90–92; Frederick W. Whitridge, "Zola, Dreyfus and the French Republic," *Political Science Quarterly* 13 (June, 1898):265, 271–72; John T. Morse, Jr., "The Dreyfus and Zola Trials," *Atlantic Monthly* 81 (May, 1898):589–90; H. C. Foxcroft, "The 'Dreyfus Scandal' of English History," *Fortnightly Review* 72 (October, 1899):565.

8. *Washington Post*, November 27, 1898; Dos Passos, *Anglo-Saxon Century*, pp. 52–53.

9. Campbell, *Anglo-American Understanding*, pp. 346–47; Reuter, *Anglo-American Relations*, pp. 169, 176. For additional discussion, see *Boston Evening Transcript*, April 19, April 20, 1898; Charles Davis to Chauncey M. Depew, February 7, 1898, Chauncey M. Depew Papers, Yale University Library.

10. *Fashoda Reconsidered: The Impact of Domestic Politics on French Policy in Africa, 1893–1898* (Baltimore: Johns Hopkins University Press, 1969), pp. 13, 59, 61–65, 77–81, 86–88; E. Malcolm Carroll, *French Public Opinion and Foreign Affairs, 1870–1914* (New York: Century Company, 1931), pp. 169–76, 179–82.

11. Barclay, *Thirty Years*, p. 137. See also the *Times* of London for October 29, 1898; *Boston Evening Transcript* for May 2, 1898.

12. Brown, *Fashoda Reconsidered*, pp. 119, 129–31. See comments in *Washington Post*, October 11, October 12, October 13, October 16, October 21, October 23, October 24, October 25, November 6, 1898.

13. Barclay, *Thirty Years*, pp. 139, 162–63. See also *New York Tribune*, December 4, 1898; *Kansas City Star*, December 11, 1898.

14. Richard Hofstadter, *The Paranoid Style in American Politics and Other Essays* (New York: Vintage, 1967), pp. 150, 158–59.

15. *Boston Evening Transcript*, April 30, 1898. See also Henry Wickham Steed, *Through Thirty Years, 1892–1922: A Personal Narrative* (New York: Doubleday, Page, 1924), pp. 131–32; Georges M. Paleologue, *An Intimate Journal of the Dreyfus Case* (New York: Criterion Books, 1957), pp. 143, 145, 168–69; Henry Demarest Lloyd to Samuel Bowles, May 7, 1898, Series I, Box 9, Henry Demarest Lloyd Papers, State Historical Society of Wisconsin, Madison.

16. Quotations are from Louis M. Sears, "French Opinion of the Spanish-American War," *Hispanic American Historical Review* 7 (February, 1927):25–44. See also Henry Blumen-

thal, *France and the United States: Their Diplomatic Relations, 1789–1914* (Chapel Hill: University of North Carolina Press, 1970), pp. 192–95.

17. Quoted in Elsie P. Mende, with Henry G. Pearson, *An American Soldier and Diplomat: Horace Porter* (New York: Frederick A. Stokes, 1927), pp. 169–77, 205–7, 224–25; "Unhappy France," *Boston Globe*, October 27, 1898. See also Carol Lloyd to Mrs. Henry Demarest Lloyd, September 2, 1899, Series I, Box 10, Henry Demarest Lloyd Papers, State Historical Society of Wisconsin, Madison. Also R. B. Bradford to William McKinley, November 1, 1898, and Harold M. Sewall to Mr. Credler, September 15, 1899, William McKinley Papers, Library of Congress.

18. Turner, *Unique Partnership*, p. 29; Barclay, *Thirty Years*, pp. 135–36, 139; "English Comments on the Dreyfus Case," *American Law Review* (March–April, 1898):256.

19. See the discussion in Lawrence M. Friedman, *A History of American Law* (New York: Simon and Schuster, 1973), p. 349.

20. R. Barry O'Brien, *The Life of Lord Russell of Killowen* (London: Smith, Elder, 1901), pp. 159, 173, 265–66, 270, 275.

21. *Ibid.*, pp. 283–85. See also Francis Rawle, "Address of the President," *Report of the Twenty-Sixth Annual Meeting of the American Bar Association Held at Hot Springs, Virginia, August 26, 27, and 28, 1903* (Philadelphia, 1903), p. 263.

22. O'Brien, *Lord Russell*, pp. 286–89, 309, 314–16, 318–19, 321–22.

23. "Letter from Joseph H. Choate," *Report of the Twenty-Second Annual Meeting of the American Bar Association Held at Buffalo, New York, August 28, 29, and 30, 1899* (Philadelphia, 1899), p. 11; *St. Louis Post-Dispatch*, September 8, 1898.

24. "The State Punishment of Crime," *Report of the Twenty-Second Annual Meeting of the American Bar Association, Held at Buffalo, New York, August 28, 29, 30, 1899* (Philadelphia, 1899), p. 377. See also Addison C. Harris, "Procedure Abroad and at Home," *Report of the Ninth Annual Meeting of the State Bar Association of Indiana Held at Indianapolis, July 6 and 7, 1905*, p. 26.

25. James Bryce, "The Influence of National Character and Historical Environment on the Development of the Common Law," *Report of the Thirtieth Annual Meeting of the American Bar Association, Held at Portland, Maine, August 26, 27, 28, 1907* (Baltimore: Lord Baltimore Press, 1907), p. 444.

26. *Ibid.*, pp. 462–63.

Notes to Chapter IV

1. Henry S. Commager, *The American Mind. An Interpretation of American Thought and Character since the 1880's* (New Haven, Conn.: Yale University Press, 1959), p. 20.

2. For such public sentiments see *New York Times*, September 11, September 12, 1899; *New York Tribune*, September 10, September 11, 1899; *New York Sun*, September 10, 1899; "France before the World," *New York Times*, September 13, 1899; William Harding, *Dreyfus: The Prisoner of Devil's Island* (New York: Associated Publishing Company, 1899), pp. 340–41.

3. *The Origins of Totalitarianism* (New York: World, 1958), p. 91.

4. "The Dreyfus Dénouement," *Nation* 58 (January 8, 1899):432–33; "Let in the Light," *New York Times*, March 2, 1899. For similar views see "France Sees a Great Light," *New York Journal*, June 5, 1899; "The Dreyfus Story," *Literary World* 30 (August 5, 1899):247; "The Dreyfus Verdict," *Nation* 58 (September 14,1899):200; "Current History," *American Monthly Magazine* 15 (October, 1899):519.

5. Roscoe Pound, "The Need of a Sociological Jurisprudence," *Green Bag* 19 (October, 1907):608, 610; George W. Kirchwey, "Respect for Law in the United States," *Annals of the American Academy of Political and Social Science* 36 (July–December, 1910):217.
6. Edmund R. Spearman, "Legal Anthropometry," *Green Bag* 7 (January, 1898):34–35, 53 (italics in original).
7. Quoted in *St. Louis Post-Dispatch*, July 9, August 25, August 29, 1899; *Chicago Tribune*, August 28, 1899. For ridicule of Bertillon see Finley Peter Dunne, *Mr. Dooley in the Hearts of His Countrymen* (New York: Greenwood Press, 1969), pp. 270–75.
8. Quotations from Seymour D. Thompson, "The Revision of the Dreyfus Case," *Green Bag* 11 (January, 1899):12–13. For similar comments see *Pittsburgh Catholic*, February 22, 1899; *St. Louis Post-Dispatch*, July 9, 1899; *Washington Post*, August 13, 1899; *Boston Evening Transcript*, August 25, August 26, 1899; *Atlanta Constitution*, August 26, August 29, September 3, 1899.
9. "A Review of Bertillon's Testimony in the Dreyfus Case," *American Law Review* 35 (May–June, 1901):389–91.
10. *Ibid.*, pp. 395–99.
11. *New York Times*, June 22, 1906.
12. For critical comments about French judicial behavior see *Atlanta Constitution*, January 16, 1898; *New Orleans Daily Picayune*, February 19, 1898; *Washington Post*, January 10, January 11, January 12, 1899; "Elimination in the Dreyfus Case," *New York Tribune*, January 8, 1899.
13. *St. Louis Post-Dispatch*, September 5, 1899. See also *Washington Post*, September 10, 1899.
14. "The Dreyfus Burlesque," *Albany Argus*, August 22, 1899. See also *New York Herald*, August 22, 1899; Finley Peter Dunne, *Mr. Dooley in Peace and in War* (Boston: Small, Maynard, 1898), pp. 244ff.; *New York Journal*, August 22, 1899.
15. "France's Infamy," *Outlook* 63 (September 16, 1899):146. For a criticism of the Rennes proceedings, see also "The Mystery at Rennes," *New York Times*, August 9, 1899.
16. William Wirt Howe, "Address," *Report of the Twenty-Second Annual Meeting of the American Bar Association, Held at Buffalo, New York, August 28, 29, 30, 1899* (Philadelphia, 1899), pp. 567–69. See also Emlin McClain, "The Evolution of the Judicial Opinion," *Report of the Twenty-Fifth Annual Meeting of the American Bar Association, Held at Saratoga Springs, New York, August 27, 28, and 29, 1902*, pp. 373, 375.
17. "The Influence of National Character and Historical Environment on the Development of the Common Law," *Report of the Thirtieth Annual Meeting of the American Bar Association, Held at Portland, Maine, August 26, 27, 28, 1907* (Baltimore: Lord Baltimore Press, 1907), pp. 449–57.
18. McClain, "Evolution of Judicial Opinion," pp. 376–77, 379–82.
19. Thompson, "Revision of the Dreyfus Case," p. 9.
20. "The Latest Developments in the Dreyfus Case," *American Law Review* 33 (January–February, 1899):128–30. For public perplexity about the Dreyfus trials, see *New York Times*, January 11, 1899; *Washington Post*, October 30, 1898; *Boston Evening Transcript*, May 27, May 28, 1899; *St. Louis Post-Dispatch*, May 29, May 30, June 4, 1899; *Kansas City Star*, May 27, June 3, 1899. For a description of the French judicial system see Lawrence Irwell, "The Judicial System of France," *Green Bag* 14 (November, 1902):527–30, 533.
21. Irwell, "Judicial System of France," pp. 530–31.
22. Joel Benton, "French Law and Law Courts," *Green Bag* 10 (September, 1898):417–20. For comments on French courts see also *St. Louis Post-Dispatch*, August 21, 1899.

23. A. G. Sedgwick, "Fruits of Militarism," *Nation* 67 (August 18, 1898):126.
24. "The Recent Zola Trial," *Green Bag* 10 (May, 1898):187, 189–91; Frederick W. Whitridge, "Zola, Dreyfus and the French Republic," *Political Science Quarterly* 13 (June, 1898):269–70.
25. Whitridge, "Zola, Dreyfus and the French Republic," pp. 259–60.
26. *Ibid.*, pp. 269–70.
27. "The Trials of Dreyfus and Zola," *American Law Review* 32 (May–June, 1898):443–44; Joseph H. Choate, "The Annual Address," *Report of the Twenty-First Annual Meeting of the American Bar Association, Held at Saratoga Springs, New York, August 17, 18, 19, 1898* (New York: n.p., 1898), p. 289. For similar comments see "The Law in the Case," *New York Times*, September 9, 1899; *Chicago Tribune*, August 28, 1899.
28. Editorial, *Nation* 69 (August 24, 1899):142–43; *New York Times*, August 28, September 9, 1899.
29. "The Release of Dreyfus," *New York Times*, September 12, 1899; V. M. Rose, "Trial by Jury in France," *American Law Review* 35 (January–February, 1901):18–21, 24–26.
30. "Dreyfus and the Jewish Question in France: French and American Democracy," *Conservative Review* 2 (August, 1899):15–16.
31. *New York Evening Journal*, December 5, 1898.
32. Eustis, "Jewish Question," pp. 15–16.
33. H. L. Nelson, "French Absolutism and the Dreyfus Case," *Harper's Weekly* 32 (October 29, 1898):1070.
34. See, for example, "The French Judiciary and the Chamber of Deputies," *New York Sun*, January 15, 1899; "Progress of the Dreyfus Trial," *ibid.*, August 14, 1899; Richard W. Hale, *The Dreyfus Story* (Boston: Small, Maynard, 1899), pp. 58–59, 63, 65–66; "France and the Dreyfus Case," *Harper's Weekly* 43 (May 13, 1899):468.
35. Choate was deeply moved by French events. See his "Annual Address," p. 289. For various points of view, see *Report of the Twenty-Second Annual Meeting of the American Bar Association, Held at Buffalo, New York, August 28, 29, 30, 1899* (Philadelphia, 1899), pp. 76–80.
36. "Correspondence," *American Law Review* 34 (May–June, 1900):459–60.
37. "The Trials of Dreyfus and Zola," *American Law Review* 32 (May–June, 1898):444.
38. Choate, "Annual Address," pp. 289–90.
39. Nelson, "French Absolutism," p. 1070. For comments on French legal behavior see also *New York Evening Telegram*, August 17, 1899; "At Rennes Yesterday," *New York World*, August 23, 1899; "Dreyfus and the Law in France," *New York Times*, September 12, 1899.
40. "The Release of Dreyfus," *New York Times*, September 12, 1899; G. W. Steevens, "France as Affected by the Dreyfus Case," *Harper's New Monthly Magazine* 99 (October, 1899):794–95.
41. *New York Times*, February 25, 1898.
42. Sedgwick, "Fruits of Militarism," p. 126; "To Protect Foreigners in France," *New York Times*, September 10, 1899.

Notes to Chapter V

1. Robert L. Beisner, *Twelve against Empire: The Anti-Imperialists, 1898–1900* (New York: McGraw-Hill, 1968), pp. x–xiii, 9–10.

2. *Ibid.*, pp. 219–20.

3. *Ibid.*, p. 225; Van Wyck Brooks, *New England Indian Summer, 1865–1915* (New York: E. P. Dutton, 1940), p. 419; William Dean Howells, "The Modern American Mood," *Harper's New Monthly Magazine* 95 (July, 1897):201–4.

4. See Oswald Garrison Villard, *Fighting Years: Memoirs of a Liberal Editor* (New York: Harcourt, Brace, 1939), pp. 137–40; David L. Jordon to Edward A. Ross, January 30, 1899, and William Jennings Bryan to Edward A. Ross, December 22, 1899, Box 2, Edward A. Ross Papers, State Historical Society of Wisconsin, Madison; see also R. Heber Newton's 1898 sermon, "International Morality," R. Heber Newton Papers, New York Public Library. Pettit is quoted in Russel F. Weigley, *Towards an American Army: Military Thought from Washington to Marshall* (New York: Columbia University Press, 1962), p. 157; see also pp. 149–50.

5. Quoted in Weigley, *American Army*, p. 160. See also the complaints of Henry Demarest Lloyd, who supported American military action, in his letters to Samuel Bowles, September 10, 1898, and to Arthur Brisbane, September 16, 1898, and the letter to him from William J. Abbott, October 20, 1899, in Series 1, Box 10, Henry Demarest Lloyd Papers, State Historical Society of Wisconsin, Madison.

6. Samuel P. Huntington, "The Dark and the Bright," in *American Defense Policy in Perspective: From Colonial Times to the Present*, ed. Raymond G. O'Connor (New York: John Wiley & Sons, 1965), pp. 110–11.

7. Richard D. Challener, *Admirals, Generals, and American Foreign Policy, 1898–1914* (Princeton: Princeton University Press, 1973), pp. 23–24, 78, 401–5. See also Ernest R. May, *American Imperialism: A Speculative Essay* (New York: Atheneum, 1968), p. 179.

8. *The Tragedy of Dreyfus* (New York: Harper & Brothers, 1899), p. 191.

9. "The Dreyfus Drama," *Boston Evening Transcript*, February 26, 1898, quoted in *Atlanta Constitution*, September 17, 1899; see also *Washington Post*, July 9, 1899; John R. Dos Passos, *The Anglo-Saxon Century and the Unification of the English-Speaking People* (New York: G. P. Putnam's Sons, 1903), pp. 30–31.

10. "France's Humiliation and Shame," *Washington Post*, June 12, 1899. See also *St. Louis Post-Dispatch*, August 30, 1899.

11. "Elimination in the Dreyfus Case," *New York Daily Tribune*, January 8, 1899.

12. *New York Evening Journal*, April 1, 1899; *New York Evening Post*, April 8, 1899. The *Times* article is "Insubordination in the French Army," see *New York Times*, July 7, 1899. On Dewey, see the clipping in the Lee Max Friedman Papers, Houghton Library, Harvard University.

13. James B. Eustis, "Dreyfus and the Jewish Question in France: French and American Democracy," *Conservative Review* 2 (August, 1899):7; "The Present Status of the Dreyfus Affair." See also *New York Sun*, September 20, 1898; *Boston Globe*, September 27, 1898. For a similar view, see "The Troubles of France," *New York Journal*, October 8, 1898. For the *Nation* comment, see R. Ogden, "Dreyfus and No End," *Nation* 67 (September 8, 1898):181.

14. "France Sees a Great Light," *New York Journal*, June 5, 1899; "The Honor of the Country," *New York World*, August 17, 1899; "The Scene at Rennes," *New York Times*, August 19, 1899.

15. Quotations are from Steevens, *Tragedy of Dreyfus*, pp. 191–92. See also Steevens, "France as Affected by the Dreyfus Case," *Harper's New Monthly Magazine* 99 (October,

1899), p. 796; "The Real Defendant at Rennes," *New York Times*, August 21, 1899; "France and Her Army," *New York Herald*, September 2, 1899.

16. Finley Peter Dunne, *Mr. Dooley in the Hearts of His Countrymen* (New York: Greenwood Press, 1969), p. 230; "Honor of the Army," *Boston Evening Transcript*, September 16, 1899. See also Washington Gladden, "One Against Many," September 18, 1898, Microfilm Roll 29, Washington Gladden Papers, Ohio Historical Society, Columbus.

17. The quotations are from *Washington Post*, September 10, 1899, and "Victims of Militarism," *St. Louis Post-Dispatch*, September 12, 1899. See also Walter Willis, "The Dreyfus Revision," *Cosmopolitan* 36 (June, 1904):235.

18. "Is a Dreyfus Case Possible in America?" *Independent* 61 (July 19, 1906):167.

19. Arthur A. Ekirch, Jr. *The Civilian and the Military* (New York: Oxford University Press, 1956), pp. vii, ix, 14ff.

20. *St. Louis Post-Dispatch*, September 12, 1899.

21. "The Zola Trial," *American Monthly Review of Reviews* 17 (April, 1898):471; Frederick W. Whitridge, "Zola, Dreyfus and the French Republic," *Political Science Quarterly* 13 (June, 1898):260, 270–71.

22. "Fruits of Militarism," *Nation* 67 (August 18, 1898):126–27.

23. Editorial, "The Danger in France," *Outlook* 60 (October 1, 1898):270, 271; H. L. Nelson, "French Absolutism and the Dreyfus Case," *Harper's Weekly* 42 (October 29, 1898):1070; *New York World*, November 7, 1898. For similar concerns, see "Will the Civil Power Assert Supremacy in France?" *New York Sun*, November 27, 1898; "Why France Trembles," *ibid.*, December 4, 1898; "France and the Dreyfus Case," *Harper's Weekly* 43 (May 13, 1899):468.

24. Clipping, Lee Max Friedman Papers, Houghton Library, Harvard University.

25. Richard W. Hale, *The Dreyfus Story* (Boston: Small, Maynard, 1899), pp. 65–68; Eustis, "Dreyfus and the Jewish Question," p. 16.

26. R. Ogden, "The Dreyfus Verdict," *Nation* 69 (September 14, 1899):200.

27. "Why We Feel It," *New York Times*, September 15, 1899.

28. "American Opinion and the Affair," *American Hebrew* 65 (September 15, 1899):581–84.

29. "France's Infamy," *Outlook* 63 (September 16, 1899):146–47.

30. Julian Ralph, "The Dreyfus Verdict," *Harper's Weekly* 43 (September 16, 1899):982. On the Esterhazy trial, see "Zola and the Dreyfus Case," *New York Times*, January 14, 1898.

31. Quotations are from a clipping from the *Hartford Courant*, Lee Max Friedman Papers, Houghton Library, Harvard University, and *New York Evening Telegram*, August 20, 1899. For other comments see *St. Louis Post-Dispatch*, August 19, August 21, 1899; *New York World*, August 30, 1899.

32. E. L. Godkin, "French Military Justice," *Nation* 69 (November 9, 1899):349.

33. "Courts-Martial," *Washington Post*, September 10, 1899.

34. Arthur Ameisen, "The Effect of Judgments of Courts-Martial in France and in America: A Comparative Study of the Dreyfus Case," *American Law Review* 33 (January–February, 1899):75–83.

35. Quotation from *New York Times*, August 27, 1899. See also Nelson, "French Absolutism," p. 1070; Ameisen, "Judgments of Courts-Martial," pp. 75–78, 145; Godkin, "French Military Justice," p. 349.

36. John I. Rogers, "Military Law and Its Tribunals," *Report of the Eighth Annual Meeting of the Pennsylvania Bar Association Held at Cambridge Springs, Pennsylvania, June 30 and July 1 and 2, 1902* (Philadelphia: n.p., 1902), p. 389.

37. *Ibid.*, pp. 363, 369. See also Villard, *Fighting Years*, p. 138.

38. Edgar S. Dudley, *Military Law and the Procedure of Courts-Martial* (New York: John Wiley & Sons, 1907), pp. 258–60, 265.

Notes to Chapter VI

1. Elbert F. Baldwin, "Georges Picquart," *Outlook* 62 (July 1, 1899):528. For a description of Picquart, see also *St. Louis Post-Dispatch*, August 18, 1899.
2. Baldwin, "Picquart," p. 528; *New York Sun*, December 11, December 13, 1898; *New York Times*, September 22, December 11, 1898; *New York World*, December 9, 1898.
3. American newspapers and magazines followed the story of Picquart's investigations. See, for example, *New York Sun*, December 11, 1898; "The Case of Col. Picquart," *ibid.*, December 12, 1898. Especially helpful are Baldwin, "Picquart," pp. 529–31, and "The Danger in France"; *Outlook* 60 (October 1, 1898): 270–71. See also *St. Louis Post-Dispatch*, June 4, 1899.
4. Baldwin, "Picquart," pp. 531–32.
5. Undated clippings, Lee Max Friedman Papers, Houghton Library, Harvard University.
6. *Boston Evening Transcript*, March 5, 1898; *New Orleans Daily Picayune*, February 12, 1898; Baldwin, "Picquart," p. 537.
7. See comments about Picquart in correspondence of Carol Lloyd to Mrs. Henry Demarest Lloyd, September 2, 1899, Series I, Box 10, Henry Demarest Lloyd Papers, State Historical Society of Wisconsin, Madison. On American attitudes toward Zurlinden, see *New York Herald*, March 2, 1898; *Boston Globe*, March 3, 1898; *New York Sun*, March 6, 1898; *New York Times*, March 6, 1898.
8. Baldwin, "Picquart," pp. 532–34; *New York Times*, September 22, 1898.
9. *New York Times*, September 22, 1898; *Outlook* 60 (October 1, 1898). See also "The Dreyfus-Picquart Case," *Philadelphia Press*, November 29, 1898.
10. *New York Sun*, November 25, November 26, December 12, 1898. For De Blowitz' remarks, see Baldwin, "Picquart," p. 534. See also *Washington Post*, November 26, November 28, 1898; *Philadelphia Press*, November 29, 1898; clipping, Lee Max Friedman Papers, Houghton Library, Harvard University.
11. Baldwin, "Picquart," p. 534; *New York Journal*, December 8, 1898; *New York Sun*, December 9, December 12, 1898. On the courtmartial, see also "Picquart and the Court," *New York Herald*, December 10, 1898; *Washington Post*, December 9, 1898.
12. *New York Sun*, December 31, 1898; "The Case of Col. Picquart," *ibid.*, March 16, 1899.
13. Quoted in Baldwin, "Picquart," p. 534. See also, *Washington Post*, April 17, June 14, 1899; *Boston Evening Transcript*, May 11, June 9, 1899; *St. Louis Post-Dispatch*, June 13, 1899.
14. "The Story of a Hero—Will Col. Picquart Be Reinstated?" *New York Sun*, July 18, 1899.
15. *New York Evening Journal*, August 19, 1899. For Picquart at Rennes, see also *Chicago Tribune*, August 6, August 19, 1899; *St. Louis Post-Dispatch*, August 15, August 17, 1899; *Atlanta Constitution*, August 18, 1899; *Washington Post*, August 18, 1899; *Nation* 69 (August 24, 1899):143.
16. For Picquart's later career, see *New York Times*, December 3, 1903. For his disillusionment, see Guy Chapman, *The Dreyfus Case: A Reassessment* (New York: Reynal & Company, 1955), p. 342, and Nicholas Halasz, *Captain Dreyfus: The Story of a Mass Hysteria* (New York: Simon and Schuster, 1955), pp. 243, 246, 342–44, 349.
17. *New York World*, July 10, 1906; "General Picquart, Hero," *New York Times*, July 19, 1906. Americans of the day would not have accepted Hannah Arendt's estimate of Picquart.

She writes: "Picquart was no hero and certainly no martyr. He was simply that common type of citizen with an average interest in public affairs who in the hour of danger (though not a minute earlier) stands up to defend his country in the same unquestioning way as he discharges his daily duties" (*The Origins of Totalitarianism* [New York: Meridian Books, 1958], p. 107). Neither would American observers have agreed with Guy Chapman's judgment that "Picquart was a brave and honourable man, but he was also a prig" (*Dreyfus Case*, p. 355).

18. "The Recent Zola Trial," *Green Bag* 10 (May, 1898):190–94.

19. *Ibid.*, p. 194; *New Orleans Daily Picayune*, February 23, February 24, 1898.

20. *Green Bag* 10 (May, 1898):194.

21. *New Orleans Daily Picayune*, February 23, 1898; clipping, Lee Max Friedman Papers, Houghton Library, Harvard University.

22. John de Morgan, "Maître Fernand Labori: A Character Study," *Green Bag* 11 (December, 1899):541. For other biographical sketches, see *New York Journal*, August 9, 1899; *New York Tribune*, August 7, 1899; *Atlanta Constitution*, January 16, 1898; *Chicago Tribune*, August 4, 1899.

23. *Chicago Tribune*, August 4, 1899; De Morgan, "Labori," p. 543.

24. De Morgan, "Labori," pp. 543–44.

25. *Ibid.*, p. 544.

26. *St. Louis Post-Dispatch*, August 15, August 17, September 1, September 8, 1899; *New York Herald*, August 15, 1899; *New York Evening Telegram*, August 15, 1899; "The Shooting of Labori," *Chicago Tribune*, August 14, 1899; *Washington Post*, August 15, 1899.

27. *New York Evening Journal*, August 15, 1899. For other descriptions, see *Atlanta Constitution* August 14, 1899; *Washington Post*, August 14, 1899; *Boston Evening Transcript*, August 14, 1899; *St. Louis Post-Dispatch*, August 14, 1899. See also G. W. Steevens, "Scenes and Actors in the Dreyfus Trial," *McClure's Magazine* 13 (September, 1899):519; *New York Herald*, August 14, 1899.

28. *St. Louis Post-Dispatch*, August 15, 1899.

29. William Randolph Hearst, "One More Dreyfus Crime," *New York Evening Journal*, August 15, 1899. See also "France's Tragic Drama," *St. Louis Post-Dispatch*, August 14, 1899.

30. *New York Evening Journal*, August 15, August 16, August 17, 1899; *St. Louis Post-Dispatch*, August 15, 1899.

31. *New York Herald*, August 14, 1899; *St. Louis Post-Dispatch*, August 16, 1899.

32. *Atlanta Constitution*, August 15, 1899; *New York Evening Journal*, August 15, August 16, 1899.

33. *New York Herald*, August 21, 1899.

34. *New York Evening Journal*, August 16, August 17, 1899. See also *Washington Post*, August 15, 1899.

35. *New York Evening Journal*, August 15, 1899; *Chicago Tribune*, August 16, August 19, 1899.

36. *New York Evening Journal*, August 24, 1899. See also *New York World*, August 22, 1899.

37. *New York Evening Journal*, August 22, August 23, 1899. See also *Chicago Tribune*, August 22, 1899; *Boston Evening Transcript*, August 17, 1899; *Washington Post*, August 21, 1899.

38. *New York Evening Journal*, August 24, 1899.

39. *New York Times*, August 23, 1899, September 5, 1899; *New York World*, August 23, 1899; *St. Louis Post-Dispatch*, August 23, 1899; *Nation* 69 (August 31, 1899):160–61. For other descriptions of Labori at Rennes, see *Chicago Tribune*, August 23, 1899; *Boston Evening Transcript*, August 23, August 24, August 26, 1899; *Atlanta Constitution*, August 24,

1899; "Honor to Labori," *ibid.*, August 28, 1899; *Washington Post*, August 23, August 24, August 27, 1899.

40. *Report of the Twenty-Second Annual Meeting of the American Bar Association, Held at Buffalo, New York, August 28, 29, 30, 1899* (Philadelphia, 1899), p. 28. The resolution was offered by Everett P. Loheeler, chairman of the A. B. A. Committee on International Law. See also *ibid.*, pp. 70, 77–78.

41. *Ibid.*, 74–77, 80–81; *Washington Post*, August 31, 1899.

42. De Morgan, "Labori," p. 541; George Rountree, "Annual Address of the President," *Report of the Eighth Annual Meeting of the North Carolina Bar Association, Held at Wrightsville Beach, June 27, 28, 29, 1906* (Raleigh, 1906), p. 19; "London Legal Letter," *Green Bag* 13 (June, 1901):317.

43. *New York Times*, March 4, 1906.

44. Alvin F. Sanborn, "Ten Years Later: The Most Celebrated Case in History," *Bookman* 28 (September–October, 1908):41.

Notes to Chapter VII

1. For these and similar comments, see Carol Lloyd to Mrs. Henry Demarest Lloyd, September 2, 1899, Series I, Box 10, Henry Demarest Lloyd Papers, State Historical Society of Wisconsin, Madison; *New York Times*, January 16, 1898; *Atlanta Constitution*, August 18, 1899; J. H. A. McDonald, "The Negative Ruler of France," *Blackwood's Edinburgh Magazine* 165 (January, 1899): 1055; "Student Life in Paris: Its Perils," *St. Louis Post-Dispatch*, January 15, 1899.

2. J. H. A. McDonald, "France Today," *Blackwood's Edinburgh Magazine* 166 (October, 1899): 550–51.

3. *New York Evening Journal*, August 22, 1899. See also "France's Infamy," *Outlook* 63 (September 16, 1899):146.

4. Quoted in Louis J. Budd, *Mark Twain: Social Philosopher* (Bloomington: Indiana University Press, 1962), pp. 172–73; Arthur L. Scott, *Mark Twain at Large* (Chicago: Henry Regnery Company, 1969), p. 249.

5. Quoted in Ralph Barton Perry's *The Thought and Character of William James* (Cambridge, Mass.: Harvard University Press, 1948), p. 208, and in his *The Thought and Character of William James, as Revealed in Unpublished Correspondence and Notes, Together with His Published Writings*, Vol. II: *Philosophy and Psychology* (Boston: Little, Brown, 1936). In the latter volume, see William James to Carl Stumph, September 10, 1899, pp. 195–96; William James to E. P. Gibbons, August 22, 1899, pp. 97–98; William James to William M. Salter, September 11, 1899, pp. 100–101.

6. Clippings, Lee Max Friedman Papers, Houghton Library, Harvard University.

7. *Philadelphia Bulletin*, November 30, 1898.

8. Barbara W. Tuchman, *The Proud Tower: A Portrait of the World before the War, 1890–1914* (New York: Bantam Books, 1966), p. 205; *New York Times*, January 16, 1898; *Nation* 69 (August 31, 1899):160. See also *Boston Evening Transcript*, April 30, 1898.

9. G. W. Steevens, "France as Affected by the Dreyfus Case," *Harper's New Monthly Magazine* 99 (October, 1899):797; H. C. De Blowitz, "The French Press and the Dreyfus Case," *North American Review* 169 (October, 1899):578–80.

10. Quoted in Scott, *Mark Twain at Large*, pp. 249–50.

11. "The Woman in the Dreyfus Case," *New York Sun*, September 27, 1898.

12. *New York Sun*, January 17, 1899.

13. *Ibid.*

14. *New York Sun,* September 27, 1898, January 17, 1899. See also *Boston Evening Transcript,* January, 8, February 5, 1898; "The Dreyfus Trial," *Atlanta Constitution,* August 18, 1899.

15. For Faure's political position, see Norman James Clary, "French Anti-Semitism during the Years of Drumont and Dreyfus, 1886–1906" (Ph.D. diss., Ohio State University, 1970), pp. 276–77; George D. Painter, *Proust: The Early Years* (Boston: Little, Brown, 1959), p. 288; W. F. Lonergan, *Forty Years of Paris* (London: T. Fisher Unwin, 1907), pp. 233–35; Joseph Reinach, *Histoire de l'affaire Dreyfus,* Vol. *IV: Caviagnac et Félix Faure* (Paris: Libraire Charpentier et Fasquelle, 1905), pp. 552–53; *Boston Herald,* February 26, 1899. For discussions about his death, see *Washington Post,* February 17, 1899; *St. Louis Post-Dispatch,* February 26, 1899; *New York World,* February 26, 1899.

16. *Philadelphia Bulletin,* November 19, 1898.

17. See, for example, *Atlanta Constitution,* January 16, January 20, October 10, October 15, October 26, 1898; *New York Times,* February 27, 1898; *New York Sun,* September 18, September 25, September 27, 1898, January 15, January 30, 1899; *Boston Globe,* September 25, September 27, 1898; *New York Herald,* September 25, 1898; "The Danger in France," *Outlook* 60 (October 1, 1898):271–72; *Washington Post,* January 8, February 27, 1899.

18. "Napoleon the Fifth?" *Puck,* January 18, 1899.

19. For reports of French civil disorders, see *New York Sun,* February 18, 1899; *New York Herald,* February 18, February 19, February 20, February 23, 1899; *Boston Herald,* February 20, 1899; *Washington Post,* February 19, 1899.

20. *Boston Herald,* February 23, February 24, February 26, 1899; *Washington Post,* February 20, February 25, 1899; "Paul Déroulède's Hard Luck," *New York Sun,* June 3, 1899; *Boston Evening Transcript,* May 31, June 13, 1899.

21. *New York Herald,* February 26, 1899.

22. *Ibid.,* February 26, 1899; *Washington Post,* January 8, February 19, 1899; *St. Louis Post-Dispatch,* February 19, 1899; *New York Times,* September 7, 1899.

23. See comments on French behavior in David L. Jordan to Edward A. Ross, January 30, 1899, Box 2, Edward A. Ross Papers, State Historical Society of Wisconsin, Madison; *New York Times,* January 28, 1898; *New York Journal,* October 2, December 13, 1898, February 5, February 16, 1899; *Boston Herald,* October 3, 1898; *Boston Globe,* October 26, December 13, 1898.

24. *Philadelphia Bulletin,* November 30, 1898; "Once More the Barricades in Paris," *New York Evening Journal,* August 22, 1899.

25. *New York Journal,* August 21, 1899. For other descriptions, see *New York Sun,* July 31, 1899; "The Paris Mob," *Chicago Tribune,* August 22, 1899; *Chicago Tribune,* August 21, 1899.

26. *New York Herald,* August 21, 1899.

27. For the story of "Fort Chabral," see Guy Chapman, *The Dreyfus Case: A Reassessment* (New York: Reynal and Company, 1955), pp. 282–84; and Hannah Arendt, *The Origins of Totalitarianism* (New York: Meridian Books, 1958), p. 111. Arendt sees in Guérin the prototype of the modern fascist tough upon whom the respectable classes depend to keep order. The daily events can be followed in *New York Journal,* August 14, 1899; *New York Sun,* August 14, 1899; *Atlanta Constitution,* August 16, 1899; *Boston Evening Transcript,* August 15, 1899; *St. Louis Post-Dispatch,* August 12, August 15, August 23, 1899.

28. *Mr. Dooley in the Hearts of His Countrymen* (New York: Greenwood Press, 1969), p. 263. For another caricature, see "A Delightful Performance," *St. Louis Post-Dispatch,* August 29, 1899.

29. For attempts to dislodge Guérin, see *Chicago Tribune*, August 17, 1899; *New York Sun*, August 14, 1899; *New York Evening Journal*, August 15, August 16, August 17, 1899; *New York Evening Telegram*, August 15, August 17, 1899; *St. Louis Post-Dispatch*, August 16, 1899.
30. "The Humiliation of France," *New York Journal*, August 18, 1899.
31. "Dreyfus and Guérin," *Washington Post*, September 22, 1899.
32. "Monsieur Guérin," *St. Louis Post-Dispatch*, September 21, 1899.
33. Edwin P. Hoyt, *The Goulds: A Social History* (New York: Weybright and Talley, 1969), pp. 63, 71–72, 105, 118–19, 126–27, 129–30. On American attitudes toward great wealth, see, for example, William Dean Howells, "The Modern American Mood," *Harper's New Monthly Magazine*, 95 (July, 1897):202.
34. Hoyt, *The Goulds*, pp. 138, 147.
35. *Ibid.*, pp. 147–48; Ernest Paul Boniface de Castellane, *How I Discovered America: Confessions of the Marquis Boni De Castellane* (New York: Alfred A. Knopf, 1924), pp. 13–17.
36. Howells, "Modern Mood," p. 202; Hoyt, "The Goulds," pp. 148–59, 163–65, 167. See also Emile de Jumonville Coulon, *Realistic Descriptions of American Life and Instructions: Prophetic Letters on the Dreyfus Affair* (New York: D. V. Wiem, 1905), pp. 17–18; Lonergan, *Forty Years of Paris*, pp. 137–38; Castellane, *Confessions*, pp. 46–50.
37. See Painter, *Proust*, pp. 192, 265.
38. Castellane, *Confessions*, pp. 127, 182–85.
39. Clipping, Lee Max Friedman Papers, Houghton Library, Harvard University. For Castellane's support of anti-Semitic causes, see also Edward R. Tannenbaum, *The Action Française: Die-Hard Reactionaries in Twentieth Century France* (New York: John Wiley & Sons, 1962), pp. 34–44; Joseph Reinarch, *Histoire de l'affaire Dreyfus*, Vol. IV: *Caviagnac et Felix Faure* (Paris: Librairie Charpentier et Fasquelle, 1905), pp. 589–90.
40. *New York Journal*, June 5, June 6, June 18, 1899; *Atlanta Constitution* June 5, June 6, 1899; *Washington Post*, June 5, June 6, 1899; *Boston Evening Transcript*, June 5, 1899; *Kansas City Star*, June 5, 1899.
41. Undated clipping, Lee Max Friedman Papers, Houghton Library, Harvard University.
42. *New York Journal*, June 6, 1899; *St. Louis Post-Dispatch*, July 9, 1899.
43. *New York Journal*, June 6. 1899; *Washington Post*, July 9, 1899, and *St. Louis Post-Dispatch*, July 9, 1899. See also *New York World*, June 6, 1899; *Washington Post*, June 5, 1899.
44. *New York Journal*, June 8, 1899.
45. Alabama correspondent, quoted in *New York Journal*, June 8, 1899.
46. Hallie Ermine Rives, "The Foolishness of an American Woman," clipping, Lee Max Friedman Papers, Houghton Library, Harvard University; *Washington Post*, June 6, 1899.
47. "A Tale of Two Sisters," *New York Journal*, June 6, 1899; "One of the Trials of Real Americans," *ibid.*

Notes to Chapter VIII

1. For good summaries of Dreyfus' early life, see Nicholas Halasz, *Captain Dreyfus: The Story of a Mass Hysteria* (New York: Simon and Schuster, 1955), pp. 19–28; Wilhelm Herzog, *From Dreyfus to Pétain: The Struggle of a Republic* (New York: Creative Age Press, 1947), p. 59; Donald C. McKay, trans. and ed., *The Dreyfus Case: By the Man—Alfred Dreyfus and His Son—Pierre Dreyfus* (New Haven, Conn.: Yale University Press, 1937), pp. 27–30.

2. For suspicions about Dreyfus' first courtmartial, see *New York Sun*, December 23, 1894, January 6, 1895; *New York World*, January 6, 1895; *New York Times*, January 6, 1895; *New York Herald*, January 6, 1895.

3. For accounts of Dreyfus' public degradation, see *New York Journal*, March 21, 1897, August 8, 1899; Walter Littlefield, "Dreyfus the Man," in *The Letters of Captain Dreyfus to His Wife*, translated by L. G. Moreau (New York: Harper & Brothers, 1899), pp. vii–ix.

4. "Leaves from the Autobiography of Captain Alfred Dreyfus, Including Passages of His Devil's Island Diary," *McClure's Magazine* 17 (May, 1901):25–26.

5. *New York Times*, September 25, 1898; *New York Journal*, December 11, 1898.

6. Douglas Johnson, *France and the Dreyfus Affair*, (London: Blandford Press, 1966), pp. 70–71; Louis L. Snyder, ed., *The Dreyfus Case: A Documentary History* (New Brunswick, N.J.: Rutgers University Press, 1973), pp. 70–74.

7. The suggestion is made in George C. Musgrave, *Under Three Flags in Cuba: A Personal Account of the Cuban Insurrection and Spanish-American War* (Boston: Little, Brown, 1899), pp. 101–7.

8. *New York Evening Journal*, December 11, December 22, 1898.

9. *Ibid.*, December 11, 1898.

10. *Ibid.*, November 13, 1898.

11. *New York World*, July 6, August 17, 1899. See also *New York Herald*, March 2, 1898, August 8, 1899.

12. G. W. Steevens, "France as Affected by the Dreyfus Case," *Harper's New Monthly Magazine* 99 (October, 1899):793.

13. *New York Evening Journal*, September 4, 1898. Comments about Dreyfus' health are found in *New York Sun*, May 2, 1898; *Washington Post*, April 21, 1899; Theron C. Crawford, "The Dreyfus Mystery," *Cosmopolitan* 24 (March, 1898):492; *Chicago Tribune*, August 17, 1899.

14. *Brooklyn Citizen* quoted in "American Opinion on the Affair," *American Hebrew* 65 (September 15, 1899):581. For examples of poetry in his honor, see Henry Robinson Palmer, "Dreyfus," *Current Literature*, 61 (September, 1906):343; Edwin Markham, "Dreyfus," *McClure's Magazine* 13 (September, 1899):387; Robert Underwood Johnson, "To Dreyfus Vindicated," *Harper's Weekly* 50 (August 11, 1906):1129.

15. *New York Times*, September 4, 1898. See announcement in *New York World*, July 14, 1899. For Zola's comment, see *ibid.*

16. "Keep It from the French People," *New York World*, July 6, 1899. See also "The Dreyfus Letters," *Outlook* 62 (July 29, 1899):727; "Lettres d'un Innocent," *Literary World* 30 (August 5,1899):254; "The New Books," *American Monthly Review of Reviews* 20 (October, 1899):502; "Dreyfus Literature," *Boston Evening Transcript*, June 10, 1899.

17. The Dreyfus case is reviewed in the obituary notice of Walter Littlefield (*New York Times*, March 26, 1948). See also Littlefield's introduction to *Letters of Captain Dreyfus to His Wife*, pp. ix–x, xv–xvi.

18. "Leaves from the Autobiography," pp. 28–34.

19. *Nation* 72 (May 30, 1901):440; "Dreyfus' Own Story," *Current Literature* 30 (June, 1901):645–49. For similar sentiments see "At Devil's Island," *The Living Age—Supplement* 229 (June 1, 1901):589–92.

20. *New York World*, September 4, 1898.

21. *New York Evening Journal*, March 21, 1897, November 27, 1898. See also *New York Times*, July 17, 1898; *Boston Evening Transcript*, August 31, 1899.

22. James Creelman, *On the Great Highway: The Wanderings and Adventures of a Special Cor-*

respondent (Boston: Lothrop, 1901), pp. 11, 174; *New York Evening Journal*, November 27, 1898.

23. "A Talk with Madame Dreyfus," *New York World*, December 11, 1898, June 4, 1899. For other comments, see "An Angel-Wife," *New York Evening Journal*, July 2, August 8, 1899; "A Modern Heroine," *New York World*, July 4, 1899; *St. Louis Post-Dispatch*, June 4, 1899. For the general reaction of the French Jewish community toward anti-Semitism, see Michael R. Marrus, *The Politics of Assimilation: A Study of the French Jewish Community at the Time of the Dreyfus Affair* (Oxford: Clarendon Press, 1971).

24. For Madame Dreyfus' acknowledgments of support, see *New York Evening Journal*, August 8, 1899; *Atlanta Constitution*, September 10, 1899; *St. Louis Post-Dispatch*, September 20, 1899.

25. Great concern was shown even about the condition of the *Sfax*, the vessel that would return him to France. See, for example, *Washington Post*, May 12, May 13, May 29, June 5, 1899; *New York Herald*, June 5, 1899; *New York World*, June 6, 1899; *Boston Evening Transcript*, June 7, 1899.

26. *New York Evening Journal*, June 7, June 8, 1899. See also *Atlanta Constitution*, July 5, July 7, July 8, 1899; *Washington Post*, June 6, June 9, 1899.

27. *New York Evening Journal*, June 19, June 23, 1899.

28. For Hay correspondence, see Microfilm Edition, 1971, Reel 12, John Hay Papers, Library of Congress, Washington, D.C.; *New York Journal*, June 28, 1899.

29. *New York Evening Journal*, July 2, 1899.

30. *New York Evening Journal*, July 2, 1899. Descriptions of Dreyfus' arrival are found in *New York Herald*, July 2, 1899; Guy Wetmore Carryl, "Arrival of Dreyfus," *Harper's Weekly* 43 (July 22, 1899):729. For a pictorial account, see "Before the Dreyfus Trial," *ibid.*, (July 29, 1899):739.

31. *New York Evening Journal*, July 2, 1899.

32. *New York World*, July 3, 1899.

33. Creelman is quoted in *New York Evening Journal*, July 3, 1899. See also *Atlanta Constitution*, July 3, July 4, July 5, 1899.

34. *New York Evening Journal*, July 13, 1899; *Chicago Tribune*, August 9, 1899; *Atlanta Constitution*, July 3, 1899; *New York World*, July 5, July 6, 1899.

35. "Max Nordau on Dreyfus," *Washington Post*, September 6, 1899.

36. "The Wonderful Machine," *New York World*, July 6, 1899.

37. *New York Evening Journal*, July 13, 1899. See also *Washington Post*, July 3, 1899.

38. *New York World*, August 8, 1899. The opening of court is also described in Julian Ralph, "Dreyfus on Trial," *Harper's Weekly* 43 (August 26, 1899):831.

39. Julian Ralph, "The Chances for Dreyfus," *Harper's Weekly* 43 (September 2, 1899):866.

40. *New York Times*, September 1, 1899. For the court proceedings, see *Washington Post*, August 17, August 19, 1899; *Atlanta Constitution*, August 17, 1899; *Boston Evening Transcript*, August 16, 1899.

41. Julian Ralph, "The Dreyfus Verdict," *Harper's Weekly* 43 (September 16, 1899):982; *New York Times*, September 11, 1899.

42. Quoted in McKay, trans. and ed., *Dreyfus Case*, pp. 270–72.

43. "The Freeing of Dreyfus," *New York Times*, September 20, 1899; *American Monthly Review of Reviews* 20 (October, 1899):395–96.

44. *New York Times*, September 21, 1899; *Atlanta Constitution*, September 21, 1899; clippings, Lee Max Friedman Papers, Houghton Library, Harvard University.

45. For these invitations, see *St. Louis Post-Dispatch*, September 14, 1899, and *New York Times*, September 22, 1899.

46. "The Vindication of Dreyfus," *New York Times*, July 13, 1906.
47. "Settled But Not Ended," *New York Times*, July 19, 1906.
48. "A Modern Tragedy," *Outlook* 83 (July 21, 1906):640–41.

Notes to Chapter IX

1. Hannah Arendt, *The Origins of Totalitarianism* (New York: Meridian Books, 1958), pp. 45–47, 92.
2. See *ibid.*; Norman Cohn, *Warrant for Genocide: The Myth of the Jewish World-Conspiracy and the Protocols of the Elders of Zion* (New York: Harper and Row, 1969), pp. 21–25; Robert F. Byrnes, *Antisemitism in Modern France* (New Brunswick, N.J.: Rutgers University Press, 1950), pp. 105, 107, 114–15; Max Geltman, "On Socialist Anti-Semitism," *Midstream: A Monthly Jewish Review* 23 (March, 1977):20–30.
3. James B. Eustis, "Dreyfus and the Jewish Question in France: French and American Democracy." *Conservative Review* 2 (August, 1899):8.
4. Arendt, *Origins of Totalitarianism*, pp. 96–97, 99; Byrnes, *Antisemitism*, pp. 92, 110–11ff.; W. F. Lonergan, *Forty Years of Paris* (London: T. Fisher Unwin, 1907), pp. 161–64; Norman James Clary, "French Anti-Semitism during the Years of Drumont and Dreyfus, 1886–1906" (Ph.D. diss., Ohio State University, 1970), pp. 75, 312, 318–19; Wilhelm Herzog, *From Dreyfus to Pétain: The Struggle of a Republic*, trans. Walter Sorell (New York: Creative Age Press, 1947), pp. 30–40, 102–3, 195. Guy Chapman, in *The Dreyfus Case: A Reassessment* (New York: Reynal & Company, 1955), pp. 27, 64–66, minimizes, in my opinion, the degree of anti-Semitism in Drumont's *La France juive*; see, for example, Edward R. Tannenbaum, *The Action Française: Die-Hard Reactionaries in Twentieth Century France* (New York: John Wiley & Sons, 1962), pp. 25–26.
5. Eustis, "Dreyfus and the Jewish Question," p. 8; Zosa Szajkowski, "Socialists and Radicals in the Development of Antisemitism in Algeria (1884–1900)," *Jewish Social Studies* 10 (July, 1948):257–66, 272–73; Clary, "French Anti-Semitism," pp. 235–50.
6. Albion W. Tourgée to William McKinley, November 23, 1898, William McKinley Papers, Library of Congress, Washington D.C. For news of anti-Jewish uprisings, see *New York Times*, December 26, 1894, January 15, January 19, January 28, 1898; *New York Journal*, September 21, October 30, 1898; *New York Sun*, November 19, December 23, 1898; *Washington Post*, January 28, 1899.
7. "The Case of Captain Dreyfus," *Forum* 23 (June, 1897):450, 454–55, 462.
8. Quoted in Robert H. Sherard, "M. Zola on French Anti-Semitism," *American Monthly Review of Reviews* 17 (March, 1898):318–20.
9. Nordau is quoted in Robert H. Sherard, "Dr. Nordau on the Jews and Their Fears," *American Monthly Review of Reviews* 17 (February–March, 1898):315, 317. For Nordau's background see Michael R. Marrus, *The Politics of Assimilation: A Study of the French Jewish Community at the Time of the Dreyfus Affair* (Oxford: Clarendon Press, 1971), pp. 265–66.
10. "Why Stand Ye Here Idle?" *New York Journal*, August 16, 1899. See also Max Nordau, *Max Nordau to His People: A Collection of Addresses to Zionist Congresses together with a Tribute to Theodor Herzl* (New York: Scopus, 1941).
11. Byrnes, *Antisemitism*, pp. 103–4; Nelly Jussem-Wilson, "Bernard Lazare's Jewish Journey: From Being an Israelite to Being a Jew," *Jewish Social Studies* 26 (July, 1964):148–50, 154–55, 160–62; Hannah Arendt's introduction to Bernard Lazare's *Job's Dung-Heap*

(New York: Schocken Books, 1948), pp. 7–11, and Lazare's chapters, "Jewish Nationalism" and "Judaism's Social Concept and the Jewish People."

12. Bernard Lazare, "France at the Parting of the Ways," *North American Review* 169 (November, 1899):647, 652.

13. See, for example, the following selections in Leonard Dinnerstein, ed., *Antisemitism in the United States* (New York: Holt, Rinehart and Winston, 1971): Oscar Handlin, "American Views of the Jew at the Opening of the Twentieth Century," pp. 48–57; Richard Hofstadter, "The Folklore of Populism," pp. 58–62; and John Higham, "American Antisemitism Historically Reconsidered," pp. 63–77. See also Egal Feldman, "The Social Gospel and the Jews," *American Jewish Historical Quarterly* 58 (March, 1969):308–22.

14. Peter Wiernik, *History of the Jews in America* (New York: Jewish Press Publishing Company, 1912), pp. 428–29; Max Margolis to Gottard Deutsch, October 12, 1898, Box 2239e, Gottard Deutsch Papers, American Jewish Archives, Cincinnati; Oscar Handlin, "American Views of the Jew at the Opening of the Twentieth Century," *Publications of the American Jewish Historical Society* 40 (June, 1951):325.

15. Quoted in Albert Bigelow Paine, ed., *Mark Twain's Letters* (New York: Harper & Brothers, 1917), p. 647. See also Mark Twain, "Concerning the Jews," *Harper's New Monthly Magazine* 99 (September, 1899):535.

16. John Bell Sanborn, "The Jew in Modern Europe," *Arena* 23 (May, 1900):492, 497–98; Eustis, "Dreyfus and the Jewish Question," p. 8.

17. Fabian Franklin, *People and Problems: A Collection of Addresses and Editorials by Fabian Franklin, Editor of the Baltimore News, 1895–1908* (New York: Holt & Company, 1908), pp. 129–30.

18. Carl Schurz, "France after the Zola Trial," *Harper's Weekly* 42 (March 12, 1898):243.

19. "Persecuting the Jews," *Outlook* 61 (January 7, 1899):3.

20. "Jew-Baiting in Algeria," *New York Sun*, July 13, 1899.

21. *New York Journal*, July 16, 1899; H. C. de Blowitz, "The Dreyfus Case," *Harper's Weekly* 43 (August 19, 1899):828; Julian Ralph, "The Chances for Dreyfus," *ibid* (September 2, 1899):866.

22. *New York Journal*, August 20, 1899; *St. Louis Post-Dispatch*, September 3, 1899; Julian Ralph, "The Dreyfus Verdict," *Harper's Weekly* 43 (September 16, 1899):982. See also *New York World*, August 18, 1899.

23. *Washington Post*, September 11, September 13, 1899; *St. Louis Post-Dispatch*, September 11, September 12, September 14, 1899.

24. Ronald C. White and C. Howard Hopkins, eds., *The Social Gospel: Religion and Reform in Changing America* (Philadelphia: Temple University Press, 1976), pp. xvii, 5–12; Richard Hofstatder, *The Age of Reform* (New York: Knopf, 1955), p. 152.

25. R. Heber Newton, "Individual Responsibility for National Wrongs" (sermon), 1898, R. Heber Newton Papers, New York Public Library, New York.

26. Walter Rauschenbusch, *Christianity and the Social Crisis* (New York: Macmillan, 1907), pp. 1–3, 7–9, 11–13, 21–22, 26–27.

27. Merriam is quoted in Feldman, "Social Gospel," p. 310; Edward C. Baldwin, *Our Modern Debt to Israel* (Boston: Sherman French, 1913), pp. i, 200, 205–9; Lyman Abbott, "America's Debt to Israel," *Outlook* 83 (December 9, 1905):857–58; Washington Gladden, "The Afternoon of Life" (sermon), October 16, 1898, and "The Lord Our God Is One" (sermon), October 23, 1898, Microfilm Edition, Roll 29, Washington Gladden Papers, Ohio Historical Society, Columbus.

28. "Persecuting the Jews," *Outlook* 61 (January, 7, 1899):3; *New York Times*, September 11,

1899; "American Opinion on the Affair," *American Hebrew* 45 (September 15, 1899):582–83.

29. Robert E. Matthews to John Hay, September 23, 1899, and George Schuyler to John Hay, September 11, 1899, Microfilm Edition, 1971, Reel 12, John Hay Papers, Library of Congress, Washington, D.C.

30. Washington Gladden, "One against Many" (sermon), September 18, 1898, Microfilm Edition, Roll 29, Washington Gladden Papers, Ohio Historical Society, Columbus.

31. "France and the Jews," *Outlook* 58 (February 12, 1898):410–11.

32. *Ibid.*, p. 411.

33. Alvin F. Sanborn, "French Workingmen and the Dreyfus Affair," *Outlook* 62 (June 10, 1899):340.

34. Washington Gladden, "The Comprehensive and Manifold Work of the Christian Church" (sermon), September 18, 1898, and "Justice and Kindness" (sermon), November 20, 1898, Microfilm Edition, Roll 29, Washington Gladden Papers, Ohio Historical Society, Columbus.

35. John T. Morse, Jr., "The Dreyfus and Zola Trials," *Atlantic Monthly* 81 (May, 1898):589–90.

36. Leo B. Levy, "Henry James and the Jews," *Commentary* 26 (September, 1958):249.

37. Quoted in Barbara W. Tuchman, *The Proud Tower: A Portrait of the World before the War, 1890–1914* (New York: Bantam Books, 1972), p. 231.

38. Michael N. Dobkowski, "American Anti-Semitism: A Reinterpretation," *American Quarterly* 29 (Summer, 1977):177. See also Dobkowski, *The Tarnished Dream, the Basis of American Anti-Semitism* (Westport: Greenwood Press, 1979), especially chs. 1–3.

39. *New York Sun*, September 3, 1898; "A Specimen Anti-Semite," *New York Journal*, June 22, August 14, August 24, 1899; *New York Herald*, September 3, 1899. See also *Boston Traveller*, September 23, 1899.

40. Dobkowski, "American Anti-Semitism," pp. 174–75.

41. "American Attitude towards Dreyfus," *Atlanta Constitution*, August 19, 1899.

42. N. S. Shaler, *The Neighbors: The Natural History of Human Contacts* (Boston: Houghton, Mifflin, 1904), p. 113.

43. "Is a Dreyfus Case Possible in America?" *Independent* 61 (July 19, 1906):166–67.

44. "A Modern Tragedy," *Outlook* 83 (July 21, 1906):641.

45. "Clericalism and the Dreyfus Case," *Current Literature* 41 (August, 1906):144–45; "Justice to Dreyfus at Last," *American Monthly Review of Reviews* 34 (August, 1906):146–47; "The Vindication of Dreyfus," *Arena* 36 (September, 1906):314–15; A. Maurice Low, "Foreign Affairs," *Forum* 38 (October, 1906):182; "The Dreyfus Affair Continued," *Independent* 64 (June 11, 1908):1359.

Notes to Chapter X

1. Hannah Arendt, *The Origins of Totalitarianism* (New York: Meridian Books, 1958), pp. 51, 117–18.

2. Quoted in Michael R. Marrus, *The Politics of Assimilation: A Study of the French Jewish Community at the Time of the Dreyfus Affair* (Oxford: Clarendon Press, 1971), pp. 115, 141, 162, 205, 212–15; *New York Journal*, August 16, 1899.

3. See Ronald A. Urquhart, "The American Reaction to the Dreyfus Affair: A Study of Anti-Semitism in the 1890's" (Ph.D. diss., Columbia University, 1972), pp. 195–98. See

also Rose A. Halpern, "The American Reaction to the Dreyfus Case" (master's thesis, Columbia University, 1941), pp. 65, 78–82.

4. *New York Times*, September 8, 1899.

5. James G. Heller, *Isaac M. Wise: His Life, Work and Thought* (Cincinnati: Union of American Hebrew Congregations, 1965), pp. 482–83, 613–14; *Washington Post*, December 8, 1898.

6. All quotations are from *Yiddishes Tageblatt*, February 11, February 16, 1898.

7. *Ibid.*, February 11, 1898.

8. See "American Opinion on the Affair," *American Hebrew* 45 (September 15, 1899):582–84; *New York Sun*, September 4, 1899; *New York Times*, September 8, 1899; *Washington Post*, September 10, 1899.

9. Henry Berkowitz, "Why I Am Not a Zionist," *Year Book of the Central Conference of American Rabbis*, Vol. III (Cincinnati: Central Conference of American Rabbis, 1899), pp. 168–69.

10. *Ibid.*, p. 173. See also *New York Herald*, June 12, 1899; *New York Times*, June 11, 1899; William Harding, *Dreyfus: The Prisoner of Devil's Island* (New York: Associated Publishing Company, 1899), p. 340.

11. "The Dreyfus Case—A Blessing to Humanity," *American Hebrew* 65 (December 22, 1899):608–9.

12. *Ibid.* (September 1, 1899), p. 515.

13. *Washington Post*, September 11, 1899.

14. For these quotations, see the summary of Rabbi Hirsch's opinion survey on the question of anti-Semitism in *Yiddishes Tageblatt*, April 3, 1898.

15. De Leon is quoted in Urquhart, "American Reaction," pp. 208–9. See also Irving Howe, *World of Our Fathers* (New York: Harcourt Brace Jovanovich, 1976), p. 523; Abraham J. Karp, ed., *Golden Door to America: The Jewish Immigrant Experience* (New York: Viking, 1976), pp. 194–5.

16. *Jewish Daily Forward*, November 23, 1897.

17. *Yiddishes Tageblatt*, January 16, 1898; Alfred Gordon, "Anti-Semitism in France," *ibid.*, February 8, 1898.

18. *Ibid.*, January 18, January 19, January 23, January 24, January 25, February 2, May 18, 1898; *Jewish Daily Forward*, January 24, 1898; *Das Abend Blatt*, January 18, January 19, January 21, January 24, January 25, January 27, January 31, April 24, 1898.

19. *Yiddishes Tageblatt*, March 12, March 13, March 18, March 20, March 22, March 31, April 5, 1898, July 24, July 26, 1899; *Das Abend Blatt*, October 1, November 14, November 17, December 12, December 30, 1898; January 3, January 9, March 17, May 1, June 5, June 6, June 7, June 8, June 27, June 28, June 30, July 3, July 4, July 5, July 6, July 7, July 10, July 16, July 17, July 19, July 27, 1899.

20. *Das Abend Blatt*, January 14, January 19, January 20, January 21, January 22, February 7, February 8, February 9, February 10, February 11, February 12, February 13, February 14, February 15, February 17, February 18, February 19, 1898; *Jewish Daily Forward*, November 26, December 8, December 13, 1897; January 12, January 15, January 21, January 27, February 7, February 8, February 9, February 11, February 12, February 13, February 18, February 19, February 22, February 23, February 24, February 25, 1898; *Yiddishes Tageblatt*, January 17, February 6, February 7, February 8, February 9, February 10, February 13, February 15, February 23, 1898.

21. *Yiddishes Tageblatt*, July 31, August 14, 1899. See also *Das Abend Blatt*, September 21, September 22, September 23, September 24, September 29, October 3, November 24, November 25, November 26, November 27, November 29, December 1, December 2,

December 5, December 9, December 12, December 13, December 22, 1898, March 4, March 14, June 10, June 14, August 18, August 19, 1899; *Jewish Daily Forward*, August 14, August 15, August 22, August 25, 1899.

22. *Yiddishes Tageblatt*, February 11, 1898.

23. *Ibid*. See also issues of January 25 and February 16.

24. *Das Abend Blatt* September 3, September 9, September 10, October 3, October 31, 1898, February 18, February 20, February 21, February 22, February 24, February 25, February 27, June 5, August 16, August 26, August 30, 1899; *Yiddishes Tageblatt*, August 18, August 21, 1899; *Jewish Daily Forward*, August 21, 1899.

25. All of the major Yiddish dailies devoted front-page stories to the Dreyfus trials on September 10 and 11, 1899.

26. *New York Times*, August 17, September 21, 1899: *Chicago Tribune*, September 3, 1899.

27. *New York Times*, September 27, 1898.

28. *Ibid*., September 15, 1899.

29. Abraham Cahan, "The Ghetto's Grief," *Harper's Weekly* 43 (September 23, 1899):947–48.

30. *New York Times*, September 20, 1899.

31. Quoted in Alex Bein, *Theodor Herzl: A Biography*, translated by Maurice Samuel (Cleveland: World; Philadelphia: Jewish Publication Society of America, 1962), pp. 112–16. Herzl's writing on Dreyfus can be followed in Ludwig Lewisohn, ed., *Theodor Herzl, a Portrait for This Age* (Cleveland: World, 1955), pp. 194–220; *New York Times*, September 20, 1899.

32. *New York Times*, September 20, 1899.

33. *St. Louis Post-Dispatch*, September 24, 1899. See also *New York Times*, August 17, 1899.

34. "Dreyfus," *American Hebrew* 65 (May 19, 1899): 72.

35. "Editorial Notes," *ibid*. (September 22, 1899), p. 600.

36. *Yiddishes Tageblatt*, February 24, 1898; Joseph Jacob, "The Jew in Europe," *American Jewish Year Book, 5660, 1899–1900* (Philadelphia: Jewish Publication Society of America, 1899), pp. 22, 32–33.

37. Henrietta Szold, "The Year 5660," *American Jewish Year Book, 5561, 1900–1901*, (Philadelphia: Jewish Publication Society of America, 1900), p. 17; Julius H. Greenstone, "The Year 5666," *American Jewish Year Book, 5667, 1906–1907*, (Philadelphia: Jewish Publication Society of America, 1906), pp. 237, 256.

Notes to Chapter XI

1. See, for example, *Pittsburgh Catholic*, March 9, 1898, February 15, 1899; *Catholic Telegraph*, September 14, 1899; *Catholic Citizen*, September 23, 1899.

2. It was an irrational fear, since most Catholics opposed the Spanish acquisitions; see *Iowa Catholic Messenger*, December 17, 1898.

3. R. Heber Newton, "Causes of Spain's Decline" (sermon), 1898, R. Heber Newton Papers, New York Public Library, New York. See also letter of Henry Demarest Lloyd, April 18, 1899, Series I, Correspondence, Henry Demarest Lloyd Papers, State Historical Society of Wisconsin, Madison.

4. For Eliot's views, see Charles L. Sewrey, "The Alleged 'Un-Americanism' of the Church as a Factor in Anti-Catholicism in the United States, 1860–1914" (Ph.D. diss., University of Minnesota, 1955), pp. i–iii, 3, 7–12. For Theodore Roosevelt's statement, see Charles A. Beard and Mary R. Beard, *The Rise of American Civilization* (New York: Macmillan, 1947), Vol. II, p. 400; Theodore Roosevelt to William McKinley, June 8, 1899, Microfilm Edition, 1961, Series I, William McKinley Papers, Library of Congress,

Washington, D.C. For Theodore Roosevelt's admiration for Archbishop John Ireland, see, for example, Theodore Roosevelt to Thomas O'Gorman, March 1, 1895; for his opposition to Catholic-baiting, see Theodore Roosevelt to Archbishop John Ireland, August 19, 1895, Archbishop John Ireland Papers, St. Paul Seminary, St. Paul, Minnesota.

5. William Croswell Doane, "The Roman Catholic Church and the School Fund," *North American Review* 158 (January, 1894):37–40.

6. Quoted in Henry Blumenthal, *American and French Culture, 1800–1900. Interchange in Art, Science, Literature, and Society* (Baton Rouge: Louisiana State University Press, 1975), pp. 122–23; Sewrey, "'Un-Americanism,'" pp. 116–17, 202, 373–74.

7. *The Letters of William James and Theodore Flournoy*, ed. Robert C. LeClair (Madison: University of Wisconsin Press, 1966), p. 76

8. Donald L. Kinzer, *An Episode in Anti-Catholicism: The American Protective Association* (Seattle: University of Washington Press, 1964), pp. 47–49, 93–94, 179, 189–90, 212–13, 243–45.

9. Joseph Reinach, *Histoire de l'affaire Dreyfus*, Vol. III: *La Crise* (Paris: Librarie Charpentier et Fasquelle, 1905), p. 636; *New York Sun*, January 20, 1899; "The Dreyfus Case," *Literary World* 30 (February 4, 1899), pp. 36–37.

10. Quoted in "The Papal Letter and the 'Outlook,'" *Catholic World* 69 (April, 1899):1–3, 5.

11. "The Dreyfus Case," *American Monthly Review of Reviews* 20 (October, 1899):464–65.

12. *St. Louis Post-Dispatch*, January 1, 1899. See also *ibid.*, September 14, 1899; *New York Journal*, February 12, 1898; Hannah Arendt, "From the Dreyfus Affair to France Today," in *Essays on Anti-Semitism*, ed. Koppel S. Pinson (New York: Jewish Social Studies, 1946), p. 209.

13. Quoted in Robert H. Sherard, "Dr. Nordau on the Jews and Their Fears," *American Monthly Review of Reviews* 17 (March, 1898):317.

14. *New York Journal*, October 1, 1898, August 15, August 18, 1899; *New York Sun*, March 16, 1899.

15. The *Congregationalist* is quoted in "The Neutrality of the Pope," *American Hebrew* 65 (October 13, 1899):705–6. For Vatican silence, see *Washington Post*, September 11, 1899; *New York Times*, September 10, September 16, 1899.

16. "A Significant Silence," *Outlook* 68 (November 11, 1899):624–25.

17. *Ibid.*, p. 625.

18. According to Father John J. Tierney, archivist of the Archdiocese of Baltimore, the card index to Cardinal Gibbon's correspondence does not contain any references to Jews in the years 1896–1901 (letter to the author, January 19, 1977).

19. *Pittsburgh Catholic*, January 6, January 26, September 10, 1898, January 11, February 22, March 1, July 12, August 9, 1899; *Iowa Catholic Messenger*, February 25, September 10, 1898, June 10, 1899; *Pilot*, September 10, 1898.

20. *Pilot*, August 10, 1899. See also *Iowa Catholic Messenger*, August 19, 1899.

21. "Dreyfus Again Condemned," *Pilot*, September 16, 1899; "France Disgraced," *Iowa Catholic Messenger*, September 16, 1899.

22. John Ireland to the editor of *Donahoe's Magazine*, May 11, 1898, Archbishop John Ireland Papers, St. Paul Seminary, St. Paul, Minnesota. For Catholic views of American expansionism, see *Pilot*, June 25, 1898; "Catholics and Imperialism," *Iowa Catholic Messenger*, December 17, 1898.

23. *Pilot*, February 4, 1899; *Irish World*, June 10, September 23, 1899.

24. For a sample of such views see *Catholic Citizen*, November 20, 1897; *Pilot*, May 7, 1897,

January 15, 1898; *Irish World*, April 30, July 30, August 6, September 10, 1898, June 3, 1899.

25. *Irish World*, May 21, November 19, 1898; *Iowa Catholic Messenger*, June 4, July 2, 1898.

26. *Catholic Mirror*, May 20, July 8, August 12, 1899; *Pilot*, September 2, 1899.

27. *Irish World*, September 30, 1899; *Pilot*, January 15, June 4, 1898.

28. *Pilot*, June 10, September 2, 1899.

29. *Pittsburgh Catholic*, September 13, 1899; *Catholic Citizen*, September 16, 1899; *Iowa Catholic Messenger*, September 23, 1899.

30. *Pittsburgh Catholic*, February 3, February 23, 1898.

31. *Ibid.*, March 2, 1898.

32. *Ibid.*, March 5, 1898.

33. *Pittsburgh Catholic*, March 23, 1898.

34. *Pilot*, March 12, September 10, 1898.

35. *Pittsburgh Catholic*, September 6, 1899; *Catholic Telegraph*, September 7, 1899.

36. Quoted in *Catholic World* 69 (April, 1899):128.

37. "Anna Gould's Charity Blessed," *Catholic Columbian and Record* 16 (April 28, 1900):1.

38. *Catholic Mirror*, August 26, 1899. For similar comments see "The Dreyfus Case," *Sacred Heart Review* 22 (August 26, 1899):131–32; "Shameful Performance in Paris," *ibid.*, p. 131; *Pilot*, "Disgrace in France," August 26, 1899; *Catholic Citizen*, August 26, 1899.

39. Thomas T. McAvoy, *The Americanist Heresy in Roman Catholicism, 1895–1900* (Notre Dame, Ind.: University of Notre Dame Press, 1963), p. 152; Patrick H. Ahern, *The Life of John J. Keane: Educator and Archbishop, 1839–1918* (Milwaukee, Wis.: Bruce Publishing Co., 1954), pp. 120–21, 149.

40. Robert D. Cross, *The Emergence of Liberal Catholicism in America* (Cambridge, Mass.: Harvard University Press, 1958), pp. 193–95. See also Ahern, *Keane*, pp. 179, 188–90.

41. *Pittsburgh Catholic*, January 13, 1898, September 13, 1899; "Catholics and Dreyfus," *Catholic Mirror*, February 18, 1898, September 9, 1899.

42. "The Dreyfus Affair," *Pittsburgh Catholic*, August 30, 1899.

43. "The Dreyfus Affair," *Catholic Citizen*, January 29, 1898.

44. "Dreyfus a Free Mason," *Catholic Telegraph*, September 7, 1899.

45. *Catholic Mirror*, September 23, 1899; *Catholic Citizen*, September 23, 1899.

46. *Catholic World* 67 (May, 1898):280. See also *ibid.*, 66 (December, 1897):420.

47. George McDermot, "Mr. Chamberlain's Foreign Policy and the Dreyfus Case," *ibid.*, 67 (September, 1898):769–75, 779; "Editorial Notes," *ibid.*, 68 (January, 1899):571.

48. See Norman James Clary, "French Anti-Semitism during the Years of Drumont and Dreyfus, 1886–1906" (Ph.D. diss., Ohio State University, 1970), p. 101.

49. "Editorial Notes," *Catholic World* 68 (October, 1898):135.

50. "Catholic Thought and Events in Foreign Lands," *Sacred Heart Review* 21 (December 31, 1898):6; "The Endless Dreyfus Case," *ibid.* (February 18, 1899):144.

51. "Dreyfus Gets a Pardon," *ibid.* (September 23, 1899):195; *ibid.* (November 4, 1899):292; *Catholic World* 70 (October, 1899):139.

52. *Catholic Columbian and Record*, 16 (October 28, 1899):4; James R. Randall, "Randall's Letter," *ibid.* (January 13, 1900):1.

53. Randall's column was featured in a number of Catholic periodicals. See his "letter" in *Catholic Columbian and Record* 16 (January 20, 1900):1; *ibid.* (June 9, 1900):1.

54. Wallace K. Hermes, "Non-Catholic Regard for Archbishop Ireland," *Records of the American Catholic Historical Society* 19 (September, 1948):190–94.

55. Quoted in James H. Moynihan, *The Life of Archbishop John Ireland* (New York: Harper & Brothers, 1953), pp. 275–76. See also *Boston Evening Transcript*, May 22, 1899.

56. *St. Louis Post-Dispatch*, September 14, 1899; *Boston Evening Transcript*, September 18, 1899.
57. Émile de Jumonville Coulon, *Realistic Descriptions of American Life and Institutions: Prophetic Letters on the Dreyfus Affair* (New York: D. V. Wiem, 1905), p. 43.
58. Quoted in Allen S. Will, *Life of Cardinal Gibbons* (New York: E. P. Dutton, 1922), Vol. II, p. 797.
59. Quoted in Robert F. Byrnes, *Antisemitism in Modern France* (New Brunswick, N.J.: Rutgers University Press, 1950), pp. 303–4. The *Catholic Mirror* of February 18, 1898, states that it is the official organ of Cardinal Gibbons. For efforts to excuse French behavior, see *Catholic Mirror*, September 9, 1899.
60. Blumenthal, *American and French Culture*, p. 143.
61. See, for example, Ferdinand Brunetière, "Le Catholicisme aux États-Unis," *Revue des deux mondes* (November, 1898), pp. 140–81. Archbishop Ireland is quoted in *Iowa Catholic Messenger*, March 28, 1898; *Pilot*, May 28, 1898; and in "Our Attitudes," *Pilot*, May 28, 1898. In a letter to the author, January 19, 1977, Father John J. Tierney, archivist of the Archdiocese of Baltimore, comments on Archbishop Ireland's patriotism. For the archibishop's efforts on behalf of peace, a task which he undertook at the behest of the pope, see correspondence and newspaper clippings, Archbishop John Ireland Papers, St. Paul Seminary, St. Paul, Minnesota.
62. The letter was translated in and commented upon in all American Catholic periodicals. See also Ireland to Gibbons, September 13, 1898, James Cardinal Gibbons Papers, Archdiocese of Baltimore, Baltimore, Maryland; *Catholic Citizen*, April 22, 1899.
63. Cross, *Liberal Catholicism*, p. 193.
64. *Pilot*, October 7, 1899. See also *Catholic Mirror*, September 2, September 16, 1899; *Catholic Citizen*, September 16, 1899; *Sacred Heart Review* 22 (October 7, 1899):288.
65. "Catholic Protection of the Jews," *Sacred Heart Review* 21 (February 11, 1899):124; Elizabeth Raymond-Barker, "The Holy See and the Jews," *Catholic World* 70 (December, 1899):394–97.
66. "Nordau Denies," *Pittsburgh Catholic*, March 9, 1898; *Pilot*, September 2, September 16, 1899; "French Catholics and Dreyfus," *Sacred Heart Review* 12 (July 5, 1899):35; *ibid.* (October 14, 1899):245; *ibid.* (October 24, 1899):261.
67. *Pittsburgh Catholic*, February 15, 1899.
68. Sydney F. Smith, "The Jesuits and the Dreyfus Case," *Month* 93 (February, 1899):113–30; Joseph Smith, "Jew-Baiting and A.P.A.ism," *Pilot*, September 2, 1899; "The Church on Dreyfus," *Catholic Citizen*, September 23, 1899.
69. "France and the Concordat," *Catholic World* 78 (October, 1903):382. See also "Imminent Persecution of the Church in France," *Pilot*, November 4, 1899.
70. Manuel de Moreira, "The Church in France and the Briand Bill," *Catholic World*, 78 (December, 1903):382–85.
71. "France and Religion," *Catholic World* 78 (December, 1903):418.
72. Thomas J. Shahan, "The Catholicism of France," *Conservative Review* 3 (1900):286–88.
73. James J. Fox, "Some Notes on the Dreyfus Case," *Catholic World* 83 (August, 1906):664–66.
74. W. L. S., "Some Causes and Lessons of the French Crisis," *ibid.*, 80 (March, 1905):733–39.
75. Fox, "Some Notes," pp. 672–77.

Selected Bibliography

Manuscript Collections

Baltimore, Maryland. Archdiocese of Baltimore. James Cardinal Gibbons Papers.
Boston. Massachusetts Diocesan Library. William Lawrence Papers.
Cambridge, Massachusetts. Houghton Library, Harvard University. Lee Max Friedman Papers.
Cincinnati, Ohio. American Jewish Archives. Gottard Deutsch Papers.
Columbus. Ohio Historical Society. Washington Gladden Papers.
Madison. State Historical Society of Wisconsin. Henry Demarest Lloyd Papers.
Madison. State Historical Society of Wisconsin. Edward A. Ross Papers.
New Haven, Connecticut. Yale University Library. Chauncey M. Depew Papers.
New York. New York Public Library. John Durand Papers.
New York. New York Public Library. R. Heber Newton Papers.
St. Paul, Minnesota. St. Paul Seminary. Archbishop John Ireland Papers.
Washington, D.C. Library of Congress. John Hay Papers.
Washington, D.C. Library of Congress. William McKinley Papers.

Annual Reports

American Jewish Year Book. Philadelphia: Jewish Publication Society, 1899–1907.
Report on the Annual Meeting of the American Bar Association. Philadelphia, 1898–1900.
Report of the Eighth Annual Meeting of the Pennsylvania Bar Association. Philadelphia, 1902.
Report of the Ninth Annual Meeting of the State Bar Association of Indiana Held at Indianapolis, July 6, and 7, 1905. Philadelphia, 1905.
Year Book of the Central Conference of American Rabbis. Cincinnati: CCAR, 1898–1906.

Unpublished Works

Clary, Norman James. "French Anti-Semitism during the Years of Drumont and Dreyfus, 1886–1906." Ph.D. dissertation, Ohio State University, 1970.
Halpern, Rose A. "The American Reaction to the Dreyfus Case." Master's thesis, Columbia University, 1941.
Sewrey, Charles L. "The Alleged 'Un-Americanism' of the Church as a Factor in Anti-Catholicism in the United States, 1860–1914." Ph.D. dissertation, University of Minnesota, 1955.
Urquhart, Ronald A. "The American Reaction to the Dreyfus Affair: A Study of Anti-Semitism in the 1890's." Ph.D. dissertation, Columbia University, 1972.

Newspapers

Das Abend Blatt (New York), 1897–1900
Atlanta Constitution, 1897–1906
Boston Evening Transcript, 1897–1900
Boston Globe, 1898–1899
Catholic Citizen (Milwaukee), 1898–1900
Catholic Columbian and Record (Indianapolis), 1899–1900
Catholic Mirror (Baltimore), 1898–1900
Catholic Telegraph (Cincinnati), 1898–1899
Chicago Tribune, 1895–1900
Iowa Catholic Messenger (Davenport), 1897–1899
Irish World (New York), 1898–1899
Jewish Daily Forward (New York), 1896–1906
Kansas City Star, 1898–1899
New Orleans Daily Picayune, 1898–1899
New York Evening Journal, 1897–1906
New York Evening Telegram, 1897–1899
New York Herald, 1895–1906
New York Journal, 1898–1906
New York Sun, 1895–1906
New York Times, 1894–1914
New York Tribune, 1897–1900
New York World, 1895–1906
Philadelphia Bulletin, 1898–1899
Philadelphia Inquirer, 1897–1899
Philadelphia Press, 1898–1899
Philadelphia Public Ledger, 1897–1899
Pilot (Boston), 1898–1900
Pittsburgh Catholic, 1897–1898
Sacred Heart Review (Boston), 1898–1899
St. Louis Post-Dispatch, 1896–1904
Washington Post, 1898–1899
Yiddishes Tageblatt (New York), 1897–1900

Articles

Abbott, Lyman. "America's Debt to Israel." *Outlook* 83 (December 9, 1905):857–58.
Ameisen, Arthur. "The Effect of Judgments of Courts-Martial in France and in America: A Comparative Study of the Dreyfus Case." *American Law Review* 33 (January-February, 1899):75–83.
"American Opinion on the Affair." *American Hebrew* 65 (September 15, 1899):581–92.
Baldwin, Elbert F. "Georges Picquart." *Outlook* 62 (July 1, 1899):528–34.
Benton, Joel. "French Law and Law Courts." *Green Bag* 10 (September, 1898):417–20.
Berkowitz, Henry. "Why I Am Not a Zionist." *Year Book of the Central Conference of American Rabbis*. Cincinnati: Central Conference of American Rabbis, 1899. Pp. 167–73.
Blair, Frank P. "A Review of Bertillon's Testimony in the Dreyfus Case." *American Law Review* 35 (May-June, 1901):389–401.
Blowitz, H. C. de. "The French Press and the Dreyfus Case." *North American Review* 169 (October, 1899):577–92.
Brunetière, Ferdinand. "Le Catholicisme aux États-Unis."*Revue des deux mondes* (November, 1898):140–81.

Bryce, James. "The Influence of National Character and Historical Environment on the Development of the Common Law." *Report of the Thirtieth Annual Meeting of the American Bar Association, Held at Portland, Maine, August 26, 27, 28, 1907*, Baltimore: Lord Baltimore Press, 1907. Pp. 444–62.

Cahan, Abraham. "The Ghetto's Grief." *Harper's Weekly* 43 (September 23, 1899):947–48.

Carryl, Guy Wetmore."Arrival of Dreyfus." *Harper's Weekly* 43 (July 22, 1899):729–38.

Choate, Joseph H. "The Annual Address." *Report of the Twenty-First Annual Meeting of the American Bar Association, Held at Saratoga Springs, New York, August 17, 18, 19, 1898*. New York: N.p., 1898. Pp. 285–314.

Crawford, Emily. "Émile Zola." *Contemporary Review* 55 (January, 1899):94–113.

Crawford, Theron C. "The Dreyfus Mystery." *Cosmopolitan* 24 (March, 1898):486–92.

Doane, William Crosswell. "The Roman Catholic Church and the School Fund." *North American Review* 158 (January, 1894):34–40.

Dobkowski, Michael N. "American Anti-Semitism: A Reinterpretation." *American Quarterly* 29 (Summer, 1977):166–81.

Eustis, James B. "Dreyfus and the Jewish Question in France: French and American Democracy." *Conservative Review* 2 (August, 1899):7–21.

Feldman, Egal. "American Editorial Reaction to the Dreyfus Case." In *Michael. On the History of the Jews in the Diaspora*, edited by Lloyd P. Gartner. Tel Aviv: Diaspora Research Institute, 1975. Pp. 101–24.

———. "The Social Gospel and the Jews." *American Jewish Historical Quarterly* 58 (March, 1969):308–22.

"Five Years of My Life." *Nation* 72 (May 30, 1901):440–41.

Fox, James J. "Some Notes on the Dreyfus Case." *Catholic World* 83 (August, 1906):664–79.

Foxcroft, H. C. "The 'Dreyfus Scandal' of English History." *Fortnightly Review* 72 (October, 1899):563–75.

Geffroy, Gustave. "Émile Zola, His Literary and Social Position." *International Quarterly* 6 (December-March, 1902):366–85.

Geltman, Max. "On Socialist Anti-Semitism." *Midstream: A Monthly Jewish Review* 23 (March, 1977):20–30.

Godkin, E. L. "French Military Justice." *Nation* 69 (November 9, 1899):349.

Goldberg, Harvey. "Jean Jaurès and the Jewish Question: The Evolution of a Position." *Jewish Social Studies* 20 (April, 1958):67–94.

Greenstone, Julius H. "The Year 5666." *American Jewish Year Book, 5667, 1906–1907*. Philadelphia: Jewish Publication Society of America, 1906. Pp. 237–75.

Handlin, Oscar. "American Views of the Jew at the Opening of the Twentieth Century." *Publications of the American Jewish Historical Society* 40 (June, 1951):323–44.

Hermes, Wallace K. "Non-Catholic Regard for Archbishop Ireland." *Records of the American Catholic Historical Society* 19 (September, 1948):190–94.

Howells, William D. "The Modern American Mood." *Harper's New Monthly Magazine* 95 (July, 1897):199–204.

Irwell, Lawrence. "The Judicial System of France." *Green Bag* 14 (November, 1902):527–33.

Jacob, Joseph. "The Jew in Europe." *American Jewish Year Book, 5660, 1899–1900*. Philadelphia: Jewish Publication Society of America, 1899. Pp. 20–47.

Jussem-Wilson, Nelly. "Bernard Lazare's Jewish Journey: From Being an Israelite to Being a Jew." *Jewish Social Studies* 26 (July, 1964):146–68.

Kennedy, William R. "The State Punishment of Crime." *Report of the Twenty-Second Annual Meeting of the American Bar Association, Held at Buffalo, New York, August 28, 29 and 30, 1899*. Philadelphia: N.p., 1899. Pp. 359–77.

Lazare, Bernard. "France at the Parting of the Ways." *North American Review* 169 (November, 1899):640–60.

"Leaves from the Autobiography of Captain Alfred Dreyfus." *McClure's Magazine* 17 (May, 1901):21–34.

McDermot, George. "Mr. Chamberlain's Foreign Policy and the Dreyfus Case." *Catholic World* 67 (September, 1898):768–79.

McDonald, J. H. A. "The Negative Ruler of France." *Blackwood's Edinburgh Magazine* 165 (January, 1899):1052–68.

Mead, Sidney E. "American Protestantism since the Civil War, I. From Denominationalism to Americanism." *Journal of Religion* 36 (January, 1956):1–15.

Moreira, Manuel de. "The Church in France and the Briand Bill." *Catholic World* 78 (December, 1903):382–85.

Morgan, John de. "Maître Fernand Labori: A Character Study." *Green Bag* 11 (December, 1899):541–44.

Morse, John T., Jr. "The Dreyfus and Zola Trials." *Atlantic Monthly* 81 (May, 1898):589–602.

"The Neutrality of the Pope." *American Hebrew* 65 (October 13, 1899):706–9.

Poliakov, Leon. "The Catholic Church and the Jews: The Vatican's New Guidelines." *Midstream: A Monthly Jewish Review* 22 (October, 1976):29–35.

Pound, Roscoe. "The Need of a Sociological Jurisprudence." *Green Bag* 19 (October, 1907):607–15.

Ralph, Julian. "The Dreyfus Verdict." *Harper's Weekly* 43 (September 16, 1899):982.

Raymond-Barker, Elizabeth. "The Holy See and the Jews." *Catholic World* 70 (December, 1899):394–409.

"The Recent Zola Trial." *Green Bag* 10 (May, 1898):187–95.

Rogers, John I. "Military Law and Its Tribunals." *Report of the Eighth Annual Meeting of the Pennsylvania Bar Association Held at Cambridge Springs, Pennsylvania, June 30, and July 1 and 2, 1902.* Philadelphia: n.p., 1902. Pp. 362–90.

Rose, V. M. "Trial by Jury in France." *American Law Review* 35 (January-February, 1901):17–26.

Sanborn, Alvin F. "French Workingmen and the Dreyfus Affair." *Outlook* 62 (June 10, 1899):340–43.

———. "Ten Years Later: The Most Celebrated Case in History." *Bookman* 28 (September-October, 1908):31–42, 154–62.

Sears, Louis M. "French Opinion of the Spanish-American War." *Hispanic American Historical Review* 7 (February, 1927):25–44.

Sedgwick, A. G. "Fruits of Militarism." *Nation* 67 (August 18, 1898):126–27.

Shahan, Thomas J. "The Catholicism of France." *Conservative Review* 3 (1900):278–98.

Sherard, Robert H. "Dr. Nordau on the Jews and Their Fears." *American Monthly Review of Reviews* 17 (February, 1898):315–17; (March, 1898):316–17.

———. "M. Zola on French Anti-Semitism." *American Monthly Review of Reviews* 17 (March, 1898):318–20.

Spearman, Edmund R. "Legal Anthropometry." *Green Bag* 7 (January, 1895):33–35.

Steevens, G. W. "Scenes and Actors in the Dreyfus Trial." *McClure's Magazine* 13 (September, 1899):515–23.

Szajkowski, Zosa. "Socialists and Radicals in the Development of Antisemitism in Algeria (1884–1900)." *Jewish Social Studies* 10 (July, 1948):257–80.

Szold, Henrietta. "The Year 5660." *American Jewish Year Book, 5661, 1900–1901.* Philadelphia: Jewish Publication Society of America, 1900. Pp. 12–30.

Thompson, Seymour D. "The Revision of the Dreyfus Case." *Green Bag* 11 (January, 1899):9–13.
Twain, Mark. "Concerning the Jews." *Harper's New Monthly Magazine* 99 (September, 1899):527–35.
Whitridge, Frederick W. "Zola, Dreyfus and the French Republic." *Political Science Quarterly* 13 (June, 1898):259–72.

Books

Adams, Henry. *Letters of Henry Adams 1892–1918*. Edited by Washington C. Ford. Boston: Houghton Mifflin Company, 1938.
Ahern, Patrick H. *The Life of John J. Keane: Educator and Archbishop, 1839–1918*. Milwaukee, Wis.: Bruce Publishing Company, 1954.
Allen, Gay Wilson. *William James: A Biography*. New York: Viking Press, 1967.
Arendt. Hannah. *The Origins of Totalitarianism*. New York: Meridian Books, 1958.
Armstrong, William M. *E. L. Godkin and American Foreign Policy, 1865–1900*. New York: Bookman Associates, 1959.
Baldwin, Edward C. *Our Modern Debt to Israel*. Boston: Sherman French, 1913.
Barclay, Thomas, *Thirty Years: Anglo-French Reminiscences (1876–1906)*. Boston: Houghton Mifflin, 1914.
Beard, Charles A. and Beard, Mary R. *The Rise of American Civilization*. 2 volumes. New York: Macmillan, 1947.
Bein, Alex. *Theodor Herzl: A Biography*. Translated by Maurice Samuel. Cleveland: World; Philadelphia: Jewish Publication Society of America, 1962.
Beisner, Robert L. *Twelve against Empire: The Anti-Imperialists, 1898–1900*. New York: McGraw-Hill, 1968.
Blumenthal, Henry. *France and the United States: Their Diplomatic Relations, 1789–1914*. Chapel Hill: University of North Carolina Press, 1970.
Brinton, Crane. *The Americans and the French*. Cambridge, Mass.: Harvard University Press, 1968.
Brooks, Van Wyck. *New England Indian Summer, 1865–1915*. New York: E. P. Dutton, 1940.
Brown, Charles H. *The Correspondents' War: Journalists in the Spanish-American War*. New York: Charles Scribner's Sons, 1967.
Brown, Roger G. *Fashoda Reconsidered: The Impact of Domestic Politics on French Policy in Africa, 1893–1898*. Baltimore: Johns Hopkins University Press, 1969.
Budd, Louis J. *Mark Twain: Social Philosopher*. Bloomington: Indiana University Press, 1962.
Byrnes, Robert F. *Antisemitism in Modern France*. New Brunswick, N.J.: Rutgers University Press, 1950.
Campbell, Charles S., Jr. *Anglo-American Understanding, 1898–1903*. Baltimore: Johns Hopkins University Press, 1957.
Carroll, E. Malcolm. *French Public Opinion and Foreign Affairs, 1870–1914*. New York: Century Company, 1931.
Castellane, Ernest Paul Boniface de. *How I Discovered America: Confessions of the Marquis Boni De Castellane*. New York: Alfred A. Knopf, 1924.
Catalog of Books Represented by Library of Congress Printing Cards, A. Paterson, N.J.: Rowman and Littlefield, 1963.
Challener, Richard D. *Admirals, Generals, and American Foreign Policy, 1898–1914*. Princeton, N.J.: Princeton University Press, 1973.

Chapman, Guy. *The Dreyfus Case: A Reassessment*. New York: Reynal and Company, 1955.

Cohn, Norman. *Warrant for Genocide: The Myth of the Jewish World-Conspiracy and the Protocols of the Elders of Zion*. New York: Harper and Row, 1969.

Coulon, Émile de Jumonville. *Realistic Descriptions of American Life and Institutions: Prophetic Letters on the Dreyfus Affair*. New York: D. V. Wiem, 1905.

Creelman, James. *On the Great Highway: The Wanderings and Adventures of a Special Correspondent*. Boston: Lothrop, 1901.

Cross, Robert D. *The Emergence of Liberal Catholicism in America*. Cambridge, Mass.: Harvard University Press, 1958.

Desmond, Robert W. *The Press and World Affairs*. New York: D. Appleton-Century, 1937.

Dinnerstein, Leonard, ed. *Antisemitism in the United States*. New York: Holt, Rinehart and Winston, 1971.

Dos Passos, John R. *The Anglo-Saxon Century and the Unification of the English-Speaking People*. New York: G. P. Putnam's Sons, 1903.

Dreyfus, Alfred. *Five Years of My Life, 1894–1899*. New York: McClure, Phillips & Company, 1901.

———. *The Letters of Captain Dreyfus to His Wife*. Translated by L. G. Moreau. New York: Harper & Brothers, 1899.

Dudley, Edgar S. *Military Law and the Procedure of Courts-Martial*. New York: John Wiley & Sons, 1907.

Dunne, Finley Peter. *Mr. Dooley in the Hearts of His Countrymen*. New York: Greenwood Press, 1969.

———. *Mr. Dooley in Peace and in War*. Boston: Small, Maynard, 1898.

Ekirch, Arthur A., Jr. *The Civilian and the Military*. New York: Oxford University Press, 1956.

Franklin, Fabian. *People and Problems: A Collection of Addresses and Editorials by Fabian Franklin, Editor of the Baltimore News, 1895–1908*. New York: Holt & Company, 1908.

Friedman, Lawrence M. *A History of American Law*. New York: Simon and Schuster, 1973.

Friedman, Lee M. *Zola and the Dreyfus Case: His Defense of Liberty and Its Enduring Significance*. Boston: Beacon Press, 1937.

Halasz, Nicholas. *Captain Dreyfus: The Story of a Mass Hysteria*. New York: Simon and Schuster, 1955.

Hale, Richard W. *The Dreyfus Story*. Boston: Small, Maynard, 1899.

Harding, William. *Dreyfus: The Prisoner of Devil's Island*. New York: Associated Publishing Company, 1899.

Hearst, William R. *Selections from the Writings and Speeches of William Randolph Hearst*. San Francisco: Privately published, 1948.

Heller, James G. *Isaac M. Wise: His Life, Work and Thought*. Cincinnati: Union of American Hebrew Congregations, 1965.

Herzog, Wilhelm. *From Dreyfus to Pétain: The Struggle of a Republic*. Translated by Walter Sorrell. New York: Creative Age Press, 1947.

Hofstadter, Richard, and Wallace, Michael, eds. *American Violence: A Documentary History*. New York: Vintage Books, 1971.

Hoyt, Edwin P. *The Goulds: A Social History*. New York: Weybright and Talley, 1969.

James, William. *The Letters of William James*. Edited by Henry James. 2 vols. New York: Kraus Reprint Company, 1969.

Johnson, Douglas. *France and the Dreyfus Affair*. London: Blandford Press, 1966.

Karp, Abraham, J., ed. *Golden Door to America: The Jewish Immigrant Experience*. New York: Viking, 1976.

King, Willard L. *Melville Weston Fuller: Chief Justice of the United States 1888–1910.* New York: Macmillan, 1950.

Kinzer, Donald L. *An Episode in Anti-Catholicism: The American Protective Association.* Seattle: University of Washington Press, 1964.

Koppel, Pinson S., ed. *Essays on Anti-Semitism.* New York: Jewish Social Studies, 1946.

LeClair, Robert C., ed. *The Letters of William James and Theodore Flournoy.* Madison: University of Wisconsin Press, 1966.

Lewisohn, Ludwig, ed. *Theodor Herzl, a Portrait for This Age.* Cleveland: World, 1955.

Lonergan, W. F. *Forty Years of Paris.* London: T. Fisher Unwin, 1907.

McAvoy, Thomas T. *The Americanist Heresy in Roman Catholicism 1895–1900.* Notre Dame, Ind.: University of Notre Dame Press, 1963.

McKay, Donald C., trans. and ed. *The Dreyfus Case: By the Man—Alfred Dreyfus and His Son—Pierre Dreyfus.* New Haven, Conn.: Yale University Press, 1937.

Marrus, Michael R. *The Politics of Assimilation: A Study of the French Jewish Community at the Time of the Dreyfus Affair.* Oxford: Clarendon Press, 1971.

May, Ernest R. *American Imperialism: A Speculative Essay,* New York: Atheneum, 1968.

Mende, Elsie P., with Pearson, Henry G. *An American Soldier and Diplomat: Horace Porter.* New York: Frederick A. Stokes, 1927.

Morgan, H. Wayne, ed. *Making Peace With Spain. The Diary of Whitelaw Reid: September–December, 1898.* Austin: University of Texas Press, 1965.

Morison, Samuel E., Commager, Henry S. and Leuchtenburg, William E. *The Growth of the American Republic.* Vol. II. New York: Oxford University Press, 1969.

Moynihan, James H. *The Life of Archbishop John Ireland.* New York: Harper & Brothers, 1953.

Musgrave, George C. *Under Three Flags in Cuba: A Personal Account of the Cuban Insurrection and Spanish-American War.* Boston: Little, Brown, 1899.

Nordau, Max. *Max Nordau to His People: A Collection of Addresses to Zionist Congresses together with a Tribute to Theodor Herzl.* New York: Scopus, 1941.

O'Brien, R. Barry. *The Life of Lord Russell of Killowen.* London: Smith, Elder, 1901.

O'Connor, Raymond G., ed. *American Defense Policy in Perspective: From Colonial Times to the Present.* New York: John Wiley & Sons, 1965.

Paine, Albert Bigelow, ed. *Mark Twain's Letters.* Vol. II: New York: Harper & Brothers, 1917.

Painter, George D. *Proust: The Early Years.* Boston: Little, Brown, 1959.

Paleologue, Georges M. *An Intimate Journal of the Dreyfus Case.* New York: Criterion Books, 1957.

Perry, Ralph Barton. *The Thought and Character of William James.* Cambridge, Mass.: Harvard University Press, 1948.

———. *The Thought and Character of William James, as Revealed in Unpublished Correspondence and Notes, Together with His Published Writings.* Vol. II: *Philosophy and Psychology.* Boston: Little, Brown, 1936.

Peters, Madison C. *Justice to the Jew: The Story of What He Has Done for the World.* New York: Trow Press, 1910.

Rauschenbusch, Walter. *Christianity and the Social Crisis.* New York: Macmillan, 1907.

Reinach, Joseph. *Histoire de l'affaire Dreyfus.* 7 volumes. Paris: Librairie Charpentier et Fasquelle, 1901–5.

Reuter, Bertha A. *Anglo-American Relations during the Spanish American War.* New York: Macmillan, 1924.

Scott, Arthur L. *Mark Twain at Large.* Chicago: Henry Regnery Company, 1969.

Shaler, N.S. *The Neighbors: The Natural History of Human Contacts.* Boston: Houghton, Mifflin, 1904.

Snyder, Louis L., ed. *The Dreyfus Case: A Documentary History.* New Brunswick, N.J.: Rutgers University Press, 1973.

Spiller, Robert E., et al. *Literary History of the United States.* New York: Macmillan, 1953.

Steed, Henry Wickham. *Through Thirty Years, 1892–1922: A Personal Narrative.* Vol. I. New York: Doubleday, Page, 1924.

Steevens, G. W. *The Tragedy of Dreyfus.* New York: Harper & Brothers, 1899.

Tannenbaum, Edward R. *The Action Française: Die-Hard Reactionaries in Twentieth Century France.* New York: John Wiley & Sons, 1962.

Tuchman, Barbara W. *The Proud Tower: A Portrait of the World before the War, 1890–1914.* New York: Bantam Books, 1966.

Tucker, Benjamin R., ed. *The Trial of Émile Zola Containing M. Zola's Letter to President Faure Relating to the Dreyfus Case and a Full Report of the Fifteen Days' Proceedings in the Assize Court of the Seine, Including Testimony of Witnesses and Speeches of Counsel.* New York: Benjamin R. Tucker, 1898.

Turner, Arthur C. *The Unique Partnership: Britain and the United States.* New York: Pegasus, 1971.

Villard, Oswald Garrison. *Fighting Years: Memoirs of a Liberal Editor.* New York: Harcourt, Brace, 1939.

Vizetelly, Ernest Alfred. *Émile Zola, Novelist and Reformer: An Account of His Life and Work.* London: John Lane–The Bodley Head, 1904.

Weigley, Russel F. *Towards An American Army: Military Thought from Washington to Marshall.* New York: Columbia University Press, 1962.

White, Ronald C., and Hopkins, C. Howard. *The Social Gospel: Religion and Reform in Changing America.* Philadelphia: Temple University Press, 1976.

Whitehead, James L. *French Reaction to American Imperialism, 1895–1908.* Philadelphia: University of Pennsylvania Press, 1943.

Wiernik, Peter. *History of the Jews in America.* New York: Jewish Press Publishing Company, 1912.

Will, Allen S. *Life of Cardinal Gibbons.* 2 volumes. New York: E. P. Dutton, 1922.

Index

Fort Chabral. *See* Guérin, Jules
Forum, 99–100
Forzinetti, Ferdinand, 121
Fox, James J., 144–45
Foxcroft, H. C., 20
France juive, 98–99, 101
Franco-Prussian War: and anti-
Catholicism, 124–25
Franklin, Fabian, 103
Freemasons, 99, 135–36
French High Court of Appeal, 27, 48,
114–15; moves Picquart's case to civil
court, 58; organization of, 33–34;
postpones Picquart's courtmartial, 58;
recommends revision, 13; reopens
Dreyfus case, 5
French Intelligence Bureau, 1, 3–4, 28,
53, 55
French Revolution: and anti-Semitism, 98
Frye, William Pierce, 68
Fuller, Melville W., 23–24

Gambetta, Léon, 72, 136–37
Gast, Edmund, 63
Geffroy, Gustave, 8, 16–17
Gibbons, Cardinal James, 128, 134,
139–140
Gladden, Washington, 106–108, 125
Godkin, E. L., 50–51
Gottheil, Richard, 120
Gould, Anna, 76–81, 133
Gould, Jay, 76
Greenstone, Julius H., 122
Greig, D. B., 106
Guérin, Jules, 99, 118–19, 128–29, 162n;
American opinion of, 75, 76; Catholic
view of, 134; in Fort Chabral, 75–76

Hale, Richard W., 49
Handlin, Oscar, 102
Harper's Weekly, 39–40, 48, 85, 103
Hartford Courant, 50
Hay, John, 19, 90, 107
Hearst, William Randolph: on Anna
Gould's behavior, 81; on Dreyfus'
"escape," 84; on Labori shooting, 63
Henry, Hubert Joseph, 2, 46, 118, 228–29;
accuses Picquart of forgery, 56; as chief
of intelligence, 4, 55; and "secret
dossier," 4, 55; suicide of, 5
Herzl, Theodor, 114–15
Hirsch, Baron Maurice de, 106–7
Hirsch, Emile H., 112, 115
Hofstadter, Richard, 21–22, 105

"Honor," French, 42, 46
Howells, William Dean, 78
Hoyt, Edwin, 78

Immigration: from Eastern Europe,
18–19, 123–24; of Jews, 101–2; of
Roman Catholics, 123–24
Imperialism, American, 19, 21–22
Independent, 47, 96, 110, 126, 146
Iowa Catholic Messenger (Davenport), 129,
130–32
Ireland, Archbishop John, 128, 134, 138;
on Franco-American relations, 138–39;
on Jews, 139; opposes critics of France,
131–32; patriotism of, 140, 173n; and
Theodore Roosevelt, 124
Irish-Americans, 19, 129–31, 138. *See also*
Catholics, U.S.
Irish World (New York), 130–31

J'accuse, 5, 8–9. *See also* Zola, Émile
Jacob, Joseph, 121
James, Henry, 109
James, William, 42, 69, 109, 125
Jastrow, Morris, 112, 116
Jesuits, French, 126
Jewish Daily Forward (New York), 116–18
Jewish Messenger, 114
Jewish State, The, 119
"Jewish Syndicate," 4, 72, 104, 135
Jewish Voice, 114
Jews, American, 148; on anti-Semitism,
115; on Dreyfus, 117–18; from Eastern
Europe, 116–19; festivals of, 118–19; on
Picquart, 117; on pogroms, 117; on the
Pope, 117–18; on Rennes verdict,
118–20; restrained response of, 112–13;
120–22; view of German and Reform,
113–16; view of Socialist, 115–16; view
of Zionist, 119–20; on Zola, 117. *See also*
Anti-Semitism, French; Anti-Semitism,
U.S.; Anti-Semitism, Vatican
Jews, French, 112
Jones, Charles F., 95
Judicial practices, French: American
confusion about 30–36; vs. Anglo-
American practices, 20, 32, 34, 37,
39–40; courtroom behavior, 10, 147;
cross-examination, 30, 34–35; *habeas
corpus*, 37; *juge d'instruction*, 37–38;
military courts, 51–52; rules of evidence,
26, 35–36, 50, 147; treatment of
witnesses, 34–36

Egal Feldman is professor of history and dean of the College of Letters and Science at the University of Wisconsin-Superior. He holds the B.A. degree from Brooklyn College, the M.A. degree from New York University, and the Ph.D. degree from the University of Pennsylvania. He has received the YIVO Institute for Jewish Research and other awards for his scholarly contributions and has published extensively on Jewish-Christian relations in the United States in the earlier years of this century.

The manuscript was edited by Jean Owen. The book was designed by Gary Gore. The typeface for the text and for the display is Baskerville, designed by John Baskerville in the eighteenth century. The book is bound in Holliston Mills' Roxite linen over binder's boards.

Manufactured in the United States of America.